We'll
Always Have
Paris

Praise for *We'll Always Have Paris*

"I'm profoundly in love with Jennifer Coburn's memoir *We'll Always Have Paris!* From Coburn's picture-perfect travelogue to her hilarious observations, she's woven together a powerful narrative with a heartfelt and thoughtful examination of what truly makes a family. I was enthralled from the very first page and I cannot recommend this book highly enough. I want to read this again, tell all my friends about it…and then renew my passport."
—Jen Lancaster, *New York Times* bestselling author of *Bitter Is the New Black*, *The Tao of Martha*, and *Here I Go Again*

"*We'll Always Have Paris* is simply brimming with *joie de vivre*! From the very moment I embarked on Jennifer Coburn's delicious Paris memoir, I wanted to travel back in time to when my own daughter was eight years old, take her by the hand, and bring her to Paris for the adventure of a lifetime. Well, until I have a granddaughter, I have the next best thing—Jennifer Coburn's gorgeous story of love, family, and the ties that bind. I am recommending this to all my friends and family and especially to my own daughter. It's simply *fantastique!*"
—Jamie Cat Callan, author of *Ooh La La! French Women's Secrets to Feeling Beautiful Every Day*

"*We'll Always Have Paris* reads like a sweet stroll through Europe with a funny friend who shares touching stories of her parent–child relationships. A great escape."
—Janice MacLeod, author of *Paris Letters*

We'll Always Have Paris

A Mother/Daughter Memoir

JENNIFER COBURN

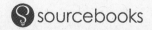

Published by Sourcebooks, Inc.

P.O. Box 4410, Naperville, Illinois 60567-4410

(630) 961-3900

Fax: (630) 961-2168

www.sourcebooks.com

Library of Congress Cataloging-in-Publication data is on file with the publisher.

Printed and bound in the United States of America.

VP 10 9 8 7 6 5

ALSO BY JENNIFER COBURN

The Wife of Reilly
Reinventing Mona
Tales from the Crib
The Queen Gene
Brownie Points
Field of Schemes

For Katie
Who makes every day a wonderful adventure

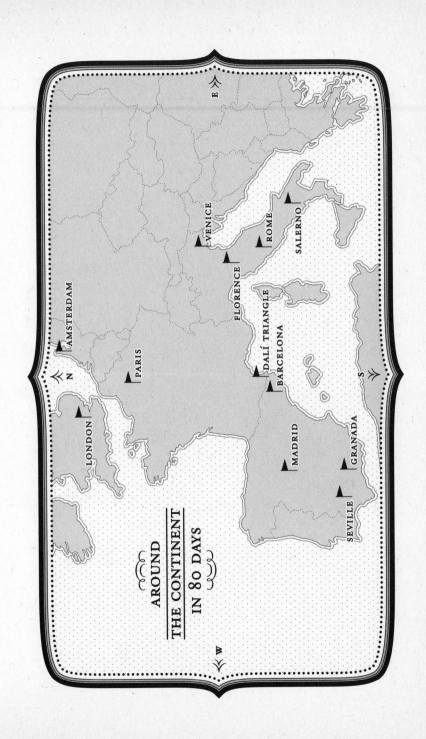

AROUND
THE CONTINENT
IN 80 DAYS

AMSTERDAM

PARIS

LONDON

VENICE

FLORENCE

ROME

SALERNO

DALÍ TRIANGLE

BARCELONA

MADRID

GRANADA

SEVILLE

N

E

S

W

INTRODUCTION

. . . .

*J*ail?!" my husband William shouted through the telephone.

"We were never actually *in* a jail cell," I explained, now safely back in our hotel room. "It was just a warning."

"A warning?" His incredulity was clear despite the crackling reception of our overseas connection. "From a police officer?"

"Yes."

"After you and Katie were arrested?"

"Detained," I replied.

He sighed audibly.

I probably should have known that climbing over a playground fence was illegal, but other families had jumped first, I explained. "I was trying to be one with the culture, do as the French were doing."

"Was there a lock on the gate?" William asked.

"Kind of."

"Listen, in any culture around the world, a locked gate

means don't enter," he said. "It's universal, got it? Locked gate equals go away. It never means hop over. How is Katie?"

"She's relieved they didn't get her name," I said. "She was concerned about having a record at eight years old."

William laughed at how similar he and his daughter were. "Did they book you? How did you get out?"

"One of the other…prisoners started yelling at the officer, and I think I kind of annoyed him by making a stupid reference to Jerry Lewis. I think he just got tired of dealing with us and decided to let the whole group of us go."

"Jen, I've got to tell you, this is not inspiring a lot of confidence."

This sentiment was one we had in common.

A trip to Paris had sounded so adventurous when I was first talking about it a year earlier. People spoke about the city with dreamy longing, as though Paris possessed a magic that could not be found elsewhere. I'd never heard anyone talk about Paris without sighing. The city was a Promised Land that held appeal for most everyone: artists, lovers, even people who just liked cheese.

Sitting across the table from the French police officer, though, I wondered what made me think I could handle an overseas trip with a child. I didn't speak French. I had practically zero travel experience. And clearly I did not understand the local customs.

It wasn't as though we had money to blow either. When I told William I wanted to take this trip, he gently reminded me of a few things. Both of our bathrooms were in serious need of repair. In one, we couldn't use the shower because the water leak would further damage the sinking floor, which was covered with a board. Our forty-year-old kitchen looked like it had parachuted in from the set of a sitcom like *The Brady Bunch* or *The Partridge Family*, complete with a mysterious metal appliance attached to the aqua blue formica splash wall. No one has ever figured out what this thing is or does, but some have guessed that it was once used to cook meat. Our oven had two temperatures: hot and off. The dilapidated louvered windows let in more air than they kept out.

And yet overseas travel was, somehow, my economic priority.

I know why, of course. My father died when I was nineteen years old. He was forty-nine, and after years of getting high with fellow musicians, lung cancer finally did him in. Marijuana was his drug of choice, but as he often said, he never met a buzz he didn't like. He also managed a two-pack-a-day cigarette habit.

Since my father's death in 1986, I've been checking my rear-view mirror to see if the Grim Reaper is tailgating.

When William and I started dating, I warned him I was kind of psychic and knew I was going to be killed in a car accident two years later. He said he'd take his chances. Whenever my doctor tells me I'm perfectly healthy, I lament the state of the American health care system. I shake my head, saddened that doctors are so inept that they haven't yet diagnosed my serious illness. Early detection is the key to survival, and these guys are clearly missing something in all the perfect blood work, the spotless MRIs, the immaculate lung X-rays I regularly request.

William says my only illness is neurosis, nothing a few monthly gab sessions with a therapist can't fix. My mother, on the other hand, becomes frenzied when I articulate my fear of dying young. "You cannot say things like that aloud!" she shrieks. "You can't even *think* them. The universe hears everything and manifests our thoughts." Then she demands I say, "Cancel, cancel," and affirm, "I am healthy and vibrant. My body is prepared to live a long life of abundant health."

As much as I love my mother, her New Age style of health insurance grates on me because at its core is the notion that people who are seriously ill caused their condition with negative thoughts. If only they would adopt a can-do attitude and chant the right fortune cookie wisdom, their cancer would run scared, like Satan from a cross. My mother argues that the power of positive thinking has helped millions of people, but it's a bit hard to swallow when you've watched someone you love be ravaged by disease and know that no positive thoughts would have saved him. When I challenge my mother's beliefs, I keep it light, telling her that I think about winning the lottery all the time. "I affirm *that* aloud," I tell her. "I creatively visualize all kinds of cool things I'll buy, and it hasn't happened yet." After these exchanges, my mother shakes her head pityingly. "That's not how it works, Jennifer."

But what if by genetic predisposition, or past habits, or just bad luck, I meet the same fate as my father and never live to see fifty? Which would Katie remember more: a trip to Europe with me or beautiful tile work in our bathroom?

My friend Evelyn was given the choice between a trip to Paris and a Rolex for her birthday. She took the watch. I thought she was out of her mind until she reminded me of her history. She was one of nine children in a working-class Puerto Rican family in Michigan. Having that watch was a reminder that she was successful. It was a symbol that she had made it. When the choice was given, Evelyn and her husband were both attorneys living in a home so well appointed that then-presidential candidate John Edwards chose to host a fundraiser there. "The trip would be over in ten days," Evelyn said, "but I will look at this watch every morning and it will make me happy." She says she'd make the same decision today.

There are no right choices. There are only our choices. As for mine, I'd take Paris.

My plan was to jam-pack Katie's mental scrapbook with beautiful memories of us walking hand-in-hand through the sepia-toned streets of Paris, stopping to listen to an accordion player whose monkey in a red beret begged us for tips. We would ride bikes, me holding a baguette, Katie a red balloon. We would see a mime and find him charming.

Whether I met my father's fate or lived a long life, I wanted to look at Katie as I lay on my deathbed and tell her it was wonderful being her mother. And with my last breath of life, I'd tell her that we'll always have Paris.

Trip One

Paris and London
2005

1

PARIS

ood morning, ladies and gentlemen. In twenty minutes, we will be landing at Charles de Gaulle Airport
in Paris where the local time is now 7:10 a.m.," a calm
disembodied voice announced. Then the flight attendant
repeated the information in French. At least I assumed she
was repeating the information. For all I knew, she could
have been saying, "On our flight this morning is a clueless
American mother and her eight-year-old daughter who is
counting on her to navigate their ten-day stay in the City of
Lights. Good luck with that."

I looked at my fellow passengers, noticing I was the only
one awake in the cabin, which always seemed to be the case
on these red-eye flights. William was back home in San
Diego flossing his teeth. In a few minutes, he would look at
the clock beside our bed and realize that Katie's and my flight

was landing. Twenty seconds later, he would be snoring. As a lifelong insomniac, I try to remember that he isn't purposely taunting me when he goes from sixty to snooze in less than a minute. Still, there are times at night when I stare at him in amazement, wondering how he can let go of consciousness so easily.

I heard the clap of lifting window shades and watched light pour into the cabin like spotlights onto a stage. *Good night, William*, I thought. *Good morning, Paris.*

Katie can sleep through earthquakes, so neither the noise nor the plummeting descent of the plane bothered her. Her brown hair was still pressed into her Eeyore neck pillow, and her white Stride Rite sandals were nestled in the space between our seats. Katie didn't even seem to notice when the flight attendant abruptly pressed the button that snapped her seat into its upright position. My daughter's delicate eyebrows lifted quizzically; she shifted her position slightly and continued sleeping.

"Katie," I whispered. "We're landing in a moment. You need to wake up." She blinked open her bleary green eyes, trying to register who I was, where we were, and what I was saying. "We'll be in Paris in a few minutes," I said, wondering if I sounded as relaxed as I hoped I did.

As the plane continued to land, I felt a slow panic rising.

Katie yawned. "Are you excited, Mommy?"

"Oh yes, Katie. I'm very, very excited," I replied, imitating the voice of a yoga instructor. "And how are you?"

"Good," she chirped.

I resisted the urge to say anything else, lest Katie know how absolutely, positively freaked out I was.

Weeks before we left, I asked Katie if she was looking forward to our trip. "Do you understand how lucky we are to be going to *Paris*? I mean, do you *get* it?" She was just finishing up second grade, and her teacher was very focused on the students' comprehension of the words they read. So Katie brought Mrs. Lunsford's lesson home.

"Well, Paris is the capital of France, and people say I'm lucky to be going, so I know it's special, but since I've never been there, I don't really understand why it's so great." Katie scrunched her mouth to the side, pondering the tough question. "So I understand it, but I guess I don't *get* it."

On the ground, I cursed my friend Maxime for telling me that Katie and I should take the train from Charles de Gaulle Airport, then delve into the Paris Metro system to find our hotel. "Eet ees easy," he told me weeks earlier as we sat at the Souplantation in San Diego. Easy for him because he is, in fact, French.

"Deed you study the vocabulary words I gave you last week?" He looked disappointed when I told him I hadn't. Sure, he was encouraging, always telling me my accent was *très magnifique,* but the French are known for being rather finicky about foreigners speaking their language imperfectly. The prospect of speaking French on their home turf was more than a bit intimidating. Maxime assured me that if I just gave it a try, they would appreciate my effort. "So," he continued, "all you know how to say ees what?"

"Hello, please, and thank you."

My friend sighed. "A writer with no words." Maxime began scribbling on a piece of paper. Writing the French words for "I have" and "I am," he begged me to try harder. He handed me a phrase book, which covered all of the basics, such as how to ask for directions, prices, and food. There was also a page on flirting. Here I was, a happily married mother on the cusp of middle age with an eight-year-old in tow. I hardly thought I'd need to know how to accept a man's dinner invitation. Still, I was charmed by the idea that pick-up lines were considered essential phrases in French. "How long will you be staying in Paris?" I read in French to my friend.

"*Ooh la la,*" he said, raising his eyebrows. "You have a knack for languages," he told me.

"How can you say that? I only speak English," I reminded Maxime.

"I am a French teacher. I can tell when someone has the ear."

Weeks later, with my suitcase stuck in the Metro turnstile, I panicked. Katie tried to pull the case through, an effort that promptly left her on her behind. I remembered Maxime's notes in my purse and vaguely recalled that some words, like "problem," just needed a French accent to translate. "Please," I called out in French, "*Je suis un problème.*" A group of maintenance men began laughing and rushed over to help. One smiled gently and corrected me. Apparently, in my haste, I'd mixed the phrases and announced to the commuters not that I have a problem, but that I *am* one. Was it possible to have a Freudian slip in a foreign language?

Katie and I exited the station and stood on the grim-looking sidewalk. With a steely ceiling of overcast, this was not the Paris I had envisioned. People rushed past us, mainly tourists with maps in hand and a few locals heading to work. No one wore a beret; no one was painting at an easel. I knew it was naïve to expect such a threshold into Paris, but I'd hoped for something a bit more visually appealing.

I stood frozen, staring at my map without a clue of which direction to walk. An elderly woman wearing a floral scarf on her head noticed that Katie and I looked lost and stopped to ask if we needed help. I shot her a pathetic look and handed her a piece of paper with the address of our hotel written on it. She grabbed my hand and patted it. "Ees close. I take you there." I heard my mother's voice warning me not to fall prey to kidnappers who would sell Katie and me into slavery, but I was pretty certain we could outrun this woman. My eyes darted in search of vans with blackened windows, but I saw none. Three blocks later, she delivered us to our hotel, kissed both of my cheeks and pinched Katie's. She said something to us in French that sounded warm and buttery.

"Mrs. Poltorak told me that French people were snooty, but I think they're really nice," Katie said, recalling the student at the airport who helped us buy train tickets and the father who commanded his sons to carry our suitcases up the Metro steps.

This was one of the many reasons I brought Katie overseas. I wanted her to experience different places and people and make her own assessments. I mentally checked the box with this life lesson jotted beside it. We had been in France for less than two hours and already my child had learned something: don't listen to Mrs. Poltorak.

I also felt that taking Katie abroad young would give her greater confidence to travel on her own someday. When my friend Laura invited me to visit her in Rome for a month during summer break in high school, I declined. The language was different. I didn't understand the money exchange. It seemed overwhelming. If Katie started traveling young, she wouldn't find international travel intimidating. She would never doubt her ability to navigate her way through the world the way I still did.

The concierge at our hotel told me that our room was not ready yet and asked if we could return in an hour. My body felt like it was midnight, and yet the clock on the wall insisted it was nine in the morning. Okay. I steeled myself. One more hour. Sixty more minutes and then even I would have no problem falling asleep. Katie shrugged and said she was fine. She'd slept on the plane and only felt "a little floopy." I, on the other hand, hadn't slept a minute, and I felt as though I had been whacked on the head with a brick and the ground had transformed into a giant waterbed.

Soon Katie and I were seated at a small, round table in a café with textured black and mocha striped wallpaper and funky hot pink chandeliers. Small black-and-white photos with gold rococo frames graced the walls with an unevenly chic flair. A bored brunette wearing capri pants and five-inch stilettos handed us menus, saying nothing. Her pouty lips conveyed that she hoped to be Europe's next supermodel, but until then she would deign to serve coffee.

"What does this mean?" Katie asked, pointing to the menu. It was a picture of a coffee mug with steam coming off the top. Beside the image were French words, including *chocolat*. I confidently announced that it was hot chocolate and suggested we each have one and share a croissant. Inside, though, a certain reality sunk in: this child trusted that I knew what I was doing. She thought I understood what things meant and how they worked. I was the adult here. That couldn't be good.

Desperately wanting to assure Katie that I was in control of the situation, I boldly thanked our coltish server. "*Merci, mademoiselle*," I said as she set down our cups.

Fuck you, appeared to be her reply. Body language always translates perfectly.

Twenty minutes later, I got my second dose of reality. Katie and I walked to the Tuileries Gardens and spotted a Ferris wheel. Taking a ride seemed like a fun, carefree thing to do, but it had the opposite effect on me. As the cart rose, the Eiffel Tower came into view. I gasped, not with joy, but sheer terror. This was not a photo of the Eiffel Tower; it was the real deal. We were unquestionably, undeniably, irreversibly in Paris. What had I done?

What did you think was going to happen when you got on a plane to Paris? Of course the Eiffel Tower is here; of course the menus are in French. What part of this is unexpected?

By the time Katie and I arrived back at our hotel, it was two in the morning San Diego time. On the way from the café, I managed to get thoroughly lost, and our grandmotherly guide was nowhere to be found. When we finally arrived at the hotel, we rode up a small elevator, and I held onto the wall for balance. The bellman opened our door, showed us in, and I promptly ran to the toilet and vomited, then collapsed on the bathroom floor. As I was throwing up, I worried that the bellman was annoyed that I hadn't tipped.

Katie rubbed my back and suggested that we take a nap. My eyes were filled with tears and my nose was running from the violent return of breakfast. Feeling the cool tiles of the bathroom floor pressed against my cheek, I hoped to God that the maid service was thorough. "It's going to be okay, Mommy," Katie offered. "I have a good feeling about this trip. I know we're going to have a lot of fun."

"You do?"

She smiled and nodded.

"Based on *this*?"

I used to comfort my mother in the same way when we were living in a studio apartment in Greenwich Village in the seventies. My parents, Carol and Shelly, had the most amicable split in the history of divorce. Even after their break-up, my father drove my mother to events in whatever five-hundred-dollar car he owned at the moment. My favorites were the tomato red Ford Pinto that demanded chilled water every few hours and the mustard yellow AMC Gremlin with cardboard floor mats. He named the first vehicle Princess Ragu, which was also his pet name for my mother because of her highbrow aspirations. In turn, my mother tolerated him bathing in our tub when the water was shut off in whatever shithole apartment he was currently renting.

As my mother describes it, during their brief marriage, my dad just wanted to get high, stare at the fish tank, and have rambling philosophical conversations with other musicians. My mother, on the other hand, wanted to go to the ballet, finish her degree at NYU, and put down wall-to-wall carpet. Each confided in me that the other was a genuinely good person, but a little bit crazy. Both were right.

Though my mother landed a secretarial job almost immediately after the divorce, the move to our new apartment left her short on funds. She always said that if my father had a million dollars, he'd give us $950,000 of it, then blow his fifty grand on drugs. The problem was that my father never had more than a thousand dollars to his name, and my mother was worried about the rent. After I'd go to bed, I could hear her weeping at the kitchen table. At the sight of her six-year-old daughter, my mother stifled her tears, embarrassed she had been caught. "Don't worry, Mommy," I told her. "I'm going to help." Far from comforting her, my declaration only made her feel worse, though at the time I couldn't understand why.

The next day, I set out a blanket in front of the Quad Cinema across the street from our apartment building and sold everything I deemed unnecessary in our home. I got a dime for a copy of The Stepford Wives, fifty cents for our salt and pepper shakers, and three dollars for a pair of my mother's leather boots. I sold half-filled bottles of alcohol to the three winos who lived in the doorway across the street. A nice woman discreetly advised me against selling my mother's diaphragm.

My mother quietly accepted the money I earned, but

the effects echoed through our apartment for months as she would notice things missing. "Where are the…" she would begin to ask before remembering that I had sold the teacups. It was years before we ever had a full set of dishes. It was even longer before I witnessed her shed a tear again.

The week after my gypsy garage sale, basking in oblivious pride, I informed my mother that I had earned forty dollars selling raffle tickets in our building. "Jennifer, honey," my mother said tentatively, "what kind of prize are you planning to give away for this raffle?" When I looked at her quizzically, she explained that I couldn't just sell raffle tickets. There needed to be a drawing and a prize as well. I assured her she was wrong; no one had asked a thing about a prize. She insisted we go to the five-and-dime, buy a glass figurine, and give it to someone who had purchased a ticket. Since there were no ticket stubs, I had to draw from memory. We delivered a frosted glass swan to the guys in apartment 2G.

The following week, my mother and I were walking through Times Square when I noticed a skeletal black man in a green fedora engaging a crowd. A dozen people gathered around his table fashioned from a cardboard box, watching his fluid hands move three cards around the surface. The cards, all face down, were switched from one spot to the next and then another. The man's voice was hypnotic, promising that players who kept track of the queen of hearts would win fifty dollars. It looked so easy. The payoff was huge. "Let's play!" I urged my mother who held my hand tight.

"No one ever wins that game," my mother explained. "At the end of the day, that guy walks off with everyone's money."

I turned to her eagerly. "Then let's watch how he does it!"

"We're going to be late," my mother clipped and quickened her pace. As we turned the corner, she smiled brightly. "Did I mention that I got a raise at work?"

"You did?!"

"Yes, a very big raise, so I've got us covered from here."

Katie and I woke up fresh and ready to take on Paris. Unfortunately it was 11:00 p.m. We went downstairs to get dinner, but because we had been so lost earlier, my confidence was low. I was determined to stay within a block of our hotel. On the street corner, a woman who looked to be at least a thousand years old with a humped back greeted Katie and me. Her chin sprouted hair and her nose looked like a pickle. She wore a black hooded cape and held out knobby fingers that were made for delivering poisoned apples. I had no idea what she was saying, but she was clearly begging for money. She was telling her story with dramatic flair, her voice fluctuating brilliantly for effect. She wept; she beat her own chest.

I wondered where her breaking point was. Had she been born into the life of a street urchin and never managed to escape? Or did she once live on a quiet street and host ladies' bridge games? What went wrong? My heart beat faster with the realization that most of us were a few strokes of bum luck away from her fate. This woman was a few bad weeks away from the grave.

"Give her some money," Katie said, breaking my trance. "Stop staring and give her some money."

"Oh, right, of course," I jolted, then reached for my wallet.

The old woman thanked us with even more drama. She beat her chest again and moaned with gratitude.

After a few steps, Katie broke the silence. "That was really sad."

"No, she was a street performer," I insisted, swallowing hard. "You know how we see people in Balboa Park playing music for tips?"

"A street performer?" Katie asked.

"Yes, a street performer," I said, repeating silently, *red balloons, mimes, and baguettes.*

After a few moments of contemplating my proposal, Katie said, "I hate to break it to you, Mommy, but that was a homeless lady."

Hours later, Katie and I lay awake, weeping in our beds. Katie sobbed that she wanted to go home. She missed Daddy. I tickled her arm and told her everything was going to be fine. "We just have jet lag," I explained as tears rolled down my face in our darkened hotel room. I tried to keep my tone calm, but my heart ached because I knew she was right. I had made a huge mistake. She was too young for a trip like this. Maybe I wasn't up to the task, either.

"Are you crying, Mommy?"

"No, my nose is just a little stuffed."

As I assured Katie that we would be fine, another part of my brain was frantically devising a plan: we would stay in our hotel room for ten days, order room service, and soon enough it would be time to leave Paris. My mind was racing in tiny circles as I planned our lockdown. Our hotel became a fallout shelter in my mind. There was food in the lobby restaurant, running water, and even a minibar with soft drinks. We had books, a sketch pad, and crayons. If we got desperate, we could channel surf until we found American sitcoms with a laugh track and a thirty-minute resolution to all problems.

Katie and I rose at noon and felt a little better. My sanity was slowly starting to return, so I suggested that since we were in Paris, we should at least walk to the Louvre, which was only six blocks away. I looked at my map and realized it was a straight shot to the museum. Even I couldn't get lost. That evening, we would have dinner with my cousin Janine, whom I'd never met, her husband Bruno, and their miracle baby, Luca.

Janine was a war correspondent. After twenty years of writing from Bosnia, Chechnya, Somalia, Rwanda, Iraq, and dozens of war zones, she married a French photographer and settled in Paris. Before Katie and I left San Diego, Janine sent an email inviting us to her flat for dinner. She asked if we could bring instant oatmeal from the United States for Luca. These were small steps we could take. We could see the *Mona Lisa*. We could show up for dinner with a variety pack of Quaker Oats. I kept the option to quarantine in my back pocket, or more accurately, in my slash-proof travel purse with multiple safety locks.

The Louvre was magnificent, but my only impression of *Mona Lisa* was that someone really ought to clean the glass box protecting the masterpiece. My Windex trigger finger reflexively extended, wishing I could wipe away all the cloudy smudging.

"It's smaller than I thought," Katie said as we bobbed and weaved our heads in order to see through the four layers of tourists in front of us. Camera shutters crackled as people frantically snapped photos. I quickly remembered the camera in my purse and reminded Katie that this shot was a must. She shrugged and continued to look at the painting, shifting and tiptoeing as needed. After taking a dozen terrible photographs of the iconic painting, I glanced at Katie, who had finally found a spot with an unobstructed view of da Vinci's girl with the enigmatic smile.

"Do you want to take some pictures?" I asked, offering her the camera.

"I see it," she chirped.

"Not impressed?" I asked.

"I want to look at it for real."

I tucked my camera back in my purse. "You're right, it's not like we won't be able to find a good picture of *Mona Lisa* on a postcard," I said.

"Or Google," Katie said, not taking her eyes off the painting.

After moving to a different area of the museum, I sat on a black leather bench and Katie began to sketch the paintings. When she finally turned her picture for me to see, it was a portrait of me with a glowing halo around my head in Crayola gold. "Wanna know why Mama Lisa is smiling?" she asked.

"Why?"

"Because I just told her a joke," Katie replied.

I considered asking her about our sob-fest the night before. My bad instincts wanted to revisit and hyperanalyze to be sure that everything was now all right. Thankfully, I realized that this would likely have the opposite effect and refrained from launching a hand-wringing talk-a-thon. Katie was coloring at the Louvre. That was my answer.

I often fretted about whether or not Katie was enjoying her childhood, or if I was screwing up as a mother. On one level, I knew her life was nearly idyllic. She was well cared for and loved. Katie had everything she needed and much of what she wanted. She got to visit Paris, for God's sake! Still, I worried that somehow I wasn't doing enough. That

I wasn't enough. Or maybe I was doing too much and that I was overbearing. I judged myself mercilessly and grew terrified that, as she got older, Katie would too. My great fear was that at the very moment she decided I was a woefully inadequate mother, I would drop dead. Life had become a series of preemptive apologies for my transgressions, both real and imagined. Every year, I placed notes for her in a file cabinet so she could read them as an adult. Ostensibly they were annual updates about her life, but the subtext was very clear: I love you. I tried my best.

That evening, Katie and I arrived at Janine's home, a sprawling fifth-floor flat flooded with sunlight. The hardwood floors were covered with soft wicker rugs, and the white couches and seats were knotted cotton, comfy chic. At the dinner table, the adults sipped red wine from thin, bulbous glasses, trying to figure out how Janine and I were related. There were several branches of the family tree separating us, though we were somehow intertwined by our grandmothers. In the end, we decided "cousin" was a close-enough classification.

I caught her up on family gossip, and we giggled over how she could not translate the word "closure" for Bruno when I told her of our cousin's "severance" ceremony with her ex-fiancé. The couple had gone into the woods, (carefully) burned their marriage license, and told each other every reason why they weren't meant to be. "They needed to have a proper ending," Janine explained to her perplexed husband, a rugged-looking guy with three-day stubble on his face. Janine tried again. "They needed to talk about what went wrong and say their good-byes."

"Why?" Bruno asked, blowing a cloud of blue cigarette smoke.

"Because they wanted *closure*," Janine said.

"Thees ees silly."

Janine had a sexy Italian look with voluptuousness that extended to her wavy brown hair. She looked as if she might roll up her linen pants and romp through a fountain at any given moment. My cousin spoke with the indefinable accent of global nomads and laughed generously before suggesting that Katie and I come to the Alps with her family for the weekend. Bruno's eyes widened with the fear that we might accept.

Janine poured another glass of wine and opened the French windows—or, I guess, just windows—and I saw Paris unfolding at dusk. From the fifth-floor balcony, the city seemed manageable, even inviting. The height made Paris look almost as the map had promised. Directly in front of us was the Tuileries Garden with its orderly rows of bushes, elegant statues, and duck pond surrounded by grass and yellow blossoms.

Pointing at a narrow body of water, I asked, "Is that the Seine River?" Janine confirmed. I watched people walking on each side of the stone-lined riverbank and crossing small bridges. *Perhaps I could do that if I remember exactly where to turn to get back to the hotel.* "And is that the train station?" I asked of the mammoth structure with arched windows and a clock.

"That is the Musée d'Orsay," Janine told me. To the right a few miles, I saw the Eiffel Tower.

I know how to get to the Louvre, I silently assured myself. *So if I just cross that bridge over the river, I could also get to the Musée d'Orsay.*

As if reading my mind, Bruno asked for my map, offering to show me the best streets for people-watching. "What are all these marks?" he asked, examining the spots of color-coded masking tape dotting the map, marking the important sites. He barely refrained from rolling his eyes and began jotting pen marks on my map, telling me which streets were truly special and which were tourist traps. "To know Paris," Bruno began, pulling on his cigarette, "you need to relax, have a glass of wine, and enjoy life." Exhale. His smoke rose like a ghost.

Enjoy life? I thought about my travel notebook filled with essential sites. Beside each one was an empty box, which I would have the immense pleasure of checking once we visited them. How would I even know if I had succeeded in the task of enjoying life? When did I get to check that box? Did I get a new box every day, or did I have to sit uncomfortably with an unchecked box until the very end of the trip when I could properly assess whether I had or had not enjoyed life?

I explained to Bruno that I am an American mother and asked if he understood what that meant. I took my daughter to art school, piano lessons, and her doctor and dentist appointments. I regularly volunteered in Katie's classroom and chaperoned field trips. I coached her soccer team and even spent one year as a Girl Scout troop leader. When I wasn't shuttling Katie from one activity to the next, I was ordering in the enrichment classes like they were Chinese food. I hired a student at San Diego State University to be Katie's study buddy on Tuesday afternoons. I even hired a show-and-tell coach when Katie was in first grade. I was a model helicopter parent.

I wanted to parent (okay, micromanage) Bruno, though he was a few years my senior. When he lit his fifth cigarette of the night, I felt like telling him that smoking could kill him, but a combination of propriety and fear stopped me. Plus, my history with my father had proven that smokers never heed the admonitions of others.

The candle on the dinner table had burned to its final inch, and yellow wax had melted onto the rustic wood table. Janine shared how she and Bruno met while covering a war in Sarajevo. During their long careers, they had each dodged bullets and survived bombing raids that left others dead. Equally painful, they had been through multiple miscarriages. They had gone through several cycles of in vitro fertilization to produce Baby Luca, who now toddled about their beautiful home playing peek-a-boo with Katie. I knew if Janine and Bruno had survived all of this and still advised me to "enjoy life," it would be utterly pathetic to lock myself in a sterile hotel room while visiting Paris.

First, though, we had to make it out of Janine's apartment building. Ten minutes after we left Janine and a very restless Bruno, we were still struggling with the main door in the lobby. We pulled it, we pushed it. We twisted the knob and jiggled the gate and still couldn't get out.

"We're locked *in*?" Katie asked.

"I know, weird." I called upstairs to Janine's apartment, mortified to have to ask for her help. She and her husband had just shared horrific stories of escaping sniper's fire, and I couldn't manage to make it out the front door.

"See the button on the left?" Janine asked patiently.

I scanned the lobby, then saw a small red button. "I see a button with the word *porte*."

"That means door. Press the button and the door will open," Janine explained.

"I feel like a dolt," I told her.

"Don't," Janine said. "Now you know." I shuddered at the thought of Bruno's reaction when he heard about the American idiot who couldn't open a door. He would snort and say, "Enjoy life, but first leave the building!"

2

PARIS

N ow fully adjusted to Paris time, Katie and I started fresh the following day. Our first errand was to stop at the post office beneath the Louvre and mail a box of Nike sneakers that a soccer coach in San Diego had given us to send to his nephews in Bordeaux. I decided I would take my friend Maxime's advice and begin every conversation with an earnest attempt to speak the language. I had my phrase book and was determined that now we would fully embrace the French experience.

"*Bonjour!*" I announced to the postal clerk. Despite Maxime's confidence in my language skills, my ability to charade was really my stronger suit. I placed my hands at each side of the box, fluttered them like wings, and said, "*À Bordeaux, s'il vous plaît.*"

The older postal clerk looked down so I wouldn't see him

suppress a laugh. I opened my phrase book and inquired about the cost. He wrote the number on a sheet of paper. After we exchanged money and my friend's package sat safely among the other outgoing parcels, I felt a ridiculously giddy sense of accomplishment. I could send packages. I could open doors. I was practically French.

When we arrived at the Musée d'Orsay, security guards told us that there had been a bomb threat and the building was closed for the afternoon. A bomb threat?! I don't know what frightened me more: the fact that there could be a terrorist attack on a tourist site or the nonchalance with which he reported it. Others casually accepted the news and began making other plans. The handful of Americans stood agape, unaccustomed to announcements like this despite our national tragedy just four years earlier.

"We weel be open in three hours," the security guard announced, hoping to shoo off the last of the lingering Americans. I admired his optimism. We weren't so sure.

Though 9/11 has been our generation's greatest tragedy on American soil, it has been relatively infrequent that terror has threatened our shores. But those who don't make their home in the United States live with the constant reality of bomb scares. The differences in our life experiences were pronounced in our reaction to the announcement at the Musée d'Orsay. The Americans were immobilized; the others moved on.

I remember watching the Twin Towers being built in the 1970s. The steel skeletons soon became glistening twins, the tallest buildings in the world at the time. On the day of my grade school talent show, my best friend Rachel told my father and me that the World Trade Center had just opened its observation deck to the public. We begged him to take us and reminded him that his favorite restaurant in Chinatown was not far. My father could not resist two fifth graders who had just belted out Fleetwood Mac and now wanted a view from the top of the world. When we arrived, though, a security guard told my father he was not dressed appropriately for the observation deck. "We expect gentlemen to wear ties, or at the very least a jacket," he sniffed.

My father was genuinely baffled as he looked down at his chocolate suede jacket with sheepskin trim. "A *suit* jacket," the security guard clarified, glancing at Rachel and me.

"Like yours?" my father asked. My father was a larger-than-life character who had grown accustomed to being able to charm anyone into nearly anything. It never crossed his mind that he would have to disappoint Rachel and me.

"Yes, like—" the guard stopped himself. "Sir, you may not have my jacket."

My father gave him his trademark look, an impish grin that made people immediately feel it was the two of them against the world. "It would be a loan. We're about the same size," my father said, removing his newsboy cap and John Lennon specs.

"Sir, I cannot loan you my security jacket."

"Fifteen minutes, man?" he asked. "You've got your tie on. Tell your boss you got hot with the jacket."

The security guard's silence encouraged my father. "My daughter and her friend really want to see the observation deck. Do you have kids?"

"Two," he said.

"You know how it is, man. Come on, help a brother out."

"Fifteen minutes," the guard implored, removing his jacket.

"We'll check out the view and come right down," my father promised.

After two elevator trips that were as exciting as any ride at Coney Island, we reached the top. Rachel and I buzzed to each corner of the outside deck and looked down at Manhattan. "Look at Central Park, Daddy!" I shouted as we spotted the sprawling green rectangle. We ran to another spot.

"Check out the Statue of Liberty!" Rachel said. Noticing my father was not following us, we looked around for him. He was stationed by the entryway with his arms crossed, looking official and informing people where the restrooms were.

I looked to the right and saw the Eiffel Tower in the distance. We couldn't get lost if I simply followed the Tower. How far could it be?

As it turned out, it was quite a hike, albeit a lovely one filled with cobblestone streets dotted with cafés and bakeries. Katie said she was hungry, so we stopped at a restaurant to grab a bite. "Look at all the dogs!" she piped with delight. Four dogs rested at their owners' feet like old slippers. I checked to see if these men were wearing dark shades and holding red-tipped white canes, but not a one was blind. Nor did the dogs wear service bibs. No one seemed at all bothered that pets were joining us for lunch, yet when a young couple walked in with their baby, the restaurant patrons let out a collective groan. I did not hear the exchange between the parents and the waiter, but it ended with the young mother and father deciding to eat elsewhere. One of the dog owners smiled victoriously and offered a piece of his meat to his shaggy friend.

When I saw the waiter approaching our table with Katie's hamburger, I knew this would be a defining moment in our travels. The burger did not look like anything we had ever seen from our grill at home or In-N-Out Burger. Atop the meat patty rested a sunny-side-up egg peeking at her, as if to say, *Didn't expect me to look like this, did you, mademoiselle?* Katie raised her eyebrows. As I opened my mouth to tell her she could order something else, Katie shrugged and said, "I guess in Paris you get breakfast with your lunch."

With this, I knew Katie would be fine on our trip. She was blessed with an easygoing nature and I, as her mother, was the incredulous, grateful beneficiary. As an eight-year-old, I might have scowled at it for a few minutes before disdainfully removing the egg. And then I would have refused to eat any of it. When I tell my mother I don't deserve a child like Katie, she always agrees. "I was looking forward to watching your daughter put you through hell," my mother teases. Once my Aunt Bernice told me that if God only gives us what we can handle, he must not have much confidence in my parenting skills.

By the time Katie and I made it to the Eiffel Tower, its pinnacle was partially obscured in fog, and rain was falling lightly. We decided to return on a clear day and hopped across the bridge to the Museum of Modern Art.

I was amazed by the contrast of the exterior and interior of the modern art museum. The outside was vandalized with uninspired graffiti and smelled like urine. Sullen, pimple-faced boys in hoodies rode their skateboards down the steps.

Inside was an explosion of colorful, dynamic political art, some of it criticism of the war in Afghanistan. One did not need an art history degree to see that Bush was regarded as the spawn of Satan here. His horned image appeared beside American flags that strangled cats. Other pieces captured different slices of political history. A life-sized statue of Angela Davis with a rifle and platform shoes was constructed from sparkling beads. A spaceship built from distressed crates hung from the ceiling with Soviet flags shooting from where flames would normally be.

Later, Katie picked up a pink beret in a shop and joined the ranks of aspiring artists in Paris. She brought a sketch pad to the Rodin Garden and drew *The Thinker* with a toilet beneath his bottom. The following day, she joined a group of art students who lined the floor at the Picasso Museum. A French woman eyed Katie's sketch of Pablo's cubist goat and raised her eyebrow at me.

She yours? her chin-nod asked.

My smile confirmed.

Not bad, she grinned before moving on, clacking her high heels against the floor.

Like all French women, the chin-nodder was beautiful, and not just because she had taken a moment to acknowledge my child. It wasn't that French women were more genetically gifted than their American counterparts, but they were always perfectly turned out and knew how to take one fabulous item and work it. It could be pistol high heels, a belt made of handcuffs, or a lavender crocodile purse, but most often it was a scarf. I studied the scarves wrapped around necks and heads, hoping I could recreate the effect. When a woman at a shop showed me how to tie the scarf, I looked positively chic. When I tried to follow the same instructions on my own, I looked like a cheap fortune-teller.

On our walk from the Picasso Museum, Katie and I passed what looked like a traditional French bakery, with enormous windows rimmed by black wood with gold letters that read *Boulangerie*. Two windows revealed not bread and pastries, however, but a bold and artistic hotel lobby. I grabbed Katie's hand and wandered into the Hôtel du Petit Moulin. Turns out the boutique hotel used to be a bakery but was now appointed with elegantly beaded lamps, brightly colored misshapen tables, billowing drapery, and a couch with various animal print pillows. All of this was set against the backdrop of a funky mural that rivaled anything we had seen in a museum.

The concierge told us that the hotel had recently been redesigned by Christian Lacroix, which explained why the two women in the lobby looked as though they were straight off the pages of *Vogue*. Typically I'd feel intimidated by a setting like this, nervous that I might break something, or worse, that people would sense I was out of my element, but desire trumped fear and I wanted to see more. This place was for people who knew how to enjoy life, and I wanted nothing more than to check in that day and treat it as my very own finishing school. I asked for a brochure, which seemed like a more genteel way of asking for the room rates.

"That table looks like a chess rook," Katie said of a piece in citrus green.

The concierge smiled and handed me a high gloss, four-color booklet with a delicate slice of onion paper that listed the room prices in fancy script. I had already braced myself not to flinch and planned to nod confidently as though the prices all seemed quite reasonable.

Much to my surprise, they *were* reasonable. Not reasonable for this trip, because the room at our hotels.com supersaver lodge was non-refundable. But the price was only around double what we were paying at Le Chain du Paris, not six times our current rate, which is what I had expected.

"Would you care to see the rooms?" the concierge asked. Moments later we were touring the eclectic mix, decorated like modern art museums, planetariums, and sloped-ceiling Parisian flats.

"*Merci beaucoup.*"

I now boldly spoke sloppy French wherever we went, borrowing simple phrases from people who answered my simple questions. On a Metro platform, two young women asked me for directions in French. *Oh my God!* I shrieked internally. *I understand enough of the words to figure out what they want. And I know the four words that will answer their question.* I answered, using exaggerated gestures just in case my remedial French didn't do the job.

"Shit, did you understand her?" the young woman asked her friend in English. "She was talking too fast for me."

"Are you Americans?!" I asked.

"Omigod!" She laughed. "Let's do this in English then, shall we?"

We laughed much harder than the situation warranted, a release of tension built up from not knowing what the hell is going on, then realizing that there are others who were in the same boat. The girls had just arrived in Paris that morning and asked if we wouldn't mind giving them some advice. We told them not to turn up their noses at the one-hour cruise up the Seine River as I had done for our first few days. Yes, it was touristy as hell, but Katie and I fell in love with it and treated ourselves to at least one ride every evening.

The Seine River cruises quickly became one of our two evening rituals in Paris. The motor of the boat purred like a kitten and lulled us into the night. The Paris skyline scrolled beside us on each side, enveloping us in its magic. "We still need to climb the Eiffel Tower," Katie announced as we rode past it. The second ritual was calling William so he could tell Katie a goodnight story. I imagined him in his white shirt and tie, closing his office door and taking off his suit jacket. "Then what happened?" Katie asked. "No way!" They laughed for nearly a half hour until Katie's questions became less frequent and her voice stopped completely. Thankfully, William had purchased an overseas calling plan to keep these marathon sessions at just a few dollars.

"How's it going?" William asked when Katie fell off.

"The only bad thing is missing you."

People often asked why William didn't join us on our travels. One day he will, and it will be wonderful. But he has a solo law practice and cannot get away to Europe even for a week. There are too many weddings and family reunions that eat away at his travel time. Plus, he's been all over the world already, so for now it's just Katie and me. Another wife might wait until William could come along, but my game clock is ticking. If I had known my father's was too, I would have stowed away in his duffel bag and joined him in Europe for a summer.

My father spent about half of his time in Europe pursuing his music career, and my mother did not allow overseas travel with him. I can't say I blame her. As much as he loved me, it would've been only a matter of days before he mistakenly left me at a hash bar in Amsterdam, his favorite of all cities.

Holland was the country of my father's greatest career success. His song "Only a Fool" went gold and ranked number three in the 1970s, beating the John Travolta–Olivia Newton-John duet "You're the One That I Want" from the movie *Grease*. His writing partner Norman tells me that today the song has been covered more than sixty times and has been translated into dozens of languages.

The only overnight visit I had with my father was a weekend in the Catskill Mountains when I was twelve years old. This part of New York typically evokes images of young Woody Allen and Joan Rivers doing their shtick at Borscht

Belt comedy clubs. This was not the case at the Sunshine Ranch, which was owned by my father's friends Morgan and Gayle. Their eight hippie houseguests described the couple as "together" because they owned a hair salon and had auto insurance. As business owners, they could have been labeled bourgeoisie, or worse, establishment. But Morgan and Gayle were members of the tribe and therefore spared of any such judgment.

They were a groovy bunch, a joint passing among them as they sunbathed nude by a small, marshy lake and talked politics, discussed music, and dissected various conspiracy theories. Some guy who called himself Treetop sat Indian-style strumming his guitar, his flaccid penis peeking out from underneath like a snail from its shell. I tried to avert my eyes, but my curiosity got the better of me. I hadn't seen such a wide variety of genitals since my friend Vickie and I leafed through her mother's copy of *Our Bodies, Ourselves*.

I primly set out a beach towel and declined the offer to remove my black Danskin leotard that doubled as a swimsuit. There was nothing sexual about their nudity; it was more like an adult version of *Free to Be You and Me*. Still, I wondered why no one questioned whether any of this was appropriate for a twelve-year-old. Before I had a chance to ponder this, the joint came my way. I held out my hand to decline. "I'm trying to cut down," I told Treetop. *And also, I'm twelve.*

My dad explained to his friend that I was "straight." He

used this label with a neutral tone, but it felt like an apology. His words yearned for mitigation.

I quickly made myself the life of the party. I may not get high, but I could pose confusing questions just like they did. I asked the group if they thought it was possible that Jimmy Carter's family was behind Elvis's death. Something to do with peanut rights on Graceland. People tilted their heads to listen to me while I pulled ideas out of thin air. I was in compensation mode, the routine that William calls my *Please Love Me Show*.

The hippies told me I was incredibly deep and complex, stifling back coughs from their last hit. Inside the house, Gayle, a Cher-like goddess, sought my assistance cleaning the bale of weed that was needed for the weekend. We stood at a table made from a barn door under a rainbow-colored parachute that hung like a cloud from the ceiling. Gayle taught me how to break up the buds and gently shake the seeds out onto a sheet of newspaper. She told me I was really good at cleaning grass but was clearly disappointed when my little fingers were incapable of rolling a decent joint. "Don't worry about it," she said, but I hated that I couldn't satisfy her. Gayle was a hairstylist who looked like it had been a decade since her last trim, with wavy brown locks that touched her beaded belt. She was counter-culture glamorous with feather earrings and bits of red bandana patching the knees of her jeans. When she wore shoes, they were suede-fringed clogs.

As a reward for helping with grass prep, Gayle took me horseback riding on their sprawling property. I had been riding for years, but this was the first time I went bareback; Gayle insisted that saddles and reins were oppressive, so I held tight to the horse's mane, secured by only my legs, and hoped this would be like the lessons my mother scrounged to afford. I was accustomed to riding in a groomed corral where the dress code was tan jodhpurs, white tops, and black velvet hard hats with chin guards. Gayle didn't even bother with a bra.

I gasped with delight when I saw a poster announcing that an American gospel choir was performing at Sainte-Chapelle, a church in Paris. Katie was too young to remember our first time hearing gospel music, when I took our family to an African-American church in San Diego. It was near Christmas and my mother was visiting from New York; our family represented four of maybe ten white faces in the large congregation. Though my mother is vampirically pale, she is able to fit in anywhere because of her willingness to simply jump in and become part of the scene, especially when hats and drama are involved. Within twenty minutes, she was shouting things like "Teach!" and "Amen!" When the reverend asked anyone who had been moved by the spirit of the Lord to please stand and come to the front of the church, she was the first to stand and begin making her way out of the pew.

"Where are you going?" I asked my mother, who had recently told us that her guru said Jesus walked to India and lived on an ashram with his wife before returning for his crucifixion.

"To the front of the church," she replied a tad smugly, as if she had been hand-selected.

"They're going to try to save you, Carol," William whispered.

"From what?"

"For God's sake, sit down, Mother."

Since Katie had no memory of this, I explained it to her on the way to the performance.

Parisians do gospel differently.

As the choir of purple-robed American singers took the stage, they greeted the audience in French. Then in English. When the choirmaster asked the audience to get on our feet and start clapping, we rose up obediently with the other half-dozen Americans. We had now been in Paris a week and could spot our fellow countrymen with ease: white sneakers and the ready smile were telltale signs.

The choirmaster barked in French, and reluctantly people began to rise and clap halfheartedly.

I felt conflicted. I wanted to clap along so the gospel choir would feel appreciated but didn't want to call attention to myself as one of a handful of rubes echoing the words to

"When the Saints Come Marching In." I looked at Katie, who was clapping her hands and bending her knees without an ounce of self-consciousness. She smiled at me.

"This is fun, Mommy. But no one is fainting," as I had promised.

"Get down on the ground!" the choirmaster sang rhythmically, then translated it into French. People began to murmur among themselves. They figured they were already being good sports with this standing and clapping nonsense.

A French woman beside me said to her friend that this man was crazy if he thought she was going to get down on the ground. "This is Chanel," she said in French, gesturing to her elegant suit.

By the following evening, Katie's enthusiasm for museums waned and she needed a playground like a monkey needs trees. When we arrived at Luxembourg Gardens, Katie's eyes gleamed at the giant rope web, the jungle gym, and the slides. Although it was past closing time and the gates to the playground were locked, four families romped about. "How?" I asked in French. "How you are here?"

A father who looked like he might have fit in well at Gayle and Morgan's Sunshine Ranch told me to hop the fence. "It is goot," he told me, speaking English with a German accent.

"We jump fence," he said, gesturing to the group. His wife, a petite woman with a mass of armpit hair peeking from her green tank top, joined him at the fence.

"Ah yes, we all jump over the fence when park closes. Eet ees what ees done," she said. Her French accent made her words more assuring. She knew the customs. Plus, there were three other families with them. Surely this was okay.

I looked at Katie, whose face was pressed against the gate like a prisoner watching a parade. "Do you want to hop the fence?" I asked.

"Will we get in trouble?" Katie asked.

"These people say it's okay."

The couple that I will forevermore think of as Gunther and Marie helped Katie over the fence, where she hit the ground running. She climbed the rope spider's web with the other children. After my more laborious entry over the iron gate, I smiled proudly. I had done it. I was in Paris doing as the French did. I was enjoying life!

Ten minutes later, our group was in a small room at a nearby police station about to be booked for trespassing. I was terrified, but Marie was irate, yelling at the officer in French at an incomprehensible speed. She slammed her fist on the desk, threw her hands in the air, and stomped her foot. The officer remained expressionless and continued smoking as he filled out our citations. I noticed a slice of baguette and cheese on a plate next to his ashtray and nervously whispered to Katie, "What, no wine?"

The tension broke. At least among the prisoners. Inspector Clouseau was not amused. "You know I speak Engleesh?" he said, raising an eyebrow.

"*Pardon, pardon*," I offered.

We are screwed!

"I *never* drink wine while serving my job!" he barked.

"*D'accord, d'accord*," I offered. "*Je suis* kidding. Um...*keeding, ze joke, ha ha,* like Jerry Lewis. *C'est bon,* Jerry Lewis?"

Clouseau looked tired of me, of all of us. He quickly scanned the room and concluded that he had neither the time nor energy to issue a dozen separate citations. He looked at Marie and spoke in rapid-fire French. She told us we were free to go. "He says that if any of us ever do the smallest wrong in Paris again, we will go to jail," she translated. We all nodded obediently and scurried from the station.

The following day, Katie and I found the Shakespeare and Company bookstore on the Left Bank across the river from Notre Dame. On rue de la Bûcherie, at the edge of the Latin Quarter, stood a seventeenth-century monastery that housed Europe's largest collection of English language books for sale.

New and used books lined every wall, cluttered and haphazardly organized. A mirrored wall included photos of authors who had visited, including Henry Miller, Anaïs

Nin, and Allen Ginsberg. A cat snuggled in the corner under a corkboard listing literary events and readings. It was a cozy haven that made me long for a pot of tea and a thunderstorm.

Painted over a threshold of the three-story bibliophilic heaven were the words "Be not inhospitable to strangers, lest they be angels in disguise." Discreetly placed in the landscape was evidence that Shakespeare and Company lived this philosophy. Small cots, bedrolls, pillows, and backpacks were tucked between bookshelves.

"Do people sleep here?" Katie asked the clerk, who was about twenty years old with Bettie Page bangs, a vintage dress, and Doc Marten Mary Janes. I imagined her name was something like Prudence or Cleo.

In a posh British accent, Cleo explained that travelers were welcome to sleep at the bookstore if they worked a few hours during the day. These guests were endearingly called "Tumbleweeds" and could stay anywhere from a few nights to several months.

Tapping on her computer, Cleo continued, "Or, if you're a writer, you can stay as our guest in the studio."

"My mom's a writer!" Katie exclaimed, standing on the toes of her white sandals. "Google her."

Katie's face begged for the sleepover.

Fear of dying young isn't an altogether bad thing. Sometimes it makes you try what you might otherwise delay.

I found myself agreeing to Katie's requests, justifying that my indulgence would solidify fond memories.

"Check-in is at midnight," Cleo told us before returning to her work.

At the appointed hour, Katie and I sat on a bench next to a half-dozen disaffected youth with pierced faces and unnaturally black hair. Their stained canvas backpacks sported logos of bands with names like Blistered Anus.

"Ouch," Katie commented to a fellow Tumbleweed.

"They're crap since they lost their drummer," he returned in a sweet English accent.

In her pigtails and bedazzled tank top, Katie shrugged. "That can happen." She had absolutely no idea about how a change of musician could affect a group, but pursed her lips as though she'd been through it a few times herself. I admired her immediate acceptance of and connection to life around her.

Another mother and her young daughter knocked on the locked door, apologizing for being late for check-in. Looking like characters from *Les Misérables*, the mother and barefoot Cosette explained they lost track of time in the Bastille Day festivities.

As we were shown to the Writer's Studio, I had three thoughts about spending the night in the same bed where Henry James slept. One, they hadn't changed the sheets since. Two, Katie's bed was actually a yoga mat on top of a door that was resting on two file cabinets. These cabinets, I should add, were not of equal height. And three, Andy Griffith looked awfully young on that box of Ritz crackers in the corner.

A tornado of gnats came from the water spigot. Our window did not open more than a few inches. The room was situated directly above a row of trash receptacles.

Katie squealed with delight, "We have a view of Notre Dame!"

I, on the other hand, just smelled hot garbage. "Don't touch a thing!" I warned Katie.

"Isn't this the best, Mommy?"

After fifteen minutes, I decided it was time to return to our hotel room.

I tried to wake Katie, but after a full day, she was down for the count. "Katie, wake up," I said in full volume. "Katie, honey, you need to get up."

Who was this alien I had produced? Like her father, she could easily drift off to sleep and slumber through the night. Didn't they count worries? Didn't they imagine their fondest dreams coming true? Weren't they afraid that if they lost control, something terrible might happen?

For as long as I can remember, it's taken me at least an hour to fall asleep, although I never realized this was unusual until my first year at sleep-away summer camp. As I lay in my bed at six years old, I heard my cabin mates' breathing change as they fell asleep. By the second week, I could identify the sound of each friend drifting off. There went Vickie. Off went Kim. Debbie and I were always last, but she would still drop off a good half hour before I even felt drowsy. None of these girls seemed to be creatively visualizing their goals. My mother insisted on this practice long before the first book by Shakti Gawain showed up in our apartment. In the early seventies, she hung glass beaded curtains and displayed framed pictures of Indian gurus. My mother said that if, right before falling asleep, I could see a clear image of my heart's desire, it would manifest by spiritual magic. This was a comforting thought for my mother, but for me it was the beginning of lifelong sleep problems.

It was more than creative visualization that kept me up nights, though. I saw newspaper headlines that made me painfully aware of the myriad of possible disasters that could happen. There was no more vulnerable place to be than unconscious in a bed. I never feared that bad people would confront me when I was selling teacups alone on the sidewalk, but asleep I was easy prey.

Even the Angel of Death knew sleep was a good time for a hit. My Catholic grandmother, Aggie, made me say prayers before sleep. To me, the rote lines were no more meaningful than a game of Pat-a-Cake, but I stopped in my tracks the first time I really heard the line "If I die before I wake." I looked at my grandmother, who was kneeling at the other end of her bed we were about to share. An enormous crucifix hung from the otherwise stark wall behind her. "I could *die* before I wake?" I asked her.

"If that's God's plan."

"I don't like that plan," I protested. "I'm six, why would God plan for me to die?" Grandma Aggie shushed me and kept up her rapid murmur of prayer. "I think I want to be Jewish like Daddy's side of the family. I've never heard of their God letting a kid die."

My grandmother opened a single eye. "I had you baptized when you were a baby, you're Catholic, there's no undoing it. Your parents don't know about it and we're going to keep it that way. But just so you know, you're Catholic so you'd better say your prayers."

"I don't want to be Catholic!" I protested. "I don't like Catholic God. He has plans where children die." I looked at the crucifix behind her and remembered my grandmother explaining that Jesus was the son of God. And there *he* was, hanging from a cross with nails in his hands and feet. Catholic God meant business.

"Mommy said I could choose my religion, and I'm going to be Jewish. Their God seems nicer."

"Next time you're at your Aunt Bernice's Passover Seder, pay attention to the part where God sends an angel to kill all the Egyptian babies. God has his reasons for killing children, but he doesn't do it very often. Besides, you're baptized, Jennifer, so there's nothing you can do about it." She smiled gently and began, "Our Father, who art in heaven." After a few minutes of prayer, Grandma Aggie crawled into bed and drifted to sleep effortlessly.

I watched my grandmother in bed that night, wondering how she could just surrender to slumber, especially knowing about God's sneaky plans for killing us in our sleep. I wondered the same thing about the girls at camp.

Often I'd drift into a state of semi-conscious light sleep where I wasn't quite sure if I was awake or dreaming. Sometimes in the morning at Camp St. Regis, I'd share stories with my cabin mates. "I had the weirdest dream last night," I began. "Our counselors had boys visit in the middle of the night and they were giggling and smoking and—" I was quickly interrupted by our head counselor, Mary, who told me that my dream was not polite breakfast conversation.

I was also struggling to fall asleep one night in summer camp when I heard my father's voice burst through the door. "Is she okay? Is Jennifer in the hospital?" he asked, panicked. This was an impossible scenario, though, because my father had been in London since April.

"Hospital? Why would Jennie be in the hospital?" Mary asked.

Then my eyes popped open. *Oh no. He didn't fly back from England because of my letter, did he?*

About ten days earlier, I had been dealt the biggest blow in all of my six years. The camp was putting on a production of *The Wizard of Oz* and there was no doubt in my mind that I would be cast as the Wicked Witch of the West. No one could cackle like me. I got daily requests from other campers—and even counselors—to cackle like a witch. As a bonus, I curled my hands menacingly, promising that I'd get that Dorothy and her mangy little dog. Stella Adler herself would have said I was fully committed to the role. Everyone assumed I would play the witch, no one more than I, who secretly knew I held superpowers like Samantha on *Bewitched*.

When the cast list was posted, I was stunned. I was to play the Mayor of Munchkinland? How could this be? The director explained that fourteen-year-old Dorothy was five feet five inches tall. How would the audience believe that she was frightened by four-foot me?

Was this guy out of his mind? Dorothy and the witch didn't do hand-to-hand combat. The witch had magical powers and cast spells. She rode a flying broom while Dorothy had to skip down a yellow brick road. The witch had monkeys to do her bidding. She could be two feet tall and scary as shit. Just look at trolls. Or leprechauns. I explained this to the director, but he remained unmoved. He said it was an honor to be the Mayor of Munchkinland because it meant the other Munchkins had elected me. I stormed out and launched the greatest political campaign of my life. Within hours, I had allies who were willing to negotiate on my behalf. Even the cast Wicked Witch signed my petition. Since it was letter-writing day, I decided to tell my father about what had just happened and how I was starting a hunger strike until this situation was remedied. No justice, no peas.

I dropped my letter in the green wooden mailbox outside the mess hall and proceeded in for dinner where macaroni and cheese was being served. My hunger strike was over.

The next day, the director said he'd given the matter more thought and written a new part called the Little Witch. I was to play the Wicked Witch of the West's younger cousin who was visiting Oz from down south. "Can you do a southern accent?" he asked.

"Why goodness gracious, yes," I said, delighted. "Do I get to cackle?"

"Yes," he replied.

The next week, all was forgiven. I was even helping paint sets, trying to prove to the director that I was a team player.

I still had smatterings of yellow brick road on my fingers the night I heard my father's voice in Cabin One. "Why would Jennie be in the hospital?" the counselor asked. I closed my eyes tight, wishing I were asleep like the rest of my friends. *Holy crap, he flew back from England over this.* Thankfully my father sounded relieved when he heard the story. I came out to the counselor's room in my Holly Hobby nightgown and stared at my dad, whom I hadn't seen in four months. Beside him were two grocery bags filled with my favorites, things my mother would never buy, like Cap'n Crunch, Hershey Bars, and Tang.

"That was a hell of a hunger strike, Gandhi," he said with a laugh.

"I'm sorry," I said.

"It was time for me to come home, I guess," he said.

Early the following morning, Quasimodo rang the bells of Notre Dame, jarring Katie and me from our beds—or in Katie's case, her door. Her face was covered with dirt. Next to me were three fresh rodent turds. We couldn't get out fast enough.

We raced through the narrow, cobblestone streets of the Latin Quarter. Restaurant staff swept broken white plates and poured buckets of water on the streets to rinse away the sins of the past evening's festivities. "Can we get some chocolate bread?" Katie asked as we passed a bakery with a yellow awning.

"Yes, yes, of course," I said, stopping. This wasn't a Bruce Willis action flick where we had to escape from the filthy bookstore. We just had to close the door behind us and wipe the soot off Katie's cheek. I ordered a cup of coffee and stopped for a moment to see a truly amazing sight: a tourist area absolutely barren. This only happens before seven in the morning. Remembering Bruno's advice about enjoying life, we lingered and absorbed the scene across the street. Though I could not understand the words, a younger waiter was clearly sharing his exploits with the restaurant owner, who seemed proud of his protégé Lothario. Exhausted, they finally sat at a table outside and lit cigarettes.

When Katie and I arrived at our hotel at seven-thirty, our hotel concierge couldn't help tease. "*Bonjour, madame et mademoiselle,*" he lilted, giving us the raised-eyebrow once-over. It was then I caught my first glance of myself in the hotel lobby mirror. I looked like an ad for the morning-after pill.

"I realize how this seems," I said sheepishly.

He grinned and told me I owed him no explanations. I half expected him to wink and tell me that what happens in Paris stays in Paris.

On our final day in Paris, I promised Katie that we would go to the top of the Eiffel Tower no matter how long the line was. If it was raining, so be it. Nothing was going to stop us.

"We're climbing to the top, right?" Katie asked, craning her neck to see the tip.

"Of course. First we take an elevator up and then we climb the last few flights to get to the very top."

Katie shook her head with disapproval. "No, we need to climb all the way."

"From the ground?" I gasped.

Noting my reluctance, Katie assured me, "It's like a French StairMaster. You can do it."

"How many flights is that thing?" I asked, now as disgusted with the landmark as any self-respecting Parisian.

Katie shrugged, then pointed to it. "It's *that* many flights."

Great. Sometimes Katie appears to be the Dalai Lama in pigtails and it doesn't always work out so well for me.

I kept up with Katie's bouncy pace to the first platform. I was breathless and sweaty when we arrived at step 347, but I was there, if not enjoying life, then at least surviving. I suggested we stop and look at the panoramic view of Paris, as the details would start to fade as we reached the top. We looked at the rows of white buildings ornately adorned with arches, vaults, domes, and rococo. The city was an architectural pastry shop. Rows of sugary white apartment buildings lined the streets adorned with what looked like marzipan gargoyles. Rooftops were frosted with copper; red blossoms spilled from window boxes like sprinkles.

We looked down to see a soccer match being played in the field beside the Seine River. An expanse of lawn and neat green rows of hedges opened to a circular path then continued into a tree-lined corridor to the military academy, a wedding cake of a building.

As we climbed to the next platform, hundreds of other tourists passed, trotting in couples and packs. Every nation on earth was represented on the stairwell of the Eiffel Tower. In our climb of a thousand stairs, we crossed paths with a tall German family with wheat-colored hair and Birkenstock sandals. The parents seemed to be scolding their three boys to stop running so fast. An orderly row of Asian women ascended. A Middle Eastern couple called their children's names as they zoomed past us, the youngest boy in surfing shorts. It was like the Security Council on casual Friday.

When we reached the top, my heart was racing from the workout. Katie ran to the edge and pressed her face through the guardrail like a dog on a car ride. She was lost in the moment with her eyes half-closed.

I remembered looking out from the top of the Twin Towers with my best friend Rachel and longed for the days when I had no checklists and when building security was loose. Bruno's advice snapped me back to reality. Here I was in Paris with my eight-year-old daughter, and it was wonderful. Someday I would be nostalgic about this, so I'd better have the good sense to enjoy the present.

"Come look," Katie urged.

I joined her at the rail and looked down at the neoclassic Arc de Triomphe and the rambling Champs-Élysées. In the distance, we saw the white-domed Sacré-Coeur perched on a hill. It was like a queen waving at us from afar, aloof yet so beautiful you could not help but fall in love.

Katie smiled widely as the Paris breeze blew her hair back.

"Are you cold?" I asked. "Do you need your jacket?"

She didn't answer, simply grinning widely and shaking her head. "Wow," she said.

"I know, isn't it stunning?"

"I get it now, Mommy."

I knit my brows, seeking explanation.

"I get it," Katie said. "I get Paris."

3

LONDON

Before Katie and I left for Europe, a neighborhood parent told me that when traveling from Paris to London, we simply *must* go first class on the train that connects both cities. I've always hated the class system, not only because it is elitist, but also because I've never been quite sure where I fit. My mother had upper-deck aspirations while my father was firmly rooted in steerage.

When I was in first grade, my mother brought home a new boyfriend and announced we were all going to dinner together. She'd been on dates but until then had never included me, so I knew she was serious about this new man.

Back then, my mother was working as a secretary at the *New York Times* and sported a distinctly Mary Tyler Moore look. Her hair was silky brown with auburn highlights and flipped just above her shoulder. But unlike Mary with her one blue beret, my mother began a collection of elegant hats that belied our economic reality. Her new boyfriend seemed like something out of a movie, not because he was particularly handsome, but I'd never seen a man wearing a suit and tie when it wasn't a special occasion. The men in our family wore ties for weddings, christenings, and Passover Seders, but never for Thursday dinner at an Italian restaurant. Joseph was a sweet guy who was clearly smitten with my mother. That I came with the package was neither an asset nor a deterrent to him.

Later that week, at the end of our Sunday visit, my father told me he was craving spaghetti, so I excitedly shared that I had discovered a great new place. "Mommy's new boyfriend took us there. It's delicious!" I reported. I told him about the variety of shapes of pasta and seven different sausages the restaurant offered. I recalled the mind-blowing sauces that were a blend of several different cheeses. Our waiter proudly rattled off their names, but all I could retain at that age was the word "cheese."

"Carol's got a boyfriend?" my father asked. "Nice guy?"

Deciding to accentuate the groovy, I omitted the part about Joseph wearing a tie and told my father that my mother's new boyfriend had a car with a peace sign on it. "Doesn't sound like the kind of guy Princess Ragu would want, but good for her if she's happy."

When my father and I walked into the restaurant I'd been to a few nights earlier, we were engulfed in red-and-gold wallpaper. The back wall was covered entirely with gold-flecked mirror tiles, and a large fountain fashioned after *The Birth of Venus* marked the center of the dining room.

The host was pleasant enough, but there was none of the fanfare I had received a few nights earlier. There were no effusive handshakes and deferential greetings for my father. Another man welcomed us with stoic tolerance and showed us to a table. My father tentatively sank into a plush velvet chair as a busboy rushed to fill our glasses with icy water and placed a basket of warm bread on the table. My father must have jolted when he opened the menu, because I heard the wood sole of his clog hit the metal leg of the table.

"Don't touch a thing," he said.

"Why?" I laughed, reaching for the warm cloth napkin draped over the bread.

He reached across the table and grabbed my hand. "I'm not kidding, don't put your hands on anything. Not the bread, not the water, nothing."

"How come?"

"Listen to me, we need to get out of here," he whispered like my partner in crime. "I know a better place for spaghetti. I want to take you there instead."

"But we're already here."

"When I count to three, we're going to get up and leave, okay?" My father's eyes darted around the restaurant. "Okay, three."

As we drove across the Brooklyn Bridge, my father lit a cigarette and inquired about Joseph. "Where exactly is the peace sign on his car?"

"On the hood," I told him. "It's shiny silver and sticks up right on the front, like he's saying 'peace, everybody.'"

"He's not saying *peace*, Jennifer, he's saying *Mercedes Benz*."

"Why would he say *Mercedes Benz*?"

My father didn't answer. A half hour later, we were eating spaghetti in a restaurant in a neighborhood that later served as the setting for *Saturday Night Fever*. Girls walked down the wide boulevard wearing satin roller-skating jackets and full palettes of eye shadow. The restaurant my father chose had a cutesy name, like Tony's Macaroni. Though it was packed, a waitress noticed my father immediately and greeted him with a hearty "Ay!" She teetered over in patent leather heels and stamped his cheek with lipstick. Tables with red-and-white gingham cloth and wine bottle vases covered the sloped floor. When the kitchen doors swung open, we could hear cooks angrily shouting in Italian at each other.

"Listen, Jennifer, I can't take you to high-class places like your mother's new boyfriend," my father explained as he tucked a white napkin into the collar of his T-shirt. "See this?" My father pointed to the right column of the menu. "These are called prices. If you eat at a restaurant with your mother and Richie Rich and the main dishes cost more than three dollars, don't take me there. Those places aren't for guys like me."

Since then, I've always turned up my nose at class designations, especially in travel where they blatantly, unapologetically separate customers into first class, business, and peasant. When boarding airplanes, I'd purposefully avoid eye contact as I walked past the passengers already comfortably seated in the front. Sometimes I would put on a haughty air, as if I pitied them in their wide seats with wine and magazines while I got to keep it real in coach. No one ever noticed my preemptive snub, but it gave me some satisfaction knowing that if these strangers deigned to glance my way, they wouldn't see a look of envy.

When my friend in San Diego suggested buying first-class tickets on the train, I told her Katie and I would be fine in coach.

"Are you crazy?" she asked. "It's summer; you might not even get to sit down in second class. First class is air-conditioned. You'll get a guaranteed seat and a lovely meal. For God's sake, it's not much more." Noting my hesitation, she added, "Do you really want Katie sitting on the floor in a ninety-degree compartment? It's like twenty bucks more, for God's sake. Live a little."

We couldn't afford a five-star hotel, but I could swing a few extra euros for a better train seat, so I took my friend's advice and upgraded. The thought of what just one deodorant-free man could do to a train compartment pushed me over the edge. Plus, it wasn't as though my father ever held poverty as some great virtue; he was just broke. Whenever the finer things in life were offered to him, he gladly accepted—and stuffed a little extra in his pockets for later.

Still, standing on the first-class platform to board the train, I felt sheepish and apologetic, as Katie and I stood separate from the rest. Before I could wring my hands over this, Katie shrieked. She had spotted a man dressed as a wizard selling the latest Harry Potter book in English, which had been released just ten hours earlier. "I thought I would have to wait until London to buy it," Katie said, walking toward the wizard as if pulled by magnetic force. She reached into her pocket and began unfolding her slim stash of bills for the wizard.

"Didn't you preorder the book?" I asked.

"Yeah," Katie replied, wondering why I was still talking and delaying her transaction.

"We'll be home in a few weeks. Can't you read it then?"

She looked incredulous. "I can hardly wait till we get on this train. I'm using my own money."

"It just seems wasteful to buy it twice."

The conductor announced that first-class passengers could now board the train.

"This is the single most important book on the planet," she said earnestly. A line of like-minded people was forming behind us. The wizard looked at me and smiled as if to say, *Just buy the kid the book*. He was right. If I were going to embrace and enjoy life, I could make small splurges like a book and a train upgrade. "If it's that special, I'd like to buy it for you." *I'll inscribe it so you can read it when I'm dead.*

We were alone in first class until a striking woman and her baby boarded. She had light brown skin and the body of a ballet dancer. After she seated her cherubic baby, she placed an elegant suitcase in the overhead compartment. It was a small, hard-shelled case that women could use only when they wore size zero. I couldn't fit my lunch in that thing.

Who gets to look like that? I wondered. *Is she a model?*

"Hello," she said brightly, smoothing her full-length sundress.

You're so pretty, I did not say aloud. "Hi."

There was something very familiar about this woman. I had definitely seen her before. *Is that…? Is that the woman from the new movie* Crash?

"Will this be your first time in London?" she asked. I nodded to confirm, a bit intimidated by this perfect creature. Gorgeous women always made me a little nervous, a bit judged, as though they were secretly wondering why I couldn't have pulled myself together better. I slid my bag of colorful jellybeans out of her sight.

"London is wonderful," she said. "I spent years there." She took out a stack of white papers and set them on her lap.

That is definitely the woman from Crash, *and that is a script on her lap.*

"Are you the actress from *Crash*?" My curiosity was stronger than my self-consciousness.

"Yes, that was me in the burning car," she said with a smidge of an *aw shucks* eye roll.

Oh. My. God! Act cool, no one likes a groupie.

"The movie, um, film was amazing. My husband and I saw it before we left and it was just so powerful." *Okay, stop.* "So gripping. I just loved it." *Enough. Stop gushing.* "Really amazing."

"Thank you. It hasn't been released here yet." She smiled. "Is this your daughter?"

Holy crap, she's continuing the conversation! I nudged Katie. "Yes. Katie, this is, um…"

"Thandie," she said. "Is that the new Harry Potter?"

Katie nodded emphatically. "You know what's funny? They use the letter *S* a lot instead of *Z*, like *realise* and *organise*."

"It takes a bit of getting used to, doesn't it?" Thandie asked.

"What are you reading?" Katie asked. "Want some jelly-beans?" She yanked the bag from my hiding spot and extended her arm, offering a rainbow of sweets.

"No, thank you." Looking to her lap, Thandie answered Katie's other question. "It's a script," she said. "A Will Smith project."

I smiled and said something insipid, like "How lovely." *Lovely? Who exactly was I trying to be? And if it was a Will Smith action flick, could it really be considered lovely?* "How cool," I added.

To save myself further embarrassment, I grabbed a book

from my bag and started reading. Minutes later, Thandie looked up from her script and asked if we'd like some tips on what to do in London. She told us about her favorite shops, lunch spots, and theater. Every time Thandie tended to her baby, I mouthed to Katie: *huge movie star*. Katie smiled and nodded as if to say she was pleased for me.

"Oh my God!" Katie said, bursting into laughter.

"What, Katie?" Thandie asked.

"Ron Weasley just *ejaculated*!"

"They're having sex at Hogwarts?" I asked.

Thandie smiled as Katie figured it out. "I'm pretty sure it means 'exclaimed'; that makes more sense."

"You should take her to see *Mary Poppins*," Thandie offered. I wondered if she suggested this to purify Katie's database, or if the thought randomly popped to mind. "It's absolutely charming," she said.

Mercifully the filter between my brain and mouth stopped me from telling Thandie that we like charming things.

"*Mary Poppins* is showing here?" Katie chimed in.

Thandie explained that the production was playing at a West End theater and urged us to make a point of seeing it. "We will," I promised my daughter.

I looked out the window and watched France disappear as we entered the tunnel beneath the English Channel. The darkness would soon be replaced by the English landscape.

Less than an hour later, daylight slapped through the

windows of the train as we emerged from the tunnel into England. It was like a high-speed birth on rails.

Katie and I stayed in Kent, a forty-minute train ride from London. One of Katie's soccer friends had an aunt who lived in England, and she offered to let us stay at her home for our ten-day visit. Aunt Molly's seven-year-old granddaughter Megan came with the deal.

Within the first five minutes of their meeting, the girls were giggling uproariously in the back seat of Molly's car, delighting in their mutual misunderstandings. "Did you bring a swim costume?" Megan asked Katie.

"A *costume*?" Katie asked.

"We're taking you to Hever Castle tomorrow and we can run in the water fountains in the gardens," Megan explained.

"You mean a swimsuit?" Katie asked.

Megan squealed. "A suit?! What the…?!" The little girl had an easy laugh and a penchant for saying "what the…?!" She had golden blond hair with a smattering of freckles and huge blue eyes that looked like they belonged on a Madame Alexander doll.

My jaw clenched and I dug my fingernails into my palms as I watched the oddity of Molly driving on the wrong side of the car on the wrong side of the road. Every time we turned a corner, I flinched, certain we would have a head-on collision. But everyone seemed perfectly comfortable, so I began doing my square breathing exercises: three breaths in, hold for three beats, exhale for three, and hold for another three. *No one's killed us!* Repeat.

"A few things you'll want to learn," Molly said, her eyes on the road. "A chip is what Americans call a French fry. If you want what you call a potato chip, ask for crisps. Many Americans have declined my offer of digestives because they think they're some sort of stomach medicine."

"What are they?" Katie asked.

"They're digestives," Molly said. "But Americans call them cookies."

"*Cookies?*" Megan said, laughing. "What the…?!"

We pulled into the driveway of Molly's Tudor style home in Kent, which she shared with her adult son, Alun. Naïvely, I expected her home to look like an English cottage with a stone fireplace warming the sitting room laden with floral patterned comfy chairs. I thought her kitchen would be decked out with copper pans hanging chicly from the ceiling and a pot of porridge simmering on the Aga. In reality, it was like most American homes I'd been in, complete with the hallway filled with framed photos of family, including Alun at eight years old wearing a yellow T-shirt with his name in iridescent iron-on letters. I smiled at the familiarity of the large TV with a DVD of *Friends* beside it and a tidy desk equipped with a Mac.

I was astonished by Molly's generosity as she showed us around the kitchen, pointing out all of the snacks she'd purchased for us. She told us she planned to take us to Hever Castle and Oxford. She promised to make us a Sunday roast before we left. It was a must, she said with a lilt. I was embarrassed thinking about what an awful hostess I would be if the tables were turned. If I were kind enough to allow two strangers to stay in my home, I'd likely hand them a key, ask them to please clear their hair from the shower drain, and wish them good luck in San Diego. While Katie and I napped after our arrival in Kent, Molly washed and folded our laundry. Within an hour, she assumed the role of our auntie, and I felt terribly unworthy yet very grateful for her kindness.

"Is this where they beheaded Anne Boleyn?" I asked Molly the following day as we stood on the lush grounds of Hever Castle.

"That was the London Tower," she explained as the girls ran through the stone fountains and waterfalls laughing at nothing. We had just taken a tour of the castle, and I was trying to imagine what it was like in its heyday. Our tour guide explained that King Henry VIII had Anne Boleyn beheaded for treason and adultery, but a recent review of the evidence did not support his charge.

As Molly and I watched the girls splashing freely, we took in the grounds. It was easy to picture the king's men on horseback galloping the expansive green, ornately trimmed with a maze of bushes. Molly wasn't overly chatty, and for once I didn't feel the need to fill the silence with conversation. But after twenty minutes, the peacefulness became too uncomfortable.

"Do you think it hurts to be beheaded?" I asked Molly, who turned her head of shaggy red hair toward me quizzically. "I mean, I've always heard that it was a pretty painless way to go, but how can that be? It's got to hurt when the blade hits your neck. I hear there's a minute or two where you're still alive after your head's completely severed and your eyes can still see. Wouldn't that be awful to see your decapitated body on the guillotine?"

Molly pondered this. "Well, I don't imagine it would be terribly pleasant, Jennie." She gave me an encouraging pat on the leg. "I don't think there's much chance anyone will behead you, so I wouldn't worry too much about it."

I hear freezing is the way to go, I thought better of saying.

Katie and Megan scampered over to us, soaked from every strand of their hair to their wrinkled toes. "Aren't you coming?" Megan asked us.

"Into the water?" her grandmother replied.

"Just dip your feet," Katie suggested.

When we declined, the girls looked at each other and shrugged, unable to fathom how we could pass on such fun.

The following day, Katie and I took the train into London on our own and decided to walk to the West End to buy tickets to *Mary Poppins*. Before we could make it out of Charing Cross Station, though, a wall of images of a very familiar face hit us.

"What the…?!" Katie said, now for the second time that morning. "That's the mum from the Chunnel." We stopped dead in our tracks, taking in the multiple magazine covers. Her face was absolutely everywhere, like Thandie Newton wallpaper. Over the next week, we poked fun at ourselves every few hours by asking, in our best Thurston Howell III accent, "Isn't this the place our darling best friend *Thandie Newton* recommended?" Katie clenched her jaw to imitate an aristocrat. "My dear, *dear* friend Thandie said this loo was the finest in all of London."

After our day at Hever Castle, we didn't see sunshine for the rest of our visit. A cloud hung over London, threatening a constant burst of showers. As Katie and I walked the promenade along the Thames River, she looked at her map and pointed to the House of Commons and Big Ben. "London Bridge?" she asked, perplexed. "I thought that fell down."

As we passed landmarks, I knew my father must have laid eyes on the same sites when he lived in London thirty years earlier. I wondered if he was feeling optimistic about his music career, or if he viewed Big Ben as a giant game clock pressuring him to hit it big or go home.

When my father returned to the United States, he brought with him a British version of Monopoly, marked with the streets Katie and I were now walking. Leicester Square: coded yellow and worth £260. I wondered if Coventry Street and Piccadilly—the other yellow properties—were nearby.

Every few days, Katie and I found ourselves passing the London Eye, the enormous Ferris wheel that provided a panoramic view of London. The line for rides snaked perpetually for what seemed like miles, so we agreed to try our luck another time.

Someone handed us a coupon for the London Dungeon, which Katie and I thought sounded like oodles of fun even though it didn't have the Thandie Newton seal of approval. The London Dungeon smelled moldier than the rest of the city. London never seemed to be completely dry, which unfortunately resulted in a small but pungent population of men who smelled like socks that had been worn in the rain.

When a cast of gruesome misfits greeted us at the entrance to the London Dungeon, I knew the historical walking tour of torture and plague was going to be extraordinarily well produced. I was awed by the gorgeous costumes, though they were smattered in blood and gore. Live rats scurried behind glass as our guide began yelling at us in a thick Cockney accent. He looked like Johnny Depp playing Jack the Ripper.

"Anytime you want to leave, just say, 'Stop the ride,'" I whispered to Katie.

"It's not really a ride," she whispered back.

"But that will be our code. If it gets to be too much, just tell me it's time to stop the ride."

"Why do we need a code? Why don't I just tell you I want to leave?"

"I don't know, I thought we could have a—"

"Do I 'ear talking?!" the tour guide barked. "Why, I'll come over there and cut out yeh tongue if I 'ear another word out of yeh, ay? Yel choke to death on yer own blood and I'll feed you to the rats."

Good God, I thought. *I'm ready to cry "Stop the ride" already.*

"Don't you ever get sick of Coney Island?" my father asked as we drove toward Brooklyn. "Maybe we could spend a Sunday just hanging out and feeling each other's vibes."

"Feeling each other's *vibes?*" I asked. "Daddy, there are rides at Coney Island." My father raised his hands in surrender and lit a cigarette. He turned on the radio, which blasted

Hues Corporation's "Rock the Boat" mid-rock. "They call this music?" he scoffed.

"It's catchy," I said.

"Music is about a universal human connection," he said, sounding a bit frustrated. "Rock the boat, don't tip the boat over," he mocked. "What bullshit." He turned the knob on the radio until it landed on Cat Stevens's "Wild World." "*This* is music." Relieved that he seemed settled, I sang along with the chorus. He smiled and joined in, "Oh baby, baby, it's a wild world, and I'll always remember you like a child, girl." Absorbed in the music, he kept the beat by tapping his silver-and-stone ring on the hard plastic of his steering wheel.

"You like Cat Stevens?" my father asked. I felt proud that he assumed that I was up on the music hit makers at age eight and did not want to disappoint him, so I told him Cat Stevens was one of my favorites. I knew of the Jackson Five and Sonny and Cher, but could not name many others. Unless Cat Stevens was the guy who wrote "Time in a Bottle" or "Benny and the Jets," I had no idea whether or not I liked his music. As we saw the steel frame of the old parachute ride, my father flicked his turn signal to enter the park. He sighed. "This man writes music. There's so much bullshit and so little music these days."

Soon we were standing in the shadow of the Wonder Wheel beside the Spook-a-Rama, debating whether or not I could go in the haunted house ride solo. "I'm not a baby,"

I explained. "Plus we just went on it, I know exactly what's going to happen. I know when Frankenstein pops out, I know when the bats fly into your hair. I have the whole thing memorized."

"Then why do you need to go again?" he asked.

"Pleeeease?" I begged.

He conceded. "I'll watch you through the little window," my father said. What he hadn't remembered was that there was only one small window where people from the outside could look into the Spook-a-Rama. That window was located at the precise point when carts passed a mummy lunging out from his casket. I'd forgotten that bit, so my father got a live snapshot of me shrieking in holy terror. As he described it, my hair was standing straight in the air like uncooked spaghetti.

Moments later, I heard men shouting, one calling my name and another chasing after him. "Don't get out of the cart, JJ," my father shouted from what sounded like the inside of the Spook-a-Rama.

"Are you fucking crazy, man?!" said a man with a Brooklyn accent.

"I'm coming!" my father shouted breathlessly. The cart came to a screeching halt, and for a moment, I was alone in the pitch dark. "JJ?! JJ, where are you?"

Suddenly the place was lit up like a hospital. I could see wires, levers, switches, and lights. The so-called bats were no more than shreds of rubber hanging from overhead. I'd been in car washes more frightening than this. My father raced to the cart. "Thank God you're okay," he said, jumping in with me.

A man caught up with us a few seconds later. "Are you out of your fucking mind?! This thing is on rails, man. You could've been electrocuted."

"What could I do?" my father protested. "She was going to jump out of the cart. I couldn't let my daughter get electrocuted!"

"What could you do?!" the man shouted. "You could fucking tell me to stop the ride. I would have hit one motherfucking button and stopped the ride. You didn't have to come running in here like Captain Fucking America."

"I'm sorry," my father said. "I was so scared I didn't think. I just knew I had to get to her." Then he asked the same question he would pose to the security guard at the new World Trade Center two years later: "Do you have kids?"

The man grabbed my father and hugged him. "I know, I know, man, you do fucking anything for them, even stupid shit like this."

"Thank you for understanding," my father said.

"Next time, don't go all fucking crazy like that. I got an off switch I could hit anytime. A little girl needs her daddy around."

On the drive home, my father said I was absolutely

never going on that ride alone again, not even when I was thirty. "You could've been killed jumping out of that cart," he explained.

"Um, you know, I was never going to jump out of the cart," I said meekly.

"You weren't?"

I shook my head. My father pondered this for a moment and lit a cigarette. "Listen, I risked my life with that stunt, so do me a favor and let me think it was for a good reason."

When I returned home that evening, I told my mother about my father's heroics at the Spook-a-Rama. She knit her brow, unimpressed. "That was rather dramatic, don't you think?" I looked at her sitting at the kitchen table with papers sprawled in front of her, likely paying bills or filling out school forms. "Why didn't Shelly just tell someone to turn off the ride instead of making such a production?"

"He was scared," I explained.

"More like impulsive," she said returning to her papers. "People get themselves killed doing foolish things when there's usually a simple solution if they'd just think with a clear head."

"I was going to jump out of that cart," I lied. "I would've died of electrocution if he hadn't saved me. He saved my life."

A half hour into the tour of London Dungeon, Katie and I looked at each other in disgust. This was no fake monster ride. It was a historically accurate, excruciatingly graphic glorification of brutality. "I want to get out of here," I said.

"Me too," Katie replied in a hurry.

I tapped a woman in costume who moments earlier had been barking threats at us and told her we needed to leave. "Right then, loves," she said sweetly. "Let's get you out." She took Katie by the hand and led us away from the group. When we were out of earshot, she said to Katie, "Everything is a show in the Dungeon." We walked down a dark hallway and she continued. "We're all actors and students having some laughs, nothing to be afraid of." With that, she opened a door as the three of us flinched at the daylight. The woman extended a bloody arm, pointing the way out, and cheerfully wished us a good day in London.

Katie and I headed to a tea shop in Notting Hill with white eyelet curtains and small tables made from pinewood. I half expected Goldilocks to come walking through the door at any moment. We ate scones and leafed through the ample selection of children's books until we were ready to walk about and look at charming brick buildings with brightly painted doors and weathered shutters.

The next day, Molly took us to Oxford despite the fact that there had been a minor bombing days earlier. I was impressed that Katie was so interested in visiting the university until I found out that she only wanted to see the locations where Harry Potter was filmed. Wherever we traveled, we saw others with the book. Potter fans would give each other a knowing nod, then compare how far along they were in the tome.

As Thandie suggested, we saw *Mary Poppins* and took in a few other shows in the West End. In my mind, I'd mixed up the harmlessly campy musical *Guys and Dolls* with the dodgy sexed-up *Chicago* and purchased tickets. I couldn't wait to see Brooke Shields play Adelaide and sing about how a person could develop a cold. Katie's eyes lit up as the curtain rose and prison women in fishnet stockings and bustiers sang about how their murder victims had it comin'. At intermission, I asked Katie what she thought. I could hear a few fellow theatergoers quiet their companions because they too wanted to hear this child's take. "I totally fancy this show!" Katie said, borrowing another expression from Megan. "I just have one question."

"Hush, love, I must hear this," a woman behind us whispered to her husband.

"What the heck is it about?" Katie asked.

The woman laughed. "Precious," she said. "Has no idea what it's about, but loves it. I do long to be a child again."

I turned around and smiled at the woman.

She returned the smile, then offered, "You do know *Mary Poppins* is playing."

On our final day in England, we woke to the sound of

rain banging on the windows of Molly's house. *Oh crap*, I thought. "It's torrential out there."

Katie sat up excitedly, her hair still molded to the shape of the pillow. "I bet there's no line for the London Eye today!"

"Maybe we just…" I began, then stopped myself. "All right, let's buy some umbrellas."

After our Ferris wheel ride through a cloud, Katie spotted a bronze statue of Salvador Dalí's melting clock. "What the…?!"

A man dressed like the surrealist approached us and asked if we would like to visit Dalí Universe. Floating eyeballs, lobster phones, melting clocks—what child wouldn't love this?

Inside the museum, Katie was agape. "This guy is crazy!" she said, looking at Dalí's sculptures and paintings. "And by crazy, I mean brilliant. It's like this guy has no rules at all. In art class, I once colored my cat green, and the teacher was all, 'Cats aren't green.' I'd like to hear what she'd say about this guy."

"Clocks don't melt," I suggested.

"Elephants don't have long skinny legs," Katie added.

I wondered if Katie was simply a fan of surrealism or gearing up for a rebellion against her highly structured, possibly overregulated life.

"Can I have a Dalí-themed ninth birthday party next year?" Katie asked.

"A what?" I asked.

"A Dalí birthday party?"

"What would that even look like?"

"Definitely a melting clock cake," she said. "And we could paint surreal self-portraits and they'd be all weird and it wouldn't matter." As if reading my mind, she continued, "And we could hire an actor to play Salvador Dalí like that time Winnie the Pooh came to my party." Katie saw that I was warming to the idea and persisted, suggesting my friend. "Milo could play Salvador Dalí. I bet his accent would be better than that guy outside the museum."

"Before today, you had no idea who Dalí was," I reminded her. "Will any of your friends care about some painter they've never heard of?"

Katie shrugged. "So Milo will come and tell a story about who Dalí is and why he's cool and stuff."

"We could play Pin the Mustache on *Mona Lisa*," I suggested. "But that's really more Dada than Dalí."

"Dada? I don't know who that is and I don't care, it'll be fun," Katie said.

"If you're still excited about this idea in March, we'll do it," I told her.

She continued, "We can get candles that look like fingers."

I smiled, realizing that we were very likely having a surreal birthday party.

"And bugs on the cake," Katie whispered again.

"Bugs?"

"Yeah, plastic ants crawling across the cake like that picture we saw in the Dalí book of that lady who had a loaf of bread going through her head and bugs crawling across her boobs."

"Okay," I said. "We can put bugs on the cake."

Katie kissed my cheek and thanked me, knowing that she had closed the deal.

The second part of the deal was the one I made with myself. I silently promised that Katie and my mother-daughter trip would not be a once-in-a-lifetime adventure, but something we did as often as we could reasonably afford. Home maintenance be damned—our next stop would be Italy.

Trip Two

Italy

2008

4

ROME

The three years between our first European adventure and the next rolled along on the pleasant treadmill of middle-class suburban life: soccer tournaments, Girl Scout meetings, and elementary school science projects. I rushed to make writing deadlines and carpool pickup times; William suited up and went to his law office every day. Our lives intersected at Katie's games and events, family meals, and theater nights, briefly touching then darting off in other directions.

William was famous among the neighborhood kids for his four-cheese macaroni and cheese. I was the mom who led improv games in which we'd sing songs in divergent styles, like nursery rhyme gospel and show tune rap. Life was good, but our obligations—many of which we imposed on ourselves—left us with too little time, something I felt acutely since I was convinced that I was on the same mortality schedule as my father.

"I want to take another trip," I told William one evening as we were getting ready for bed.

"You just got back from Europe!" he said after spitting out his mouthwash.

"I'm not talking about tomorrow. I figured if I save religiously, I can afford to go when Katie finishes fifth grade."

"Or we could fix the bathrooms," William offered. "Or the kitchen, or the windows, or put the money into Katie's college fund."

"This is kind of an educational investment," I said.

"Don't insult my intelligence, Jen. If you want to take a trip, don't try to pass it off as summer school for Katie."

"Okay, I want to go to Italy."

"Italy?" William asked with a sigh.

"They seem like they've got the same *joie de vivre* as the French, but with pasta."

"And how long do you plan to *joie* your *vivre*?"

"A month."

"A month?!" he said louder than he expected.

"I want to take our time," I said. "We're living life at a breakneck speed, William. I want to take my time when we travel, you know, sit down and read a book in the park rather than trying to cram everything in." I reminded him that Katie and I could travel free on frequent flyer miles and of how frugal we were on our last trip. I promised I would pace my work so I could miss a month's pay. I looked at him hopefully. "If you really think it'll get us into hot water financially, we won't go."

"Jen, if this is important to you, you should do it, but if you have kitchen envy when one of the neighbors remodels, I do not want to hear about it."

"I will not have kitchen envy," I said.

"You have kitchen envy all the time. Every time we see someone's new kitchen."

"You will never, ever hear about my kitchen envy ever again."

"That, my dear, is a deal I will take."

On the plane ride to Rome, I wondered why I ever thought overseas travel was a good idea.

"*Signora, signora!* You must come out of the bathroom right now," the flight attendant demanded as she pounded on the door. "We are landing."

I felt the plane descending but could not muster the strength to stand, unlock the door, and return to my seat. I was vomiting, so my goals were much simpler. With one hand bracing the wall and the other being used as a ponytail holder, I squatted, my legs bent like a frog. I hoped to keep my balance so I wouldn't topple over. This had become my travel routine: fail to sleep, get a headache, then puke.

Prior to our departure, I asked my doctor to give me a mask filled with nitrous oxide, like the ones used to knock out patients before surgery, but she laughed and assured me that the sleeping pill she prescribed would do the trick. I reminded her that she'd made the same promise when I left for Paris three years earlier and I didn't sleep a wink on that trip. "You need to let go and allow the medication to work," she told me.

After twenty-three years in Southern California, I still hadn't gotten used to the New Age undertone: mechanics who ask about my automotive *issues*, a former boss who did astrological readings, and a doctor who urged me to let go, let pill.

"You must return to your seat, *signora!*" the flight attendant insisted, pounding on the door again. My eyes welled with tears as my stomach contracted. "One moment, I'm sorry," I said, offering a weak pound back.

A few minutes later, I collected myself and made it to my seat, where Katie was beside me, sleeping soundly. She had grown ten inches since our last trip to Europe, but still folded neatly into her space. She wore her hair in a long brown ponytail and sported a natural, Ivory Girl look. As the plane hit the ground, I jostled my eleven-year-old. "We're here, Katie."

As our plane sped down the runway, Katie's eyes popped

open and, with the energy of a person who already had her morning shower and coffee, she asked, "Is this Rome?"

"It is," I said, masking my discomfort.

"You look kind of…gray."

"Just a little motion sickness," I explained. *It can't be something more serious, can it? What would we do if I became sick in a foreign country? What if I die in Italy? What then?*

My stomach twisted with anxiety at the thought of William having to fly to Rome to collect Katie after she spent a day alone at Child Protective Services. Would they cremate me here and continue with the itinerary I'd set for Katie and myself, sprinkling my ashes over the Roman Colosseum and ruins of Pompeii? I hoped so. There were so many non-refundable deposits.

I wondered how William and Katie would manage without me when they got back to San Diego. I imagined a sink filled with dishes and a Vesuvian mountain of laundry, washed once a month, if that. The towels would never be properly folded again. I shuddered to think what the Christmas tree would look like without my decoration micromanagement. The idea of missing Katie's middle school and high school years became a crushing pain in my chest. Never again hearing her little voice call me *Mommy*. I gasped a sob.

"Why are you crying?" Katie asked.

"I'm just so happy that we're in Italy," I said, wiping my nose with a shirtsleeve.

Forty-five minutes later, Katie and I were in a taxi, racing through the streets of Rome, weaving around cars and pedestrians. The sharp turns slid Katie and me to one side of the back seat, then a hard left threw us to the other. The taxi wheels jumped onto the curb then pounded back down onto the road, our driver scarcely missing whatever was in his way. It didn't matter to him whether he narrowly averted another car, a pedestrian, or a dog. The road was an obstacle course, and there seemed to be no points off for casualties.

When I noticed the driver checking me out through his rearview mirror, I assumed he was concerned about my health. Instead he had other plans. "First time in *Roma*?" he asked me. When I confirmed, he smiled and placed a tattooed arm on the back of his seat. He looked in his mirror again. "You no look a so good," he said without an ounce of sympathy. In fact, he suppressed a laugh.

When the cab driver dropped us off at our bed and breakfast, he took the ten and fifty euro bills I handed him, turned away, then pivoted to face me again. He presented me with two tens. "*Signora*, you no give me enough money."

"I didn't?"

"The ten and fifty euro, they are the same color," he explained. "Honest a mistake."

At this point, there were two versions of myself battling. A small voice within squealed, *You are being swindled. Raise your hands in the air, shout and make a fuss about how he is trying to cheat you.* The larger part of me just wanted to lie down on the sidewalk and beg the world to stop spinning. The latter voice, rather unconvincingly, said, *Maybe you made a mistake. You're tired and sick and you have no way of proving anything.* The imbecilic me peeled another fifty bill from my thinning cash fold and gave it to him. With a smarmy, self-satisfied smile, the driver said, "Welcome to *Roma!*" He peeled off quickly, a tourist jumping out of the way to avoid him.

When we reached the lobby of Casa Banzo, our bed and breakfast, I counted my money. I'd left San Diego with two fifty-euro bills and several smaller ones. Now I was left with only twenties and tens. I would have to find an ATM sooner than I'd planned.

Head down, I barely noticed how utterly charming our bed and breakfast was with its dusty blue exterior and white confectionery trim. Paulo, the college boy who worked as the concierge, rolled our suitcases to our room as I told him about the taxi driver. He rolled up the yellow sleeves on his shirt and shook his head and, like a disappointed father, said, "Ah *Roma*, bad, bad *Roma*." Then turning to Katie and I, he perked up. "You see, everything else nice for you. There is bad *fru-eet* in every country."

Bad fruit? Katie mouthed behind Paulo's back. I nodded to confirm.

She smiled and mouthed, *I love Rome!*

Our room was suited for nuns. Between the twin beds, a small crucifix hung on a stark white wall. The twin beds were covered with white cotton bedspreads with orderly rows of stiff white pompoms, the same kind my grandmother Aggie had for as long as I remember. I wondered if there was some sort of *Catholic Home & Convents* magazine or if Roman Catholics just instinctively know how to create a monastic look.

As Katie and I lay in our beds for our post-flight nap, I lamented my stupidity in handing over an extra fifty euro to the taxi driver. "Maybe his mother is sick and he needs the money," Katie offered.

"*Your* mother is sick and *I* need the money," I snapped. "I feel so gullible."

Katie crawled into my bed and put her hand over mine. "What would you say if it was me who made the mistake?"

"I'd say you're an idiot."

"No, you wouldn't," Katie said. "Tell me what you'd really say?" she asked, though she knew the answer.

I yawned and closed my eyes. "I'd tell you that a person can make mistakes but then they can move on and have a wonderful time, even when there are bumps along the way."

When Katie didn't reply, I turned my head to see that she was out cold, lightly breathing beside me.

I couldn't let go, though, constantly replaying the scene in my mind, and thinking about how I should have done things differently, how I should have paid closer attention. My mind busily imagined scenes in which the cab driver regaled his friends at the bar that night with stories of his stupid American passenger. "Drinks on me!" he would say, slapping his hand on the table. He should break a finger.

Or maybe Katie was right and our cab driver was living a life of economic desperation. We were on a budget, but hardly destitute. By world standards, our life was pretty comfortable, so maybe this man really did need the fifty euro more than we did. But it wasn't really about the money; it was about the vulnerability of being in a place where our very first interaction was exploitative. I could part with money, but I was robbed of my sense of security.

As requested, Paulo knocked on our door at five o'clock sharp. Recalibrated by seven hours of sleep, I let go of the notion that Rome was a city of thieves and was ready to cautiously tackle our first evening in Italy. A mild breeze from the Tiber River swept over the cobblestone riverbank as Katie and I walked the two miles between the Jewish Quarter and the Spanish Steps.

A band of a dozen Italian men played on the steps, dressed in their ornately embroidered black hats, pants, and jackets.

We dropped a euro coin in their open guitar case and sat for a moment before realizing we were starving.

We stopped at a deli with a twenty-foot long glass case displaying marinated eggplant, *caprese*, squid, *prosciutto*, and dozens of pasta salads. A blackboard listing every imaginable type of pizza caught Katie's eye. After inquiring for the third time about the price of the salads, an older man with a plain white apron exhaled with annoyance. "What you like to eat?"

I explained that everything looked delicious, but we'd been swindled out of our daily allowance so I had to keep dinner at ten euro. "Ah, taxi steal a you money," he said, shaking his head. "You sit, I make you dinner for a ten euro."

"But—"

"I know what you like to eat, *signora*—everything you point at, ay?"

"Yes, but—"

"And *signorina* like a what kind of pizza?"

"Sausage, *per favore*," Katie offered.

Ten minutes later, the man with a gray pompadour returned with a plate piled high with all of my favorites, plus a few more he thought I would like to try. He brought Katie a generous slice of pizza with a rotund bottle of Orangina. "This is amazing, but—" I started. He walked away and returned a moment later with a glass of red wine, a basket of bread, two bowls of soup, and an enormous slice of white cake soaked in caramel syrup. I looked at him in amazement. "I can pay for this on my credit card," I said, slightly embarrassed that I'd given him the impression we were impoverished rather than simply frugal. "There's no way this was only—"

The man held up his hand and gave me a firm look that demanded my silence. He patted the table and smiled. "Welcome to Roma, *belle*."

After dinner, Katie and I walked back to our neighborhood and passed the time with two simultaneous games of *I Spy: I Spy the worst parking job ever!* And *I Spy a man wearing red pants.*

We spotted about a dozen cars that were mounted halfway onto the sidewalk. One clever driver pulled his car into a small space, nose-first, despite the fact that every other car was parked parallel to the curb. Katie pretended to be the car owner reacting to our judgment. "What?!" she bellowed. "There is a no room to park nice. I do smart thing!"

After we counted more than twenty men in red pants, we changed it to orange because the game was getting too easy.

Before long, we were back at Casa Banzo, tired, but not quite ready to turn in. "The piazza Campo de' Fiori is a block away," I told Katie. "Want to check it out?"

She gave me what we dubbed the Euro-shrug, a gesture we'd seen at least a dozen times in our first few hours in

Italy. We initially noticed it when I thanked the deli man for his generosity. He shrugged with his hands stretched wide, his head tilted to the side, mouth scrunched with a facial expression that read, *Ay, what you gonna do?* The Euro-shrug could also mean: *Why not?* or *Who really cares?* At its best, the shrug meant: *Who knows why life does these funny things?* At its worst, it meant: *Shut up and eat.*

During the day, Campo de' Fiori served as a farmers market, but in the evening, the rectangular enclosure of stone buildings became a lively piazza illuminated by yellow streetlamps. The four- and five-story buildings stood shoulder-to-shoulder with a few narrow alleys to enter and exit. In the center of the piazza was a statue of the Italian philosopher Giordano Bruno, who looked a bit like the Grim Reaper with a book instead of a scythe. At his feet sat a four-piece classical music group, hoping for tips from the hundreds of diners who filled the piazza's restaurant tables. I gave Katie a euro coin to toss into the musicians' cup and suggested we cross the street to explore Piazza Navona.

Like Campo de' Fiori, Piazza Navona was an open area, lined with outdoor restaurants and dotted with street performers. This piazza had a more magical feel because of its three marble fountains, the most famous being Bernini's *Fountain of Four Rivers.* As exquisite as the fountains were, though, our attention was immediately drawn to an old man performing a show with elaborately costumed finger puppets.

He played Michael Jackson songs and rigged the Pop King's shoes to shoot smoke when he moon-walked across the cardboard box of a stage. When the puppeteer was done, a Latin jazz quartet began playing music. Next up was a boy, no more than fifteen, who whipped out a violin and began playing and singing tourist favorites. Katie and I spent an hour clapping like fools at the ever-transforming, ever-transfixing stage of Piazza Navona.

Katie began snapping pictures not of the performers, but of the people watching or passing. She shot a business owner pulling down the metal gate of his storefront. She snapped a toddler looking at an incoming spoon with an expression that said *I am not eating that!* Katie's blurred photo caught the movement of a fashionable young man in sunglasses as he glided by, too sexy for us all.

We moved on to the steps outside the Pantheon, a majestic ancient temple built in 126 A.D. that boasted eight columns and an enormous rotunda. I had intended to snap a photo of this historic site and promptly check it off my list, but the building was hypnotic. In the evening light, the stone looked lavender. I usually bristle at descriptions of places as spiritual, but there was no other way to express how I felt about this building. It had seen so much history that I felt oddly compelled to stare, believing if I did, it might reveal the answers to life's great mysteries. The spell was short-lived, though, as a fidgety Middle Eastern guy shot a small illuminated disc into the air and whispered, "I make good price for you, *bella*."

"What?"

"Girl likes fun toy," he said, pointing to Katie, who was now shooting photographs of people's shoes.

"No, no, thank you," I said, trying not to show my annoyance.

"You need purse?"

Before I could decline, a series of whistles sounded and dozens of vendors collected their wares from display blankets and scurried off.

As we walked back to Casa Banzo, Katie told me she wanted to take "people shots" this trip. "We're digital now so it's not like I'm wasting film."

"Okay, fine with me," I told her. "I still need to document the sites, though, so we'll share the camera." She nodded in agreement.

"You know what I noticed about you today?" Katie asked, not waiting for a response. "You always give money to street musicians, even when we don't stop and listen."

"You have to support street musicians, Katie," I said. "Imagine tonight without all of the performers in the piazzas." Katie nodded, satisfied with this explanation.

"You know what I like best about Italy so far?"

"How everyone calls us *bellas*?" I answered. "How colorfully the men dress?"

"The piazzas. Who do we talk to about getting some piazzas in San Diego?"

The closest thing to a piazza I'd seen in the United States was the replica of the Arc de Triomphe in Washington Square Park, where I spent many Sundays with my father. Some days I would climb on the jungle gym in the playground while he flirted with the mothers. In the summer, we would run in the fountain despite my mother's concern that it was filled with germs.

When I was ten years old, I saw something I'd never witnessed before—and never would again. A brown upright piano and bench sat under the arch. My dad rushed over the cobblestones to reach it before anyone could assault it with the usual ear-grating version of "Heart and Soul." Whenever there was a piano, my father was ready to perform, invited or not.

Soon he had an audience tapping their feet and swaying in the sunshine. As my father's leathery hands tapped the keyboard, he belted the start of the chorus of his signature song, "Life's Lookin' Beautiful." We were both surprised to hear one of the park's drug dealers chime in with a gospel-like echo. "Life's lookin' beautiful," my father sang.

"Yes it is!" the dealer chimed in.

"Life's lookin' beautiful," my dad continued.

"Hear me now," sang the old black man with a face as wrinkled as a raisin.

"Life's lookin' beautiful since I seen you."

The crowd, which had now reached about fifty, began clapping when my father finished. In an instant, we had the same thought. Our eyes locked intently. I nodded to let him know I was on a mission.

He began playing another song, "Remember Me," always a crowd pleaser, as I bolted for the Good Humor stand.

"What do you do with your empties?" I asked breathlessly.

"Nuttin'," the Good Humor man said. "What people do with their trash ain't my problem." This was the dawn of the anti-littering movement, and he probably thought I was an overzealous do-gooder. Beside him was a thick wire garbage can, which provided a clear view of ice cream wrappers, empty Italian ice cups, and other assorted trash. Then I struck gold. I reached in elbow-deep and pulled out a blue-and-white coffee cup from a Greek diner. Unfortunately, it still had a few sips left at the bottom and a lipstick mark around the rim. I ran to the cement water fountain and quickly rinsed the cup until it was presentable.

I made it back to the arch just as my father began the chorus. As I placed the coffee cup on top of the piano, my father gave an approving smile and continued singing. "Don't you remember the love we shared? Don't you remember the way you used to care?" He made enough that afternoon to take us to Chinatown for dinner—lobster Cantonese and cold noodles with sesame sauce. We even ordered Cokes.

"'Remember Me' was a big hit in Italy," my father reminded me as he dipped a crispy chip into a small bowl of Chinese mustard. "Rita Pavone. Cute little girl with a boy haircut and a set of pipes," he said. "When that song hits the charts here, I'm going to buy a mansion on Long Island, and your mother and you can live in it with me. Think Carol would go for that if I gave her her own wing?"

"She says she's never leaving Manhattan again," I told him.

"Then I'll buy a brownstone," he said, holding his empty Coke to signal to the waiter that he'd like another. "Upper East Side. Carol can have the big apartment and I'll live upstairs and you can go back and forth as you please."

"I think she'd like that," I said.

"You did good today," my father said. "That was quick thinking with the coffee cup, JJ. We're going places, you and me."

I was well aware of the fact that wandering around Italy for a month with my daughter was an enormous privilege. Still, the reality was that our daily spending plan was slim. I told Katie to load up on the free breakfast at Casa Banzo, then casually offered her a cup of two-euro gelato at around noon so she would forget about a proper midday meal. I carried dry Fiber One cereal and water in my backpack, which I ate—or more accurately, filled up on—throughout the afternoon.

I did want to experience the food of Italy, though, so for dinner, Katie and I shared an entrée at a nice restaurant. We were always the first diners, seated for the early bird shift at 8:00 p.m. with other American tourists. Sometimes we arrived before the chef. The waiter explained that we could not order for another half hour because the kitchen staff was cutting vegetables and preparing the food. The tone was friendly, but the subtext clear: why in the world would you arrive the moment we open?

In addition to our frugal meal plan, we developed other ways of saving money. While visiting the Roman Colosseum, a young Scotsman who worked at the site told me that the price for my admission would be half if I were a European citizen. "The lass would be free," he said with a wink. "All over Italy, you'd save a load if people thought you were, say, English or Scottish."

"Really?"

I was torn. I always felt vaguely embarrassed when my mother would tell New York City bus drivers that I was six years old so I could ride for free. I gave Katie a modified explanation of what my mother shared with me: *If they can afford to let you on for free as a six-year-old, they can afford to let you on for free at nine. You're still only taking up one seat.* This translated perfectly to our situation. We weren't going to use any more resources than European families. Why should we be penalized for being Americans? The whole thing reeked of their continental discrimination. And my rationalization.

Quietly, I began practicing my accent. "The rain in Spain stays mainly in the plain. Would you fancy a cup of tea?"

After our quick tour of the Colosseum and ruins, Katie perched herself on a low tree branch and hung upside down, taking photos of passersby. She found a more comfortable position splayed across the branch like *Alice in Wonderland*'s Cheshire Cat and shot dozens of tourists and vendors as I sat underneath her in the shade and read a novel.

Katie and I walked to the Borghese Gardens to visit the Borghese Gallery, but stumbled upon a building that looked similar to the Metropolitan Museum of Art in New York. Its façade was different, but it had the same grand stature. Between the columns hung a huge banner that read "NO" in bright red letters.

"That's welcoming," I remarked.

"I want to go there! What is it?"

Looking at my map, I told Katie the building was the Museum of Modern Art and assured her we were scheduled to see it later in the week. "A *Roma* MoMA?! Can we go today?"

But…my schedule is so perfectly laid out, I thought.

"We'll be back to see it in two days," I told Katie.

"Why not switch days?" Katie asked. "See this today and the Borghese later?"

It was one thing to be flexible when emergencies arose, but to rearrange our itinerary simply because we felt like it seemed frivolous.

As I opened my mouth to tell her we couldn't, I looked at the red banner again. Rather than being an answer to Katie's question, the message seemed to be imploring me not to be so rigid.

There was no compelling reason we couldn't swap days for our visit to the Borghese Gallery and the Museum of Modern Art. There was only my discomfort, a feeling that could only be overcome by my daughter's desire.

"Okay," I said, standing still. Katie grabbed my hand and led me up the stairs. "One moment." I reached into my purse and grabbed my notebook. I began drawing scratch marks through our daily schedule, switching days for our visits to the two museums.

"What are you doing?"

"Changing our plans," I replied. Katie tilted her head quizzically. "In ink. I wanted to change our plans on the page so we…" I drifted off. I really had no idea why I needed our change of plans to be properly documented.

"You're silly sometimes, Mommy."

"I'm utterly ridiculous, Katie. Frequently."

We had seen an impressive modern art collection at the Vatican and some of the world's most important paintings at museums and churches throughout Rome, but nothing blew us away quite like the exhibition at the modern art museum, which featured an artist we'd never heard of before.

That day, Mario Schifano made our list of top ten favorite artists. The bright color and crackling energy of his post-modern pop art charged us with excitement we hadn't experienced since London when Katie discovered her love of Dalí. Schifano's large canvases looked as though they should hang beside Andy Warhol and Roy Lichtenstein's but possessed their own distinct style. Katie and I stared at a large mural, examining a series of colorful wigs floating onto different heads. At least I thought they were wigs. Katie insisted they were babies. We simultaneously burst into laughter at each other's assessment. "How could you think those are wigs?!" Katie shrieked.

"Because babies don't sit on top of human heads," I returned. "Stop laughing, we're supposed to be British."

"English people laugh, Mommy."

"Not this loud, *shhh*."

Years earlier, we had begun playing the museum game we called Pretentious Art Critic. We never needed to ask the other to play. One would just begin using the Thurston Howell III voice, and the other knew it was time to add to the drivel. "The artist is saying that we all costume our authentic selves as a survival mechanism," I began through a clenched jaw. "And colorful wigs—"

"Babies," Katie interrupted. "Colorful babies on our heads represent the innocence of our young minds."

"Which are so quickly destroyed in the commercial meat grinder of our consumer culture," I said.

"That makes no sense whatsoever, but so often the most profound insights are nonsense."

"How very right you are," I said.

Returning to her normal voice, Katie whispered, "I love this Schifano guy."

"I'm with you. There isn't a piece in here that I am not one hundred percent in love with. This man is absolutely brilliant."

"Aren't you glad we changed the days?" Katie asked.

"We didn't change the days; we let the days change us."

"That's some deep stuff, Mommy," she teased.

"I'm going to bring my new girlfriend Stella on Sunday," my father said on the phone. "She's a brilliant artist, better than Picasso."

By the time the weekend rolled around, my father's announcement had escaped my nine-year-old brain until I walked out of my apartment building door and saw a rail-thin woman leaning against my father's car. She had a mop of curly brown hair and wore a purple ribbed tank top and embroidered jeans.

As my father opened the lobby door, he pointed toward the girl in front of his beige jalopy. "That's Stella," he informed me. "She moved in Wednesday." The three of us slid into the front bench seat of my father's car and headed toward Brooklyn Heights where my father had recently rented an apartment after he returned from what was supposed to be a six-month stay in London. Rumor had it that he was evicted from the home of a music producer where he was staying. Apparently he slept with the producer's wife.

"It was an honest misunderstanding," I overheard my father explaining to his sisters, Rita and Bernice. "The guy said, 'Help yourself to anything,' and winked at me. He said, 'What's mine is yours,' and his wife was standing right there, so I figured he was giving me a signal."

"A signal?!" Rita balked. "He meant you should have a snack, not his wife."

"She was a very aggressive woman," my father defended. "I thought they had an arrangement."

"An *arrangement*," Rita spat. "Does anyone actually know a single person with one of these so-called arrangements?"

Always the peacemaker, Bernice chimed in. "There were those men from the diner."

"They were involved in a prostitution ring, Bern!" Rita said.

Bernice shrugged. "Anyway, Shelly's home and that's all that matters."

Now, three weeks later, my father had moved Stella into his ninth-floor Brooklyn Heights apartment. The home had high ceilings with an oversized arched window overlooking the downtown Manhattan skyline. His view was a straight shot across to the Twin Towers. When I stood close to the window and looked far to the left, I could see the Statue of Liberty on her private island.

After the short drive over the bridge, I discovered that my father's apartment had been transformed into the Museum of Stella. Canvases with brilliant cubist paintings hung clustered on one wall. On the adjacent wall was a mural of a crowd of people standing behind a velvet rope looking at the canvases. The third wall was solid mirror, so it became difficult to tell what was real and what was simply a reflection of the absurdity that had become my father's home.

As my father moved further off the beaten path, my mother continued her upward climb toward middle-class life. Earlier that year, she moved us from our studio apartment in Greenwich Village to a two-bedroom spread in Stuyvesant Town. We sang the theme song to *The Jeffersons* as Mother Truckers moved us on up to the East Side. Unlike George and Weezy, my mother and I weren't relocating to a luxury apartment, but a working class development, one pay grade up from *Good Times*. It didn't have the character of Greenwich Village, but we each got our own bedroom and that was a thrill for us. My mother's first purchase was plush wall-to-wall carpet more suited for Sutton Place than Stuyvesant Town.

"You finally got your wall-to-wall carpeting, Carol," my father said during his first visit. "Happy now?"

"I will be when you take off those filthy clogs," she said as she accepted my father's offering of whole wheat bagels and vegetable cream cheese. She smiled and invited him in for the full tour.

On our last day in Rome, Katie and I discovered that our tickets for the hour-long Tiber River cruise offered unlimited rides during a twenty-four-hour period. The timing could not have been better. After eight days of walking non-stop, my feet had their own heartbeat. My abnormally large pinky toes were colorless. I wondered if they'd need to be amputated when we arrived in Salerno the following day.

"Good morning," I said in my bright English accent to the man at the ticket booth. Like everyone else in Rome, he offered me a European discount and waved Katie on for free without question. "You like a music?" he asked, offering us headphones. On the riverboat, reminiscent of the *Adventures of Tom Sawyer*, Katie and I placed the headphones on our ears and listened to classics like "Santa Lucia" on guitar. The plucking of Italian songs matched the mood of the scrolling scenery so perfectly that I wondered if someone had orchestrated the playlist so the melancholy songs would play as we passed older buildings while flitty numbers began during stretches where children played by the riverbank. By our fourth river ride, I gave Katie a gentle nudge. "This is so cliché, I love it," I said. "Why do you have your nose buried in a book?"

"I watched the first two times," she said. "And I love this book."

"Are you bored?"

Katie looked up. "I'm content."

"Show-off."

The boat captain approached us. We were the only passengers and it was his job to chat us up, to be a good ambassador for Rome. He was a sweet older gentleman, and maintaining the English accent was making me feel guilty. "*Signora*, we stop the boat for a two hour to take a lunch," the captain said, gesturing to his crewman. "You come back in a two hour and ride again?"

"If that's all right," I said.

"*Belle*, to have you on our boat all day is a wonderful thing. You come back and ride the boat all day and all night."

My heart sank. "I need to confess something."

The captain sat beside us and leaned in. Katie looked up from her Kindle. "We're not British," I said sheepishly. "I used this accent to get the discount on the fare. I'm sorry."

He knit his brow. "You sound a like you from England."

"She's good at accents," Katie said.

The captain paused again, looking down. "Where you from a for real?"

"America," I said. "California."

"You can do the voices of America?" he asked. "Like John Wayne?"

"Ask her to do New York," Katie piped in.

The captain smiled and did his own impression of a New Yorker. "I break a you face," he said, smiling brightly. "Now you say like John Wayne."

Tapping into my spaghetti western, I looked him square in the eye, adjusted my cap, and told him, "I'm afraid I'm gonna have to break your face, Pilgrim."

"You stay for pizza!" the captain yelped.

I straightened up. "I reckon I'd like y'all to stay for pizza."

Katie snorted. "I think he's inviting us to stay onboard for lunch."

"*Si*," he confirmed. "You stay and eat pizza with us. I tell you things to say and you say them like America states. Can you say like the Dakota? Oh, I love the *Fargo* movie." Imitating a character, the captain continued, "Look a like the cold front is a coming." Then breaking character, he laughed. "It's a so cold already and they say the cold is a *coming*? The movie, she is so funny."

"You're not angry?"

"Angry?!" he scoffed. "All day I go up river, down river, up river again. Can you do voice like *Italiano*?"

Katie shut off her Kindle and slipped it in her backpack. She smiled mischievously. "Yup, she does all kinds of accents. Ask her to do yours."

My head whipped to face her. *Are you freaking kidding me?!* I said by way of facial expression.

"Ah yes, do my accent!" the captain said. "Marco, come listen to *Americana*. She going to make a her voice like me."

Katie smiled again and gave me the Euro-shrug.

5

SALERNO

Back home, while planning our trip, several friends asked if I'd met Claudia, an Italian urban planning professor visiting San Diego State University for the year. They said she was very Italian: warm, generous, and loved to throw parties. When I called her, she was in the midst of planning her birthday party and immediately invited my family to join.

"You come a Saturday," she insisted. "I have many Italian friends to tell you about a your trip." As it turned out, in her six months in San Diego, Claudia had collected a veritable United Nations of friends, more than I had accumulated in two decades in the city. There were German, French, Japanese, Spanish, African, and Italian grad students and professors. They spread out on the porch and lawn chairs in front of the house, a pitcher of mojitos in front of them.

Others sipped wine and played ping-pong on her garage roof. Another group ventured up a steep hill in Claudia's backyard where she had designed patio furniture from truck tires. She fashioned a canopy by spreading a bed sheet across four metal poles planted in the ground. There was a smoker's corner with liquor bottles resting in an ice-filled garbage pail. French rock blasted from a boom box tethered to the house by thirty feet of orange industrial extension cord. It was like *Sanford and Son*, Euro-style.

When Claudia saw me, she smiled broadly. "You are a Jennifer," she told me in her musical accent. She kissed both cheeks and introduced herself to William and Katie and offered them both a glass of wine. William quickly discovered the Mexican beer stash and Katie settled for lemonade.

By the evening, William and Katie were the reigning ping-pong champions and I discovered that, after several mojitos, lifting oneself out of the center of a tire was not as easy as it looked.

Weeks later, we invited Claudia to our home for dinner. She brought two guests: her aunt, Micheline, who was visiting from New York, and her friend, Andrea, who was visiting from Salerno. When I picked up the trio at Extraordinary Desserts downtown, Claudia explained that Andrea had just arrived from Los Angeles on a Greyhound bus and she could not fit him in her Fiat convertible. "I go with Jennifer," Andrea offered, striding toward my minivan in his black skinny jeans and dark fitted T-shirt. "Why you have such a big car?" he asked.

"My daughter plays soccer," I explained.

"One child?" I nodded to confirm.

"*Mama mia*," he said scanning the length of the van. "You know how Italian children go to soccer game?" I raised my eyebrows to encourage an answer. "On Papa's motorcycle."

Looking out the window at the changing scenery, Andrea had an idea. "You know what we do, Jennifer? We go somewhere else for dinner, just you and me."

I laughed. The offer was a harmless one, clearly tossed out with no more thought than a fisherman throwing his baited line into the sea. "I don't think my husband would appreciate that," I told him.

"Ah yes, the husband," he sighed. "We stop for cigarettes, no problem?"

"Not a problem," I said, smiling inside. "But you know that smoking is bad for you, right?"

"No, it's good. Everybody smoke."

"Yeah, Andrea, the jury is back on smoking. It'll kill you."

"No, no, very old people smoke and they are good," he said.

We pulled into the gas station where Andrea could chose from several brands of cigarettes. I made one last attempt. "You're only seeing the smokers who live," I pressed.

"What?"

"It's not really fair to say that you know plenty of old people who smoke because you're not accounting for the ones who never live to see old age." He stared at me. "Because they're dead."

Andrea flashed a bright smile and patted my knee. "You worry too much," he said before bolting from the passenger seat. I wanted to tell him that at thirty years old, he didn't feel the effects of daily smoking, but the habit was indeed taking its toll on his health. I wanted to tell him that one day he might have a daughter he would leave to navigate adulthood fatherless because he insisted that smoking was harmless. I wanted to tell him that after he was gone, people would ask his family how he died; when they learned it was lung cancer, they would immediately ask if he was a smoker. When it was confirmed that he was, there would be an awkward silence in which people would inevitably wonder, *What did he expect?*

There is little pity for smoking-related lung cancer. There is no Race for the Cure to raise money for smokers who suffer from lung cancer. There are no cute ribbons fashioned after a filtered cigarette. When nonsmokers are diagnosed with lung cancer, the first thing people say is that the person didn't even smoke. Everyone shakes their heads at the injustice.

Moments later, as we approached my house, I saw Claudia's car parked half in the driveway and half on the sidewalk. I imagined the neighborhood dog walkers knitting their brows as they sidestepped to avoid the Fiat.

After an hour of laughter and wine, Claudia made a declaration. "You come and a stay with me in Salerno this a summer." She broke a piece of bread from the loaf and dipped it into sauce William had made for the salmon. I thanked Claudia for the kind offer, but explained Katie and I weren't going south of Rome except for a day trip to the ruins of Pompeii. We had already made our hotel reservations and our plans were set.

"No, no," she said. "Everybody come to Italy, they go a Rome, Florence, Venice. Southern Italy is a beautiful. You visit Salerno for a few days, and I take you to a Pompeii. You give to me a phone number for your hotel in Rome and I change your reservation. You stay a with me."

This was not a request.

She sat at the dinner table and waited for me to bring her the phone number so she could call Casa Banzo, right there and then. As Claudia dialed her cell phone, I shot William a look from across the dinner table. "What am I going to do?" I whispered.

"I think you're going to Salerno," he said and poured another glass of wine.

In bed that night, I laughed incredulously, slightly tipsy. "Why am I going to *Salerno*?"

William told me that if my travels were supposed to teach me to enjoy life, I needed to embrace unexpected changes to my plans. "The whole point of these trips is to let go and live a little, so just go with it. You've got a whole month in Italy. Why *not* go to Salerno?"

"You never cease to amaze me, how you totally and completely know me better than I understand myself," I told him. "Where would I be without you?"

"Probably in jail," he replied.

Six months later, Katie and I sat on a train that had left Rome three hours earlier and pulled into Salerno station in the early evening. Claudia emailed me days earlier to let me know her husband Gianluigi would pick us up at the station. Katie and I spotted him immediately. He looked like fun, with a Hollywood smile, cropped brown hair, and—of course—red pants. He was the perfect complement to Claudia's more buttoned-up look and cemented his status as the whimsical half of the pair when he introduced himself as Gigi and tossed our bags in the back seat.

Gigi's car seemed as if it had been plucked from my father's collection. It sat unevenly in the parking lot, resting on the metal rim of a front wheel. I am not a car person. In fact, my first date with William came about after he noticed me struggling to start my car in the parking lot after leaving an improv comedy class we were both taking. His sister had enrolled him to help William overcome shyness.

I needed the creative outlet after spending the day at a desk job. In the parking lot, William opened my hood, sniffed, and asked me when my last oil change had been. I stared blankly. He looked at my odometer and asked when I'd last changed my oil. When I told him I didn't remember, he rattled a checklist of questions about my auto maintenance history. Nothing had been done since driving the car off the lot two years earlier. So if someone as clueless as me looked at Gigi's car and noticed a tire was flat, the situation was dire. "Do you want to get some air for your tire? Or, um, patch up the hole?" I asked, my eyes darting around for a service station.

"It's a good," he said, patting my back. "We are very close to home."

We arrived at the apartment a little after ten that night, where Claudia laid out a feast of pasta, squid, and marinated artichoke. By now I knew better than to feel guilty that they had delayed their evening meal for our arrival. This was the normal dinnertime for Italians. Gigi broke out a bottle of clear liquor, slammed his hand on the table, and growled, "*Grappa!*" A party had begun.

"What does *grappa* mean?" Katie asked.

As Gigi poured from the bottle, Claudia explained that *grappa* is grape liquor. Gigi finished for her, "It is insult not to a drink *grappa* when you are in *Italia*."

"So, if I politely decline…?"

"It is like you have come into my home and slapped a my face!" Gigi said, his eyes sparkling, hands pouring.

I was facing my first real parenting dilemma of our travels. I have always told Katie that, within reason, we should follow the customs of the places we visited. I have also warned her about succumbing to peer pressure, especially around alcohol, so I wanted to make it very clear that accepting Gigi's offer of *grappa* was my choice, not my forfeiture. I tried not to sound as self-conscious as I felt when I announced, "I've decided I *would* like to try *grappa*. Yes, that is what I have decided…for myself."

I watched Gigi and Claudia toss back their heads to drink the *grappa* and decided a quick shot would be the best approach, a wise decision since the drink tasted like liquefied fire. I was painfully aware of every internal organ as it heated to a different temperature in my body. Throat: 200 degrees; stomach 400; liver boiling. Gigi threw back another and Claudia declared it was time to dance. Gigi held out the bottle by way of offering another. "I'm kind of a lightweight, so one's my limit," I told him as Paul Simon and Art Garfunkel's music began to blast from the stereo speakers. Gigi nodded his head, accepting.

By now, Katie and Claudia were dancing to "Mrs. Robinson," alternating between a box step and something that looked like a modern jazz interpretation of trees blowing in the wind during a storm. They were both utterly beautiful and ridiculous, and I thought this is what happiness must look like.

After we made it through the entire three-CD collection, Claudia said that she needed to get to sleep since tomorrow was a workday for her. "Same here," said Gigi. "I have to make it an early night." It was two in the morning.

The next day, Claudia dropped us at the ferry to Positano so we could spend the day enjoying the Amalfi Coast.

Katie and I stood at the front of the boat, letting the breeze wash over us as we approached the seaside towns. White and pastel-colored villas were chiseled into steep mountainsides. On the beach were dense rows of orange umbrellas beckoning. The captain overheard Katie and me speaking in English and asked if he could practice on us. "I teach myself in the book but I like try with real American," he said. Katie and I nodded willingly.

"Tell us something about Positano," Katie said slowly. "What will we like?"

"Ah, Positano," the captain said. His uniformed chest filled with pride. "This bitch is a eunuch."

"Whoa!" I said, laughing, Katie doubled over. "We definitely need to work on your pronunciation."

Despite his fifty years, the captain looked like a little boy, sheepish. "What I say?"

"Okay, let's start with what you *want* to say," I told my student. "This *beeeeach*, not *bitch*, is *unique. Unique. You-neek.*"

"*Bitch*," he tried again.

"No, *beeeeach*. Do it with me, *beeeeach. You-neek.* Watch my mouth, *beeeeach. You-neek.*" Together we repeated the words, the phonetics lesson going on for a few minutes.

"Good! Good work, Captain, *molto buono.*"

"What is bitch and eunuch means?" he asked.

"Well, a bitch is, um, a woman who doesn't treat people very nicely."

He furrowed his brow. "What is to *treat* the people?"

"Here," I offered. Putting on a high-pitched Italian voice, I stomped my foot, folded my arms, and turned up my nose. "I love you, I hate you. Come here, go away. Buy me flowers," I said, motioning accepting the imaginary flowers then throwing them overboard. "I hate your flowers! I hate you." I batted my lashes and smiled coquettishly. "You give me necklace?"

Recognition flashed across his face. "I know the bitch!" the captain shouted victoriously.

"Lucky you. Now a eunuch is…hmmm." Katie raised her brows and smiled. Turning to my eleven-year-old daughter, I asked, "Do you know what a eunuch is?"

"Yup, read about them in an article about opera singers," she replied.

"All righty then," I said, continuing. I swaggered around

the deck and spoke in a low man's voice. "I'm a man; I'm a manly, manly tough man." Then I held up a finger to pause, made a snipping motion at the crotch, and finished in a high-pitched voice, "And now I have no testicles."

"No *pene*?!" the captain gasped.

"No, he keeps that, but no…hmmm—"

"Meatballs?!" the captain gasped. "So I say, *our bitch is a eunuch* and it mean…" The captain drifted off as he absorbed the bizarre image. "*Mama Mia!*"

My father would have loved the beach of Positano with its large stones and washing machine current. He regularly hung out at Bay One, the pothead beach where he met Stella. I went to the beach with him, but I was more like my aunts Rita and Bernice, who found comfort in the sterile containment of a pool with its aqua interior, numbers painted at every foot of depth. There were no murky surprises in a pool.

On my twelfth birthday, our trip to Jones Beach was derailed when my father and Stella had yet another blowout. The plan was to spend the day at the beach, then head to nearby Merrick for Chinese dinner with my aunts and their families. The shouting in the car got to be too much for my father, so he pulled over at a park in Long Island so they could continue the fight.

My father and Stella had been together nearly three years and now had a nine-month-old son together. But by the looks of it, they could no longer stand one another. Stella began shaving her head, wearing Christ-like robes, and roller-skating the streets of Brooklyn. My father was irate one day when he came home to find Stella holding the baby while skating figure eights in traffic. She insisted she was very careful and had been surrounded by a protective white light. While at their new apartment weeks earlier, I noticed dried dead tropical fish pinned to the wall like something you might see in a middle school classroom. Noting my horror, Stella assured me the fish died of natural causes. "I'm no fish murderer," she said. "These are for scientific research."

"What ever happened to your paintings?" I asked when I saw the walls were mostly blank.

"What ever happened to Baby Jane?" she replied.

Noticing my look of confusion, my father explained that this was the name of an old Bette Davis movie. "Today must be classic film day," he said, rolling his eyes. "Some days she only speaks in Beatles song lyrics, some days it's rhyming, sometimes it's poetry. She thinks it helps her sound artistic and offbeat, but it just makes her a pain in the ass to communicate with."

We never made it to the beach on my birthday. Instead I spent the day holding baby Leo, trying to distract him from the fighting. I placed him on a grassy hill in the park and photographed him with my new Instamatic. "I will be out of the apartment by July Fourth, Shelly!" Stella shouted. "It will be my Independence Day from *you*!"

"Good!" he bellowed back. "I'll help you pack."

"I don't need your help!"

"You need mental help!" he shouted before he began a coughing fit. He had been coughing a lot lately and seemed to constantly need to clear his throat. I suggested he quit smoking. Now that I was older, schoolteachers were taking more hardcore tactics in their antismoking campaign and showing us photos of black, cancerous lungs. My father insisted the cigarettes weren't the problem; his health would greatly improve once he quit Stella.

I wondered about Stella's departure and what it meant for me. And for Baby Leo. Would I ever see him again? Would my father see him on Saturdays and me on Sundays? Or would we double up on visiting Sundays?

Stella's shouting that meeting my father was the worst thing that had ever happened to her interrupted my train of thought.

"You ruined my life, you crazy bitch!" my father shouted back.

People were beginning to stare, so I took Leo to the other side of the grassy hill and picked dandelions. "Look at the pretty flowers," I said to the baby as I snapped his photo. He began looking around for his parents. "Look here, Leo," I urged.

From the other side of the hill, we heard shouting though I could not make out the words. Leo began crying and reached his arms in their direction. "No, let's go *this* way," I offered, walking further away. "I see ducks in the pond."

Leo wailed harder, wriggling out of my arms so he could make a crawl for it. "Okay," I conceded, carrying him back over the hill.

"If anyone told me I would meet the biggest mistake of my life, I would've never gone to Bay One that day," my father told Stella.

"I hate you!" she shrieked.

And on it went like this until the sun began to set and all thoughts of splashing around Jones Beach for my birthday had been forgotten. That evening, as my father pulled his car into Stuyvesant Oval to drop me off, he startled, remembering that he had forgotten dinner. "It's okay," I told him. "I'm not really hungry."

When I arrived home, my mother was sitting at the table eating a veggie burger and a plate filled with raw greens. "How's the birthday girl?" she asked.

"Great, really great."

She told me she went to a healing workshop and learned a new technique to release trauma. In the past few years, she had made these sorts of activities her part-time job, attending nearly every New Age lecture available in Manhattan. "Against my better judgment, I bought you a slice of *chocolate* birthday cake," she offered.

I perked up.

"Tell me about your day. What did you and Shelly do?"

"We went to the beach," I said, the lies flowing easily. "The waves were big, but not too bad. Then we went to Merrick and had Chinese food with Aunt Rita and Bernice and everyone," I reported.

"How are those two?" she asked with obvious affection. My mother smiled and returned to her veggie burger. After a moment, she looked up, "Do me a favor and take a shower before you sit at the table. I don't want sand to get in the carpet.

I rolled my eyes. "I don't have sand."

"If you were at the beach, you've got sand. We can spend five minutes arguing about it, or you can spend five minutes in the shower," my mother reasoned.

My eyes filled with tears.

"Jennifer, I have to tell you, sometimes it's hard being the parent who tells you to do your homework, do the dishes, and wash the sand out of your hair. Your father is the fun parent, I get it, but I have *chocolate cake* for you, and all you have to do is take a shower so you don't get sand all over our home, is that so hard?"

She noticed me eyeing her veggie burger and asked if I wanted her to make one for me. I jolted, reminding myself that if my mother knew the truth about the day, she would be furious with my father. If she knew about the pot smoking, she would have taken him to court to revoke his visitation rights. My mother once got a call from another parent complaining that my father had smoked pot in front of her daughter. Irate, my mother warned that if my father could not go one day without being high, he was not fit to visit me. Later he called my friend a snitch and said I needed to be more careful of friends who would rat him out. His tuning in for a day was never an option. On some level, we both understood that neither my father nor I had any idea what his baseline personality was anymore. His being high *was* normal. Clean and sober Shelly would have been a stranger to me.

"I have some extra kale too," my mother said, returning my focus to our dining room.

"I told you I had a huge dinner," I snapped. "I'm stuffed. I don't know if I even have room for your stupid cake," I said before making a swift escape to the shower.

Thirty years later, Claudia and her Italian family would unknowingly compensate for my failed twelfth birthday by laying out a lunch spread like nothing I'd ever seen before. I had no idea why her parents would host a party for someone they had never met, but was grateful for the generosity. On the table was fresh mozzarella, sliced tomatoes, *prosciutto*, breads, three different pasta dishes, and an array of grilled vegetables and roasted meats. They sang "Happy Birthday" in Italian as they presented a tricolored ice cream cake, mercifully with only one candle.

Claudia made reservations for us to tour the ruins of Pompeii at ten at night when the temperature was expected to dip below one hundred degrees. Before we left for her parents' apartment, I peeked my head out the window. "It looks like it's going to rain," I said, practically poking a low-hanging cloud. "Should we go to Pompeii after lunch before it starts?"

"It's a no going to rain," she replied.

"It looks pretty grim out there."

"You worry too much," Claudia said.

"I think you worry too little." She laughed.

Later that evening, Claudia's cell phone rang. She began speaking in rapid-fire Italian, sounding disappointed. I turned to Katie. "Ten euro says it's Pompeii cancelling our tour."

"Not taking that bet," she said.

Claudia shook her head and hung up the phone. "Jennifer, you're a never going to believe what happen."

"Pompeii is closed," Katie and I said in unison.

My daughter beamed. "Jinx, jinx, personal jinx. You owe me a soda!"

On cue, a burst of thunder erupted and the torrential downpour began as she explained that the site was, in fact, closing for rain.

"Here's what a you going to do," Claudia said, undeterred. "Tomorrow when you get on the train for *Firenze*, you transfer in a *Napoli*, yes?" I nodded. "Pompeii is a stop on the way to *Napoli*."

"If you say so."

"You hop off train in Pompeii and you will see someone in an Italian government uniform who can check your bags at the train station," Claudia said. "Then you walk across the street and the ruins are right there. Then you hop back on train and go to *Napoli*."

I looked at Katie and remembered how desperately she wanted to see the ruins of Pompeii. During the school year, when her teacher allowed students to select a topic for a report, Katie chose Pompeii. When the Pompeii exhibition was at the San Diego Natural History Museum, Katie insisted we visit in preparation for our trip.

"Um, okay," I told Claudia.

Katie clapped and jumped. "Can I do that? Am I allowed to just *hop on and off* the train?"

Claudia had already expressed outrage at how much I paid for train tickets by buying them in San Diego. She told me I paid thirty euro for a three-euro fare that I should have purchased at the train station vending machine. "*Mama mia!*" she shouted, then slapped one hand on the table and curled the other into a fist. "You tell them, I pay ten times what—"

"No, no," I interrupted. "I am not going to argue with an Italian train conductor. Just tell me, is this allowed or not allowed?"

She sighed. "No, but you go on train with a ticket. Say you make a mistake if they give you a problem. Thirty euro is a crazy."

"Oh no!" I yelped as I looked at Claudia's balcony. The rain was soaking all of our laundry on the clothesline. "This will never dry by morning."

"Of course it a will," Claudia assured me. "It will a dry overnight. You leave out a there. You worry a too much, Jennifer."

"You've mentioned that, Claudia."

She was half right. After we wrung out the laundry, we rehung it on the clothesline after the rain stopped. By five the following morning, our clothes were *almost* dry. I went out onto her tiny balcony in my nightgown and started running laps, spinning clothing in each hand like propellers, hoping to air dry them. I hardly noticed the sun rise. Or the neighbors watching, wondering what in God's name was happening on Gigi and Claudia's balcony.

Later that morning, Katie and I sat on a train headed to Pompeii. I was a bit nervous, but more proud that I was taking this leap. I was finally taking my French cousin's advice to relax and enjoy life. Besides, what could go wrong? I had all of Claudia's instructions written, including the Italian phrase for baggage check. The ruins of

Pompeii were right across the street from the station. Our plan was foolproof.

Then the train stopped.

"I don't see the station," Katie said.

"There's no station, sweetheart," I said. "The train broke down."

A half hour later, the train began moving again but at the pace of an elderly mule. Katie began making a rowing motion out the window and coaxing the train along. "Almost there, Little Italian Train That Could," she coaxed. We arrived at Pompeii station an hour and fifteen minutes late.

Calculating when the train left for Naples, I told Katie we had two hours to explore the ruins of Pompeii. "Perfect!" she said.

I wondered if she really felt it was perfect. Was I simply lucky enough to have a child with a naturally easygoing nature, or was she shielding me from her disappointment? Before I could begin my internal therapy session, Katie shrieked, "Mount Vesuvius!" as she pointed to the ominous centerpiece of the region.

Three old men sat at a small table outside the station playing dominoes. Their backdrop was a clear blue sky and mountain. "*Scusi*," I interrupted. Remembering the handy word *dov'è* for where, I asked, "*Per favore, dov'è...?*" I looked at Claudia's cheat sheet and asked where the baggage check was. They shook their heads and responded in Italian that there was no baggage check area.

"Um…*dov'è Pompeii, per favore?*"

They looked at each other amused. One man pointed at the small white sign posted over their table. It read "Pompeii." He rattled off Italian words I couldn't understand, but that clearly meant *Foolish woman*, this *is Pompeii.*

How do you say watch me, look at me? I wondered, flipping through my phrase book.

"*Guardami*," I said pointing to myself, going into charades mode. I placed my hands over my head in a point and spread my legs so my body would resemble a volcano ready to erupt.

Think about acting class. Be the volcano.

"*Io sono Vesuvius.*" I then began to grumble like the volcano getting ready to erupt. They weren't getting it. Either that, or they wanted to see how far I would go. The cost of directions was going to be a full dramatic recreation of the fateful day in Pompeii. I tilted my head back so my mouth pointed skyward and made a bubbling, spewing noise like percolating coffee. I brought my fists to my face and then lifted fluttering fingers up toward the imaginary volcano rim. Each man suppressed laughter. With my hands and arms, I imitated lava flowing down the sides of the volcano, all while grumbling and bubbling "*Sono Vesuvius*, grrr." Then I held up a finger to let them know I was doing a new scene. I pointed to myself, now a woman in the ancient city washing her laundry in a basin.

"*Mama mia, Vesuvius!*" I shrieked, placing my hands on my cheeks. I began running in place, looking over my shoulder checking to see if I was outrunning the flowing lava. "Oh no!" I gasped, then froze in the position of the statue featured on the ruins of Pompeii promotional material.

"*Brava!*" they shouted and clapped. "*Si vuole scavi.*"

Vuole? *That either means "you want" or "you go," right? And* scavi *must mean excavation site*, I thought.

"*Si scavi!*" Katie said.

The men rattled in Italian and pointed. Noticing I didn't understanding his directions, one of the men tore a piece of paper from his pad and drew a map.

Scavi was not across the street as Claudia had promised. Nor was there an Italian government official waiting to check our bags anywhere in sight.

Katie and I proceeded to walk the mile or so to the ruins of Pompeii, pulling our suitcases through sun-baked cobblestone streets. I gained a new appreciation for the delicacy of my elbows as they absorbed the shock from the suitcase wheels jumping in and out of the grooves in our path. For a moment, I considered walking in the gutter so we could enjoy a paved road. Then I remembered that something perilous occupied these streets: Italian drivers.

"Look ahead!" Katie shouted.

"It's a mirage," I said, exhausted. "Don't fall for it. There is no water."

She laughed. "It says 'Tourist Information'—in *English*!"

Printed boldly on a blue canvas tent were the welcoming, wonderful words. In fact, there was a row of about fifty tents offering maps, tours, and souvenirs.

I eagerly greeted the couple working at the blue tent and asked where the baggage check was. They looked at each other and shrugged. "Here," the man replied. "Three euro and you leave bags in back."

This was the baggage check? Where was the Italian government official? As I rolled my bags to the back of the tent, I wondered where the other luggage was. "Um, you're sure this is a baggage check?" I asked dumbly. What did I expect? If they were crooks, they weren't going to tell me.

"Yes, it's no problem," the woman assured me. "Three euro."

The further we got from the blue tent, the more my discomfort grew. My anxiety erupted when we reached the entrance of the site. A barrel of a woman in an Italian government uniform stood with her arms folded under a sign that read "*Deposito Bagagli*," the exact words Claudia had written for me.

"*This* is the *Deposito Bagagli*?" I asked the woman, switching back and forth between my natural voice and my English accent.

"How many tickets?" she replied with the energy of someone who was days from retirement.

"One child, one adult," I said.

She knit her eyebrows. "Where are you from?"

"*From?*" I asked, sheepish.

"Let me see your passports," she demanded. Obediently, I showed her the U.S. passports.

"We live in California currently," I said lamely.

She blurted the price for full-fare non-European Union members. I handed her my credit card and asked again, "If this is the baggage check, who did I give our bags to?" She did not respond. "The people in those tents? Who are they?"

"The gypsies?" she snorted.

"Gypsies?!" Didn't gypsies wear head scarves and off-the-shoulder blouses? Those two looked like an ad for Old Navy.

"They probably won't steal your things," the baggage clerk said cruelly. "You weren't stupid enough to leave money in there, right?"

"No, um, not *that* stupid."

"Next!" she shouted.

I began breathing heavily with panic, no easy task in the stagnant Italian summer air. If the gypsies stole our luggage, we would have absolutely no clothing except what was on our backs. I had our passports and train and plane tickets, but I'd grown rather attached to some of my sundresses. And all of the Vatican souvenirs I had bought for my Catholic family and friends would be lost. I had no desire to spend our first day in Florence shopping for new underwear, shirts, and shorts. Glancing at my watch, I realized that we only had forty-five minutes to explore the ruins if we were to make it back to the station in time to catch our train to Naples then connect to Florence. "Katie, we need to move quickly," I told her.

We spent the next three-quarters of an hour jogging through the ancient city, barely stopping to read any of the exhibition descriptions. I knew that this visit to Pompeii would likely be our only one together, so I rushed through, trying to cram a daylong tour into less than an hour.

The site was 160 acres, the lifeless and parched remains of the ancient walled city. There were large open lots with broken columns and statues, and small lots displaying antiquities like kitchen items, tools, and utensils. Some structures like the amphitheater remained mostly intact, while others like the Temple of Apollo were reduced to small fragments of their former selves. Some cells were once people's homes, now no more than a faint property line.

As Katie looked at the exhibits, my mind raced with worry. If the gypsies stole our suitcases, we would need to replace those too. Good God, how could I be so stupid?!

"Can you believe this was once an entire city?" Katie asked, looking at another display. "Did you see that poor dog?"

"The statue of the dog?" I asked Katie.

"Mommy, that was no statue. He was covered in lava from the eruption at Mount Vesuvius."

I wasted my time in Pompeii simultaneously trying to cover the most ground possible and fretting about gypsies selling my moisturizer on the black market. As a result, I saw very little and understood even less.

Katie and I exited the site and looked around at the completely unfamiliar area. Despite my best efforts to remember which exit was nearest to where we entered, I had lost my bearings in the sprawling site. Making a mental note to turn left at the crumbling column did absolutely no good. "If we follow the outside of the wall, we'll make it to the tents eventually," Katie suggested as she quickened her pace. I looked at my watch nervously.

"Wasn't there a church nearby?" I asked.

"Please, this is Italy," Katie said with an eye roll. "There's always a church nearby."

"No seriously, look for the cross on the steeple, that's where our bags are." *Or were.*

After twenty minutes, we saw the blue tent and sprinted toward it. "I want our bags!" I demanded breathlessly, accusing.

The man gave a Euro-shrug and led me to the back where the suitcases appeared to be untouched. I unzipped the bags, and everything was exactly as I had left it. "Oh," I said, feeling like a heel. "*Grazie.*"

He shrugged again and we were on our way. If Katie and I rolled our bags at the same pace we'd set as we walked the periphery of the ancient city, we could make it to the train station with zero minutes to spare. We bought chilled water not only to drink, but also to douse on our bodies as we raced to make the train. We arrived sweaty, breathless, and probably in need of elbow surgery, but on time.

The train, however, was not. It pulled in to the station an hour later.

When Katie and I arrived in Naples, we had an hour to spare before our train left for Florence. I spotted a pay phone. "Let's call Daddy!" I suggested. "He should be just getting to work around now."

Telling William about our day in Pompeii, I reported, "The jig is up on my European discount."

"Your what?"

"Oh, I've been using an English accent to get EU discounts on admission at tourist attractions," I said blithely.

"I'm sorry, what did you say?"

I explained again.

"That's what I thought you said," William said, irked. "Jennifer, that's stealing."

"*Stealing?*" I said, appalled by the accusation. "There's no reason they should charge European residents less than the rest of us."

"Actually, there is," William said. "They pay taxes into the system that maintains sites like the ruins of Pompeii and all of the museums you've been visiting. You don't."

"Oh," I said, deflated. "I hadn't realized."

"Here's what you need to do," William told me. "When

you're in Florence, find a museum or cultural attraction and slip some extra money in the donation box."

"Really? Can't I just stop?" I asked.

"Nope." Marrying a man who embraced the rule of law was a good deal for the most part, but there were moments like this when it was going to cost me. William and I exchanged a few more words before I handed the phone to Katie. "Be good," he said, bidding me farewell.

After Katie and I boarded the train to Florence, I finally felt the effects of the long day. I melted into my cushioned brown seat and felt a lump in my throat as the train pulled away from Pompeii station.

"I know this wasn't exactly what you had hoped for from Pompeii," I told Katie, who was looking out the window. "But you're young; you'll get to Pompeii again and you'll make that visit perfect."

She turned to face me, her long braids disheveled, freckles smattered across her nose. "A trip doesn't have to be perfect to be great, Mommy. We got to see the ruins of Pompeii. Do you know how lucky we are?"

Katie instinctively knew what I had struggled my entire life to grasp. And I still hadn't really gotten it. Eluding me was the ability to focus on what I had, rather than what I had lost or could lose.

I smiled and placed my hand over hers. "You're right."

Looking out the window, she snorted a little laugh. "People have had worse days in Pompeii, you know?"

6

FLORENCE

Visiting Florence was like attending a surprise party every day.

Katie and I arrived by train a little after nine that evening and found the city absolutely, positively barren. It was apocalyptically desolate; not a soul on the streets. We got the attention of a taxi driver by tapping on the window of his yellow cab and breaking his trance.

My childhood friend Andrew had recommended the Cimatori Bed and Breakfast because he knew we shared the same travel requirements: location and price. The Cimatori was in the center of town, the third floor of a walk-up apartment building that looked like something from the Lower East Side of Manhattan before it was hip. The lobby was lined with old white subway tile. Two bikes sat chained to a rack. A row of metal mailboxes was bolted to the wall, each bearing the name of a different bed and breakfast. As Katie and I pulled our suitcases up three flights of stairs, we read small ceramic signs for each. One bed and breakfast marked its door with a dainty oval sign that bore its name in lavender script and a trim of painted wildflowers. It seemed to be trying to convince visitors that it was the entrance to a charming country cottage.

The hostess at the Cimatori quickly showed us our room, rattled explanations of where everything was, and rushed off. She wasn't rude but clearly in the midst of doing something more important like assisting at a childbirth or fighting a wildfire. "We talk in the morning, ay?" she said, her long black hair flowing behind her.

I turned to Katie. "Let's take a little walk and get our bearings."

"Sure," she said, grabbing one of the maps on the desk.

The front door of our bed and breakfast opened onto a narrow street lined with apartment buildings. I looked left, then right, but neither direction offered any sort of visual invitation. "Let's just walk to the end of the block," I offered.

Before we made it to the end of the cobblestone street, however, we saw another small alley that led to a statue of an equestrian. "Katie, let's walk down to the horse." I hoped I wasn't leading us into the dodgy part of Florence, but ganglands weren't usually marked with Renaissance sculptures, so I figured it was probably safe. I could not imagine an Italian hoodlum challenging his rival to knife-fight behind a Botticelli.

As Katie and I got closer to the statue, we realized that the alley actually opened to a giant piazza, the largest we had seen so far after eleven days in Italy. The long corner of intricately adorned buildings was positioned like outstretched arms, the periwinkle sky maternal and soothing. The piazza was dotted with about a half-dozen sculptures, including a copy of Michelangelo's *David*. "We are at Piazza della Signoria," Katie announced, looking at her map. Pointing, she added, "That building is the Uffizi Gallery, and if we walk one more block we'll be at the Arno River."

"Should we go further?" I asked.

"Why not?" Katie returned with a Euro-shrug. Walking along the Arno, Katie and I still did not see a soul. I knew Florence wouldn't be like Rome with its constant hustle, but even Salerno had more nightlife than this. We took in the stone bridges that stretched across the narrow river and wondered why no one was out. It was worth a stroll just to watch the light from the street lamps dancing on the black water. But where was everyone?

An eruption of cheering came from every corner of Florence. People blew horns and cried out the way they might when ringing in the New Year. "*Mama Mia!*" we heard from several different directions.

"What's happening?" Katie asked, delighted.

"Goal!" someone shouted, as if to answer her question.

The next morning, all the talk at breakfast was about Spain's big win of the Euro Cup. A few women soccer players from Hong Kong sat next to an ebullient Italian couple and two deflated German men. I wondered why the victory was so personal for Italy, then the host explained that if your country isn't playing, you root for your neighbor. She glanced side-long at the Germans and said that Spain's opponent played extremely well and the victory was very hard-won.

The late-morning streets of Florence were like fresh-baked flatbread. In fact, the whole city had a warm, doughy feel that reminded me of my long-deceased grandmother Aggie. Perhaps it was the fact that the low height of the yeasty colored buildings allowed sunshine to constantly bake the streets. Perhaps it was the ever-present aroma of bread. I wasn't sure, but something about the city made me crave focaccia.

Post-soccer frenzy, Florence was amply populated with people making their way about town with unfolded maps and gelato cups. Katie's and my only plan was finding the Accademia so we would not miss our scheduled time to see the *David* sculpture the following day.

About a block before we reached the museum, we heard booming opera singing coming from a nondescript building. We looked at each other and raised our eyebrows. Without saying a word, we headed toward the giant dark wooden door. A man in red jeans pushed open the door while simultane-ously rolling up the sleeves of his aqua button-down shirt.

I managed to clumsily ask in Italian what translated to: "What is music?"

"Ah, *belle*, you are Americans." We nodded. "Music school has…ah, how you say, *esame*?"

"Exam?" Katie popped like a game show contestant.

"*Si! Esame* for the opera student. You have come to watch?"

At first I worried that he had mistaken us for expected guests. Before I could explain that we *wanted* to watch, Katie chimed in. "*Si, grazie.*"

Sporting her little red backpack, Katie stepped into the school and accepted a catalog from the man. "You use a for fan," he explained, handing me a small booklet as well.

Katie and I sat in the back row of a muggy auditorium as a twentysomething skater boy belted out *Figaro*. An elderly Italian woman with red cotton-candy hair interrupted and directed. He sang it again and again until the woman was satisfied that he had fully embodied the character. Katie and I looked at each other in amazement at how the bony young man's voice could fill the auditorium until the walls nearly shook. Wide-eyed, she asked, "Where does he get all that air?"

Katie and I now shared the experience of hearing the *Figaro* aria outside of the traditional venue of an opera house. When my mother and I lived in Greenwich Village, one of the two guys who lived upstairs sang for the Metropolitan Opera and used *Figaro* as his standard warm-up. He sang it in the shower; he sang it in the kitchen. He sang it in the morning; he sang it in the afternoon. *Figaro, Figaro, Fiiiii-garo!*

When the couple fought, the opera singer wouldn't storm out the front door. Instead he opened the window and climbed out onto the fire escape. One evening, my mother and I heard delicate, apologetic tapping on our living room window. It was Opera Guy. My mother opened the window, but before she could ask why he had climbed down onto our fire escape, he blurted, "Goddamn Frank locked me out. I needed a little fresh air and he locked the windows." With Opera Guy now inside our apartment, my mother asked if he had a key to the front door. "No," he said, primly placing his hands on his lap. "I am so steamed. Can I use your broom?"

My mother handed it to him without question. Like the diva he was, Opera Guy lifted the broom handle and began banging on our ceiling. "You're an asshole, Frank," he shouted.

Our neighbor banged a few more times and shouted, "You can smoke yourself to death up there, but I will not have you destroy my instrument!"

They were in their own world, separated only by the thin layer that divided our apartments.

"Who's Frank?" I asked my mother as our upstairs neighbor escalated the fight by stomping on his floor.

My mother was baffled by my confusion. After living in Greenwich Village for nearly a year, the idea of a gay couple shouldn't have fazed me. Two lesbians helped us move our furniture into the apartment. Most of my mother's friends were gay men.

"Yes, they live together. They're lovers," my mother explained of our neighbors.

"I thought his name was Figaro."

After the Italian student passed his opera exam, a young woman took the stage wearing a white rag on her head. She held a mop and began a soprano aria that could make people weep, even those who had no idea what the words meant. Katie reached into her backpack and took out a book. "We can leave if you're bored," I whispered.

"Bored? This is great," she said, offering me a swig from her water bottle. "I didn't know I like opera." She rested her head on my shoulder, the heat depleting us. The student hit a point in her song where she was begging the master of the house for mercy after he had just shoved her onto the floor. My eyes filled with tears, though I wasn't sure if it was because of what was happening on stage or within me. Two instructors in the front row dabbed at their eyes with handkerchiefs. Either the student's performance was excellent, or these teachers were also highly neurotic mothers overwhelmed by the joy of realizing that life's most perfect moments could not be planned, scheduled, or even expected.

"What do you think she's singing about?" I asked Katie, who lifted her head to reply.

"I think she's very unhappy at her job."

The next day, Katie and I took a walk down the Arno River before our appointment to see Michelangelo's *David*. As we crossed the Piazza della Signoria, we saw a full-size theatrical stage with ballet dancers stretching together on the *barre*. "Isn't that nice, they're giving outdoor ballet lessons. Maybe it's the ballet school's final exam," I suggested.

That night we realized that what we'd witnessed earlier was a professional ballet company practicing for a full-scale performance in the piazza. Under the stars, dancers performed on a stage the size of the Lincoln Center's. The piazza held thousands of people who gathered to watch, picnic baskets and wine bottles in hand. "What is this?" I asked someone.

"A ballet," a woman answered in a thick Eastern European accent. Her flat expression clearly indicated she thought I was an idiot. What else would it be? Women in delicate gauzy skirts and toe shoes flitted across stage into the arms of muscular men in tights.

"Where do we buy tickets?"

"You are, no doubt, Americans," she said. "You do not

buy tickets. Sit and vatch ballet. Tomorrow evening vill be symphony."

When my mother left New Jersey to move to Greenwich Village in the late 1950s, one of her great loves was studying at the Joffrey Ballet School. She was nineteen years old and bursting to escape her traditional Italian Catholic life in Newark. Her parents saw no need for a girl to attend college, so my mother applied to NYU on her own and financed her education through a work-study program for several years. She moved in with two women who took her under their wings and taught her about gender politics and the burgeoning women's movement. Her posse attended free lectures, theater, and poetry readings in warehouse basements. They dropped small bronze tokens into subway turnstiles that led to tubes marked with angry graffiti. With neither cruelty nor apology, my mother calls those days the best of her life.

Every few years, my mother and I take a walking tour of her youth in the Village where she points out her old apartment (where the buzzer now reads "Fisher"), the neighborhood Laundromat (which is now a hip bistro), and the Italian meat market (which has remained unchanged). She sighs with nostalgic delight at all of her old haunts, but the one that evokes the most emotion is when she sees the oversized windows of the Joffrey Ballet School on Sixth Avenue. "I ran from my classes at NYU straight to ballet, then went out with my friends for the evening," she says. "We never got tired."

When she married my Brooklynite father, my mother reluctantly left Manhattan. She returned soon after their divorce six years later. "I should have never left Sheridan Square," she still says more than forty years after her return to Manhattan. "Our place was rent controlled. I'd pay $600 today."

My mother is one of the old-school New Yorkers who firmly resents the transplants who moved to Manhattan only after the construction of glossy Trump residences. When women with jet-black winged hair and bedazzled running suits pass us on the street now, my mother shakes her head. "They were afraid to come to the city unless it was to see a Broadway show," she scoffs. "They'd jump into their Cadillacs, lock the doors, and complain about the noise." She furrows her brows at the sight of frat boys-turned-businessmen barking into their cell phones. "They've taken over and now young artists have to commute from Pennsylvania." Some actually do live in Pennsylvania, but when my mother refers to the state, she could mean any of the other four boroughs. She might also mean Long Island, Westchester County, or New Jersey.

Thanks to rent stabilization, she has been able to remain in Manhattan but has lost several friends to the city's gentrification. At the dawn of the Reagan Revolution, my mother's college boyfriend bought a place in Woodstock. We imagine him today with a long gray ponytail making candles and teaching yoga. In the mid-eighties, another dear friend fled to San Francisco. And the year *Wall Street*'s Gordon Gekko declared "Greed is good," my mother's roommates from NYU packed their burlap sacks and bought a Christmas tree farm in Massachusetts. The nineties brought Mayor Rudy Giuliani, and soon Times Square's triple X peep shows became Starbucks and the Olive Garden. Local pimps were replaced with latte baristas and waiters sporting apron flair.

"Maybe it's good," my mother says, now a woman who carries a senior Metrocard, wears sensible shoes, and questions the wisdom of multiple tattoos. "The kids have done wonders with Brooklyn, but I sometimes miss the old city." She says that just ten years ago, by the time the L train arrived at First Avenue—its last stop before leaving Manhattan—she was the only person left on the subway. "Now it's filled with young people with guitars and knapsacks and bicycles," she says. "The train is still packed when I get off, and they all stay on and head to Brooklyn."

Katie and I arrived at the Accademia a full hour before our scheduled time. We walked the exact route that had taken us ten minutes the day before, but I wasn't going to leave anything to chance. Seeing the *David* was important. As much as I enjoyed our afternoon of unscheduled opera, I wasn't ready to let go of my checklist mentality. And I wasn't sure abandoning it completely would be a good idea either. It would be crazy to visit Florence and miss one of its most important historical sites.

Walking through the doors to the Accademia was like stepping though the wardrobe to Narnia. I gasped seeing him, even from afar. I fully expected to be underwhelmed by the *David*, but the marble statue had the opposite effect. From the moment I saw the statue in the distance, it was as though the wind had been knocked out of me. "My God, it's…" I began, unable to complete the thought.

"Huge," Katie finished.

We quickened our pace to get closer. I had never had a reaction like this to a work of art. It was like falling in love, an inexplicable sense of euphoria just being in his presence. I had seen this image countless times in art books and on postcards, but being in the same room with the statue was something entirely different. If I wasn't certain I would've been arrested, I would have climbed up onto the pedestal and run my bare hands across every inch of his smooth, marble body. I settled for staring at *David*'s toes for twenty minutes and making my way up fourteen feet. Every muscle, every vein, and every hair was perfectly sculpted. I'd always thought of him as expressionless, but

I'd never had the chance to look directly at his eyes and notice the way his forehead furrowed with a mix of fear and determination.

Was it possible to have a crush on a statue?

Katie stared at *David* with his slingshot and wondered aloud how big the statue of Goliath would be.

"Through the roof," I replied. "Thank goodness Michelangelo was commissioned to sculpt the underdog."

My mother came to see me at Camp St. Regis on the first visiting Sunday in July. My father visited in August, which was also the day of the horse show. When I was ten years old, I won first place in my division, so my father urged me to ride in the championship. "You have to be at least thirteen," I explained, taking off my boots and hat.

"How come?"

"I don't know," I said with a shrug. "Just the rules."

We sat on a slope of dry grass that overlooked the corral as the next group rode in on their horses. "I'm not really one for just following rules that don't make sense," he told me. "Do they do anything in the championship that's dangerous for a ten-year-old?" I shook my head. "Do they do anything you haven't done before?" I shook my head again, eyes focused on the corral. "You should ride in the championship."

"I'll never win," I explained. "The girls who are riding are much, much better."

"It's not about winning, Jennifer," he said. I knew I wasn't going to get a Ward Cleaver-style speech about it only mattering how I played the game.

"It's not?" I looked at him.

"No. Everyone is going to love you when they see you on that horse."

"They are?"

"Are you kidding me?! You're a foot shorter than anyone else in that ring," he said. "You're a featherweight swinging with the heavies. I'm telling you right now, if you ride in the championship, you will come in dead last, but no one will get more applause than you."

My heart raced at the thought. "But...the rules," I said.

"I'll talk to the judge," he said. "Is that her?"

That's right, the judge is a girl, I remembered silently. *I'm going to wind up riding in this thing, aren't I?*

During the break, I watched my father from a distance. Against a backdrop of the white stable, my father smiled and introduced himself to the horse show judge. My father's hands gestured to me as he spoke for a few minutes. The judge smiled and nodded.

My father trotted back to the hillside and gave me the thumbs up. "You're in. Very cool girl. She saw no reason for the age discrimination."

"Are you sure I should?"

"Wait till you feel the rush of everyone rooting for you," he said.

As I entered the corral, I heard a collective *Awww*. Then a single voice began chanting my name. A few people joined in, and within thirty seconds, my father was leading the entire audience, shouting "Jen-nie, Jen-nie!!!"

My father's prediction was spot on. I placed last, which I found only slightly humiliating. "You're ten years old, you had to come in last," my father explained, placing his arm around me. "You were the underdog and the people loved you. That's better than any trophy."

Before the symphony in the piazza, Katie and I stopped at a local deli to pick up our dinner. Dozens of sausages hung in the window. Breads were piled high. Inside, tubs of mozzarella balls, pasta, and seafood salads sat behind glass counters. Katie opted for a piece of pizza and a bottle of Orangina. I made a meal of the octopus, squid, and mussel salad.

Katie and I sat on a blanket in the piazza for hours as the seventy-piece symphony filled the city of Florence with classical music. Wine bottles were drained as the evening went on; couples got cozy. Apartment windows opened and balconies filled with onlookers. It was like a serenade of Florence en masse and we were all smitten.

The next day was our scheduled tour of Pisa, which a travel agent back in San Diego had arranged for us. I figured if we wanted to see the Leaning Tower of Pisa, we had to go through an organized tour group. The touring company asked guests to meet at a bus station at 2:00 p.m. We spent the morning taking a long walk down the Arno River, people-watching and admiring the bridges. The hosts at the bed and breakfast told us the Ponte Vecchio was spared bombing because the Nazis could not bear to destroy such a beautiful historic site. *Oh those sweet, sentimental Nazis*, I thought silently.

Katie and I decided that we'd spend a few minutes checking email at a local cybercafé. "Oh my God!" Katie shrieked after looking at her screen for a few minutes. "Someone forgot to close their email."

"You're reading someone's personal email? You know better than that, Katie."

"Wanna know what it said?"

"No, you should close that email."

"This tour guide of a teen group got fired and the company had to write to all of the parents and tell them that Mr. Finkle had been let go for *drinking* with the students," Katie read.

"Really?"

"And that if any of the teens were caught drinking, they would be sent home immediately. No refund!"

I loved Katie's eleven-year-old innocence. Sixteen-year-olds drinking was unheard of in her world of elementary schoolyard tetherball and gold star stickers on spelling tests. "But Mr. Finkle is still traveling with the group. He's following them even though he was fired."

"Seriously?! That's odd. Does it say why he won't leave?"

"Nope."

Now intrigued with the drama, I speculated. "I bet he's in love with one of the girls he was drinking with." Our fifteen-minute tokens for email use expired, so we grabbed a cup of gelato nearby and lay on the grass for the next half hour, trying to fill in the blanks about the case of the wayward tour leader. With a mouthful of chocolate gelato, Katie continued. "Know what? I think the guy who told on Mr. Finkle is also in love with the girl. I think he squealed to get rid of him."

"This is quite an opera."

With a chocolate mustache of gelato, she sang, "Mr. Finkle must-a leave-a teen tour."

I joined with a flitty soprano number from the girl torn between the two men. It sounded a bit like the frenetic part of *Figaro*. "Finkle-a-drinker, Finkle make trouble, Finkle no leave, Finkle in love," I sang.

We improvised a duet by the girl's parents back home who worried about their drunken daughter. We called it "Oy Vey Maria." A few people glanced our way and smiled, but for the most part no one seemed fazed by the sight of a mother and daughter laughing themselves silly, trying to compose the worst opera ever.

With our hands outstretched for the grand finale, I caught a glimpse of my watch and noticed the time. "Oh no! We need to get to the bus for Pisa!"

When our bus pulled into Pisa Square at 3:00 p.m., our tour guide told us we absolutely must meet back at the bus by 6:00 p.m. so she could return us to Florence by 7:00 p.m. *But we don't need to be back so early*, I thought. "Three hours is plenty of time to do what we came for," I assured Katie.

Still on the bus, the tour guide repeated her instructions in Spanish and French through a microphone.

All Katie wanted to do was climb that tower. For days, she had been talking about how many steps it had, how high it was, and how long it might take if she jogged. "Okay, we take you to church now," our tour guide said as the bus doors exhaled open.

Church?! At this point, we had seen several dozen churches. Two days earlier, we had visited a church with a mosaic of Jesus shooting light beams from his fingers. "Is Jesus…playing laser tag?" Katie asked.

"Don't be silly, they didn't have laser tag back then," I said.

"The churches are pretty, but we've seen so many. I feel

like we've seen Jesus doing just about everything." She was right. We'd seen him as a newborn, sleeping in the manger, in his mother's arms, giving sermons, being tried for crimes, having his last supper, being crucified, and rising from the dead. And shooting light from his fingertips.

"We haven't seen his prom shots," I offered. "Those are in Venice and I hear they're *cuh-razy*. He took Mary Magdalene, and plenty of people thought her dress was way too short."

As we departed the bus, I told the tour guide we were going to skip the church visit. We could see the Leaning Tower beckoning Katie like an outstretched finger saying, *Come here, kid*. The tour guide snapped, "No, you stay with group! We go to church. It is few minute, then you go to your own."

There was no escape. If we tried to tiptoe away, we would have surely been caught. "It's okay," Katie whispered. "We've got plenty of time."

After a forty-five-minute tour of the church, the guide took us on a half-hour walk through the piazza and told us more than we ever wanted to know about a fountain.

Finally, our tour guide forced a tight smile and told us we were free to tour the rest of the square on our own. Before we could bolt, she barked, "Be back at the bus at six o'clock or there is a trouble."

Katie and I ran to the Leaning Tower, passing dozens of people posing for pictures pushing down—or holding up—the tower. Breathless, we arrived at the booth to buy a ticket to climb the tower. "*Signora*, the next ticket for climb is at six o'clock," a man told us.

"Six o'clock?!" Katie gasped, her eyes welling with tears.

This was turning into the ruins of Pompeii part two.

On the bus ride back to Florence, the tour guide finished her cell phone conversation with her boyfriend, then plastered on a big smile. Through the microphone, she asked everyone, "You like a visit Pisa?"

Fuck you.

I watched Katie stare out the window for the next half hour. "It was cool to see the Tower at least," she said, trying to convince herself that the day trip wasn't a complete loss. But I wasn't in Italy to create experiences that ended with Katie's resignation. Our troubles in Pompeii were out of my control. Because of the timing here, however, I could remedy the situation. On the one hand, it was important for Katie to learn to be flexible and roll with the punches of life. But on the other, I knew I could go back and straighten things out for us in Pisa. So fix them I would.

"I have an idea," I said, tapping her leg. "Tomorrow we have our tour of Siena and San Gimignano, but on Saturday, let's take a train and come back to Pisa on our own."

"Can we do that?"

After our visit to Pompeii, I was actually terrified at the prospect of independent day trips. But as afraid as I was to venture out on our own, I had greater fear of disappointing Katie, of her remembering me as a mother unable to deliver what was most important to her. This was critical, especially if my fate was the same as my father's. I wanted Katie to think of me as a mother who made the most of our time together, even if it was cut short.

"Yeah, how hard could it be? We'll just check out the train schedule and grab a map," I said, feigning confidence.

The next day, after a guided tour through Siena and San Gimignano, I decided we were absolutely done with high-priced organized day trips. Our guide was a direct descendant of Mussolini, controlling every move we made, including when we went to the bathroom. Katie and I got such a bad case of motion sickness on the bus ride to San Gimignano that, upon arrival, we immediately got off the bus, threw up, and found cool nooks in the stone walls in which we could curl up and cry until the world stopped spinning.

As luck would have it, we started feeling better at the exact time the fascist with the clipboard told us it was time to get back on the bus to Florence. Our bus mates told us the town was charming and shared their photos of the walled village and surrounding Tuscan olive groves. They showed us the olive wood salad bowls and flavored oils they bought. It was almost as if we had been there.

"Pisa, take two," I said to Katie, waking her for our Saturday adventure. We purchased train tickets for a few euros and hopped aboard. Although I knew the ride would take nearly an hour, I felt panic-stricken every ten minutes and was compelled to shoot my fellow passengers a pathetic look and ask, "Pisa?" The conductor assured me that he would alert us when the next stop was Pisa, but I kept worrying about what would happen if we missed our stop. How far would we go before realizing we were in another part of Italy altogether? I was sweating at the thought of the conductor announcing, "Oopsy doopsy, we are now in Austria." Instead he smiled patiently and said, "*Signora*, next stop is a Pisa."

Although we could not see the Leaning Tower from the train station, finding it was quite easy. All I had to do was ask where, *dov'è*, while holding my hands overhead and leaning—a much easier charade than Pompeii.

Katie and I filled our backpack with books, water, and snacks, knowing that we might have a very long wait to climb the tower. In front of us in line were people grumbling with disappointment. The next ticket to climb the tower was three hours away. "*Buono*," I told the ticket agent when he informed me of the wait.

"You wait till three in the afternoon?" he asked to clarify.

I gestured my head toward Katie and said, "I wait till ten at night," then gave a shrug. "You have *bambinos*?"

He smiled at Katie, "You have good mama."

For the next several hours, we sat in the shade of the Leaning Tower, moving with the sun as necessary. At our appointed time, Katie and I stood in line for the three-hundred-step climb to the top of the Leaning Tower. After about fifty steps, I started to feel as if I were on the mad teacup ride at Disney World. This tower didn't just feel like it was leaning, but swaying and spinning too. I asked a security guard if Katie could make the trip on her own.

"How old?" he asked.

Gripping the rail, I squeaked, "Eighteen?"

"*Bella*, she's a no eighteen years," he said sympathetically.

"She is here," I replied, pointing to my head.

"Don't you feel well?" Katie asked.

"I feel great. I just think you can make it faster on your own."

"Children go with the adult," I was informed.

Inhaling deeply, I began counting steps.

My mother must have felt the same way when she thought about taking me on the rides at Disney World, which had just opened in Orlando, Florida. I was eleven years old, and my mother offered to take me on a special trip for just the two of us. I could choose anywhere in the country. She tossed out a few suggestions—an ashram in New Mexico, a bed and breakfast in Provincetown, the Shakespeare Festival in Oregon.

When I told her I wanted to make the pilgrimage to Disney, her face dropped. "You don't like rides?" I asked.

"No...I—" my mother's voice trailed off. "Sure, we'll go to Disneyland."

"*World*, Ma, this is Disney *World*."

What I hadn't known at the time was that, six months earlier, my mother had just dealt with the blunt end of our family's greatest tragedy. Everyone was told that my mother's only sibling, her older brother Ernie, had been struck by an untimely heart attack on his forty-fourth birthday. It was my mother who went alone to her brother's home in Miami to face the scene where he was brutally murdered. She arranged a funeral and lied to her eighty-year-old mother about why Ernie could not have an open-casket wake. Aggie never understood why her son couldn't have a proper Catholic wake, but in a dark corner of her mind, she might have suspected that the birthday money she sent her son was the motive for a house burglary that went terribly, terribly wrong.

Returning to Florida so soon after was one of the most self-less acts my mother could have performed. She wore mouse ears and held a balloon. Mercifully, however, she was spared the rides. Waiting in the entrance line to enter Disney World, we looked at our map, selecting attractions and rides. My vote was for Space Mountain. She thought Tomorrowland looked good.

"You sound like our family," said a black woman in a red straw hat who was standing in front of us.

"Love the hat," my mother commented.

"I like yours," she replied. Gesturing to a man and a woman about her age, she said, "These two wanna go on all sorts of crazy rides, Whiplash Mountain, Pirates of Death. Honey, you can count me out."

"Aw, now Lavonne, we ain't come to Disney World to see no wax figures," said her husband.

"Mmm-hmm," the other woman agreed.

As my mother began chatting with the trio, we learned that Lavonne and Shawn were married, and Doreen and Lavonne were sisters. Shawn and Doreen were my kind of people: thrill-seekers. My mother and Lavonne were a match made in heaven: hat-lovers in search of air-conditioned, static displays.

"Why don't you two take Jennifer on the rides and Lavonne and I will go at a slower pace till lunch?" my mother suggested.

The three looked at each other tentatively. "I'm sorry," my mother said. "I've overstepped."

Shawn laughed. "Lady, you ain't from the South."

In a moment, my mother understood. Despite the recent victories of the civil rights movement, Florida still wasn't the kind of place where a black couple could walk around with a little white girl and not raise a few eyebrows.

We stood for a moment before Shawn broke the silence. "Aww, let's try it. But Carol, Lavonne, you don't see us back here at noon, you head straight to Mickey's police station, 'cause that's where we gonna be."

Our mix-and-match families split to pursue our Disney dreams. "Jennie, we run to the rides; that okay with you?" Shawn asked.

"Shawn, you are speaking my language," I said, bolting toward Space Mountain.

When we met for lunch, my mother was wearing Minnie Mouse ears over her white sunhat. Lavonne had bought herself a fan and a large bag of fudge from the Main Street candy shop. "I am so glad I met this lady!" Lavonne said. "Carol knows everything about theater and the ballet. I am gonna get myself to New York City someday soon, Carol. We're gonna see *A Chorus Line*!"

My mother and I returned to the Ramada Inn that evening and shared our highlights. We sat on a bench outside, watching palm trees and fountain water change color as tinted spotlights cycled the rainbow. It was the most exotic place I had ever seen. "I'm glad you didn't have to go on the rides," I told my mother.

"Me too," she said. "They make me light-headed."

"What if we hadn't met that family?" I asked.

"I would've been light-headed."

"I cannot believe I am on the top of the Leaning Tower of Pisa!" Katie said for the sixteenth time.

"I know, pretty incredible." Once we reached the top, Katie and I stood outside, which made a world of difference because I could focus on the horizon.

"What do you want to do tonight?" I asked Katie.

"Mom, we are on top of the Leaning Tower of Pisa right now!" Katie reminded me. "Look around." I turned to see open fields and the University of Pisa stadium. I looked down and saw the square and small shops. I even took in the line of people waiting to make the climb and gave them a little wave.

Back on the train to Florence, I asked again about our evening plans. Katie told me she wanted to walk to the bakery and get a giant meringue puff. "Then, I don't know, let's see what Florence has in store for us," she said with a shrug.

That evening, as we neared the Arno River, we saw a couple playing music at the base of the Uffizi and a crowd of nearly a hundred people gathered on the steps listening to them. "Oh Cecilia, you're breaking my heart, you're shaking my confidence daily," the man and woman sang in harmony.

"Let's stay!" Katie suggested.

We found a space on the steps, clasped hands, and swayed as we sang along to Simon and Garfunkel's song about how they've all come to look for Ameeeerica. The couple with the guitar led the group in singing about fifty ways to leave your lover and begged mama not to take their Kodachrome away.

These songs would be perfect for the slideshow at my funeral,

I had the good sense not to say. I longed for the day I would have the good sense not to even think it.

"*Ciao bella*," a handsome young man in kelly green pants said as he sat next to me.

We politely chatted for a few minutes about the music and the city before he invited me to a party. "A party?"

"*Si*, a party."

"I can't go to a party," I told him.

He pouted a full bottom lip and sank his head to accentuate his brown eyes. "Why no?"

"Umm, because I am with my child. Plus, I'm married and quite a bit older than you."

"But you are so beautiful. You put the baby to sleep and come to party with me."

"I'm sorry, that's not going to happen."

Then he pulled out the big guns. He looked deep into my crow's feet and shook his head, as though he could not believe what he was seeing. "*Mama mia*, you are the top model."

Whenever girlfriends get divorced, I urge them to get on the next plane to Italy, where they will be lavished with male attention. I realize this is very shallow. After a serious break-up, one needs a time of mourning and serious introspection. Plus, I am fully aware that Italian men are mentored—starting in nursery school—in the art of seduction. They were all charmingly full of shit, but I still enjoyed it. I hadn't felt so thoroughly beautiful in my entire life as I did during our month in Italy.

My mother's crowd subscribed to the belief that they needed to bolster children's self-esteem by telling them they were the shining center of the universe. We were told we could do anything or be anything we wanted. We weren't just smart; we were the smartest. We weren't just great; we were the greatest. And we weren't just pretty; we were the most beautiful in the entire world. What our parents didn't realize is that some of us would grow dependent on this steady stream of compliments. I was one of the superlative junkies in desperate, constant search of a fix.

Once when I was very young, my mother left me alone in her room to listen to a vinyl record of *Snow White*. The magic mirror told the Wicked Queen that someone else's beauty had surpassed hers. "This child is the most beautiful girl in all of the land," the mirror reported. Terrified, I hid under her bed, certain that a huntsman was coming to get me.

I heard my mother's voice becoming increasingly concerned the longer she searched for me, so I gave a loud *Pssst* as she passed her bedroom.

"Jennifer, why are you under there?"

"The Wicked Queen," I whispered. "She found out about me and she's really mad. She wants me dead!"

"She wants *you* dead?"

"Yeah, the mirror told her about me."

"The mirror mentioned *you*?"

"Yes, she said the fairest one of all the land. That's me, and now the queen wants me dead!"

"Sweetheart, the queen is after Snow White, not you," my mother explained. "We live in a different land, so you're the most beautiful girl in *this* world, but Snow White is the most beautiful girl where she lives."

That was the last time I ever felt such certainty about my looks.

At forty-two, I was still holding up pretty well, but my once effortlessly lean body now looked as though it belonged in a Dove firming cream ad—the one where they give women permission to have thighs. When I unbuttoned my jeans at night, I swore I heard the same sound that Pillsbury dough made when I twisted the cylindrical container. My hair was beginning to gray, and when I smiled, the parentheses around my mouth remained. My least favorite position in yoga class was the downward dog because, as I hung my head downward, I always felt like the skin from my face was about to splatter against my mat like pancake batter hitting the griddle. So being called the top model by a young Italian was a wonderful souvenir, though cheaper than the toys sold outside the Pantheon in Rome.

On our final day in Florence, there was talk of a possible train strike, but when we arrived at the station, there were no picketers or any signs of trouble. Inside, though, there were far too many people. It was clear that travelers were not boarding trains and leaving. Finally we heard that the employees of Italy's transit system were officially on strike. People milled about casually. We could sense the other Americans by their panicked expressions. We were freaking out about how we would get to our destinations.

"Excuse me, you're Americans," I said to a family of four, parents and two lanky teens. "Do you know what's going on?"

"There's a train strike," said the husband. "No one seems to care though."

"Why isn't anybody demanding answers?" the wife said in a thick New York accent. She was right. Everyone seemed so nonchalant about this strike, not the least bit anxious that they were missing their trains. No one but us seemed uncomfortable with the uncertainty.

Another American gravitated toward us and asked if we had any information. "Is anyone negotiating? Do you know anything?" he asked.

The wife got frantic. "We have reservations in Rome! How the hell are we going to get there?!"

Her teens rolled their eyes. I glared at them. *She's right, you little shits. Stop texting and panic with us!*

A man in a Trenitalia uniform and a clipboard approached us. "Where you are going?"

"When will the strike end?!" the wife asked, now shrill.

"I ask where you are going."

We all looked perplexed, so the man in the uniform filled us in. "If you go to *Milano*, then strike ends at two in afternoon; *Roma* is at five."

"The strike ends at different times for different destinations?" I asked. He confirmed with a nod. "What about Venice?"

"Seven," he told me.

"Wait a minute," the wife said, scrunching her mouth to the side unhappily. "If the strike is settled, why don't you people get back to work?"

He shrugged. "This is Italian train strike."

"A strike that ends in waves?" the woman from New York asked. "Who's heard of such nonsense?"

I turned to Katie and said it looked as though we were getting another eight hours in Florence. "This is much better than being stuck in an unfamiliar place," I said. "Let's check our bags and spend the day in Florence."

As we approached the baggage check area, a man pulled down a gate and hung a sign that read that, in solidarity with the train workers, they too were on strike. "Oh well, our suitcases have wheels; it won't be too bad."

Two blocks later, I changed my tune. "I have an idea," I told Katie as I eyed a five-star hotel. "Follow me. No gypsies this time."

"Ah *signora*, you need a room?" the older gentleman offered.

"We are leaving for Venice, but the train strike delayed our trip for eight hours," I explained. "How much would you charge to leave my bags here for the day?"

"Ah yes!" he said. "Train strike. You leave bags here for day."

"Thank you, but what is the fee for this?"

"*Bella*, no fee, you are guest of *Firenze*."

"Right, but we're not staying in *this* hotel," I explained. "We are actually *leaving*."

"I understand what you say, but you listen that I check you bags."

"I should pay you though."

"Pay me?!" he said, disgusted. "You are guest of *Firenze*, I no want money. I do good for you. *That* pay me."

"Really?" I said.

"*Si*."

"I can leave my bags here all day and you don't want to charge me?"

"Yes," he said.

"I'd be happy to pay you."

"Ahhh," he sighed. "*Americana*, you are guest of *Firenze*. I do good for you. You no pay me; you only say '*grazie*.'"

"I just say '*grazie*'?"

"*Si, bella.*" He smiled as if gently coaxing a child into the sea. I could imagine him at the beach, standing waist-high in the water, holding out his arms for his baby granddaughter. *It's okay, you safe with Papa.*

My fingers unfurled from around my suitcase handle. "Okay," I said, releasing the bag. "Katie, give this nice man your suitcase."

He wrote our names on a tag he attached to the bags and rolled them into a room in the lobby. "*Ciao, belle*, I see you when you train go. Enjoy today in *Firenze.*"

"No money?"

"*Mama mia!*"

I stood for a moment and inhaled deeply. Okay. "*Grazie*," I said.

"*Si, buona, molto buona*," he said. "Now go have nice day in *Firenze.*"

7

VENICE

By the time our train reached Venice, it was eleven at night. The sky was the color of ink, blending seamlessly with the water. Spots of streetlamp light reflected on the still waters of the Grand Canal.

I looked at my notes and saw we could catch a *vaporetto*, a waterbus, to San Marco Square, then walk five blocks to our hotel. But with the Italian transit system on strike, nothing would go as planned.

Small clusters of passengers from the train were gathered around an American woman barking instructions. "If you can understand the words I am saying, come here and we will organize taxis," she said.

Obediently, we joined the others gathered in a circle around the woman.

"What's going on?" I whispered to a fellow traveler.

"The *vaporettos* are on strike till midnight," a man said, not looking away from our fearless leader.

She continued, "All people who need to go to San Marco Square, stand here." Katie and I joined this group. "Where are you people going?" the woman asked another family. They answered and she placed them in a different group.

"Do you work for the tourism commission?" I asked her, grateful that someone was in charge.

"I'm from L.A.," she said, dismissing the question. "You're in the San Marco Square group," Hollywood told me. "Is that where you want to be?"

I nodded my head to confirm.

"Good, we'll chat later. Right now, I've got thirty people I need to get into taxis."

She is awesome, Katie mouthed before yawning.

As we began walking onto the dock, a boat pulled in. The child who was asleep on my shoulder just a half hour earlier sprang up like a jack-in-the-box, arms spread wide with a maniacal smile. "Let me get this straight," Katie began hopefully. "The taxis are boats?"

"Yes, and so are the buses. The only way to get around Venice is by boat."

She squealed, jolting the other weary travelers. "Venice is the best city in the world!" The others smiled patiently at the excitement of this child.

As the boat began gliding over the canal, I tried to borrow

some of Katie's joie de vivre and think of a boat ride as the thrill of a lifetime. I looked down at the black water moving below, but I lost my balance and grabbed the side of the small boat, realizing that I was one sharp turn away from being shark bait. Or piranha bait. Or whatever sharp-toothed killer inhabited the waters of Venetian canals. "Katie, put your hands down. This isn't a roller coaster," I advised her.

"It's so much better!"

Ten minutes later, we were checking in to our hotel, A Tribute to Music, a small building discreetly tucked into the bank of the Grand Canal. As we came through the doors, the concierge sang, "Ah, *belle*, you make it! So, so late; I pray for you." He left the registration desk to greet us, his shoes clacking against the high gloss marble floors until he reached the red rug. The lobby was wallpapered ivory and gold; ornate mirrors hung beside golden angels.

"There was a train strike," I explained.

"*Si*, I know the strike," he said, nodding. "I help you with your bags. You are on the top floor. We walk."

"Can we take the elevator?" I asked, yawning for effect.

"No elevator," he said as he began rolling our bags toward the wide stairwell. "It is short steps."

As Katie and I made it through the lobby and up the stairs, we admired the musical theme. Framed records, concert posters, and decorative instruments were mounted to the walls. On the landing of the second floor sat a dark wood baby grand piano with small flowers painted on it. I imagined the artist adorning it as I remembered the last time I thought about someone taking a paintbrush to a piano.

In the spring of my senior year in high school, my father and I had dinner at his favorite Italian restaurant, the one with the sloped floor and combative staff. After the waitress took our order, my father fidgeted with a daisy in the wine bottle on the table and told me that Stella was pregnant again.

"I didn't realize you guys were…back together," I said.

A few months earlier, my father had found an apartment in his building for Stella and six-year-old Leo. They would rent an apartment on the first floor while my father remained in his place on the sixth. As my father described it, he wanted to share the same roof, but not the same walls.

Stella had stopped painting and found a new art form, melting plastic into oddly shaped molds she created. She was now a devout believer in Christian Science and would never trust physicians or pharmaceuticals with the care of her body. But apparently toxic fumes from burning plastic were no problem. If the place accidentally caught fire, it was God's will. Stella still wore plain white robes she fashioned from bed sheets, but grew out her hair and braided it Caribbean style. She adopted a Chihuahua she called Spirit and soon got him a playmate in the form of a blue parakeet that miraculously stayed perched atop the dog's back despite his bouncy gait. When neighbors complained about the noise from Leo and the animals, Stella carpeted the place with wall-to-wall sleeping bags she bought at thrift stores.

"It was one night," my father said, inhaling a cigarette and then coughing.

"And she's keeping it?" I asked.

"What can you do?" my father asked with a shrug.

The waitress delivered our drinks. My father seemed unfazed by his own news, but perhaps it was because he had already absorbed the shock. When we were alone again, I whispered, "Haven't you ever heard of birth control?"

"I always considered myself a lucky guy," he shrugged.

"Why?"

He said nothing.

"Daddy, you should be the one telling *me* about birth control. I'm seventeen; you're the grown-up!"

"You're not having sex, are you?" He swatted the air to signal that, on second thought, he didn't want the answer.

"With all the weed you two smoke, I'm surprised your sperm had the energy to make it to Stella's fried eggs," I snapped.

My father exhaled his cigarette. "Another thing, the doctor said he wants to run some tests."

"Oh my God, you can't let her go through with it if there's something wrong with the baby. I don't mean to sound cruel,

179

but neither of you are good enough parents to raise a sick child." I immediately regretted the comment. "I mean, you're a great dad to me, but I've got Mom for the real stuff. What I mean is that you travel a lot and that leaves Leo and this new baby alone with Stella. Leo just got suspended from first grade for imitating a gorilla during his class photo. And he's healthy."

"The baby will be fine," my father said.

"That remains to be seen."

"The tests are for me," my father said, stubbing out his cigarette.

"What kind of tests do they need to run on you?"

"The kind of tests he can bill my insurance for," my father dismissed. "I've had this bronchitis for a few months and my doctor wants to test for cancer. It's nothing to worry about, just routine testing to lubricate the medical machinery with insurance money."

"They think you have cancer?! Why are you still smoking?"

"JJ, I am positive I don't have cancer. I'm just telling you because I've been thinking. If I have cancer, I'm going to marry Stella so she and the kid...*kids* can get my Social Security benefits if I die."

"So you *do* think it's possible?" I asked.

"It's a contingency plan, but I'll tell you what's more likely to happen: I'll have cancer, marry her, then go into remission and be stuck with her forever." He laughed. "That'd serve me right, wouldn't it?"

He looked at my shocked expression and assured me that everything was going to be okay. "Come on, look at me," he said. "Do I look like someone with cancer?"

He was right; he looked fine. He said doctors were always trying to find excuses to run expensive tests, but his physician was a good guy so he was going along for the ride. My father laughed and said he was really in it for the post-biopsy painkillers.

"Come on, JJ, don't look so serious," my father said. "A fortune-teller once told me I would die at eighty-six making love to a beautiful woman. That's her story and I'm sticking to it."

I reminded myself to breathe. I told myself to stop staring at him and take a bite of food or make some sort of move toward normalcy.

"Have I ever let you down, JJ?"

I shook my head.

"Then trust me," he said. "This is a case of the doctor who cried cancer."

He was dead twenty months later.

Eight weeks before he died, I sat with my father as he rested in his rocking chair, cheeks hollowed and his head bald. I was on winter break from college, and Stella had taken Leo and Baby Thor to visit her parents.

My father had lost so much weight from cancer treatments that he looked like a prisoner in a Nazi concentration camp. The cartilage in his jaw had eroded, causing his face, from the bottom lip down, to shift. Mentally, though, nothing had changed. He told stories, albeit with some struggle, and held court as I looked out of his apartment window and noticed the first snow of winter glittering in the moonlight.

"So I come home from chemo last week and Stella's painted the entire place white," he began. He sounded like Rodney Dangerfield beginning a routine.

"Yeah, I've been meaning to ask about this," I said, gesturing to our surroundings. Stella, now his wife and full-time caregiver, had painted the walls stark white with stenciled gold Bible passages in the style of the *Star Wars* opening. All of the furniture had been painted white and the fabrics reupholstered in white. Even the hardwood floors were painted white. The only thing that remained dark was my father's piano.

"Last week I get home from chemo and Stella is painting everything white, so I say to her, 'Am I dead? Is this heaven?' She tells me she thought the white would be soothing. I let her know that being able to breathe would be better. I have lung cancer, and she's spreading noxious fumes over every surface. So guess what she says?"

"I…I'm not sure," I said, uncertain of how to respond.

"She says, 'Hang out for a little while longer so I can

paint the piano.' Can you believe it? She wanted to paint my piano."

My father went on to tell Stella that she could paint the piano when he died. "I said, 'I'll be dead soon and you can paint the piano then.'" He laughed, though I wondered how he could joke about imminent death. I also laughed, half nervously and half obligatorily.

I told him what I instinctively knew he needed to hear. "I don't know anyone else who could see the humor in this situation."

"I've still got it, don't I? My lungs have surrendered to the war I waged against them, but my mind is still intact, isn't it?"

"Yes, Daddy."

When he walked me to the elevator that night, we looked at each other and hugged longer than we ever had before. The elevator arrived with two people already inside. "Let it go," my father instructed as I looked at the open door. As I let the door slide closed, the passengers sighed, annoyed that their ride to the lobby had been delayed.

"Don't go," he said.

"Back to college?"

"Don't go anywhere. Just hang out with me for these last few weeks."

I gulped. Six months earlier, I couldn't wait to return to college, but now it all seemed so pointless. Soon my father would be dead, and in a hundred years, everyone I knew and loved would be gone anyway.

I had already asked my mother if I could skip the upcoming semester, but she would not allow it. There was no callousness in her decision. She knew there was nothing for a nineteen-year-old to gain from sitting in a cramped apartment in Brooklyn watching her father suffer through his final days of life. She also knew that I would likely remain shellshocked for months, apply for a job at a grocery store near his apartment, and never return to college.

"I have to go," I told my father. In the privacy of my thoughts, I shouted, *You stay! Try Laetrile in Mexico. Go to that witch doctor Mom knows.* But the guilt of feeling anger at a dying man proved to be too much. I swallowed hard and apologized that I couldn't fulfill his dying wish. "I'm really sorry, but I have to go."

"So am I, JJ. I'm sorry that I have to go too."

Instead of hugging me again, he held my hands tight. "You know, this cancer thing really takes a bad rap," he said, his eyes glazed with tears. "If I were hit by a bus, we wouldn't have a chance to say goodbye. It's better that we're not caught off guard by death. A lot of people aren't so lucky." He forced a smile and pulled me in for a final hug. Afterward, I stepped into the elevator, and as the door slid across him like a theater curtain closing shut, he took a bow. That was the last time I saw him.

Two months later, I stood in my dorm room at the

University of Michigan and called my father as I had nearly every day since my return to school. It was so easy to talk to him by phone because I could not see the physical toll of his degeneration. I told him about boyfriends, classes, and parties. He filled me in on his sons and Stella's latest craziness. I had almost forgotten he was sick until my roommate gave me a phone message. "Your father called," she said, choking back tears. "His voice sounds really, really bad."

On the night of my final call, the phone rang about six times before Stella answered. When I asked her to put my father on the line, there was an uncomfortable silence. Finally, she spoke. "I can't do that."

"Is he sleeping?" I asked.

"He's resting."

"*Resting?* What do you mean? Is he...did he die?"

"I don't like that word," she said serenely.

"Stella!" I shouted. "Yes or no, is my father alive?"

"No."

I collapsed to the ground, clutching the phone receiver, the cord stretched to its limit. Sitting on the floor, curled against my closet door, I asked when my father had passed away.

"This morning," Stella said.

"This *morning*? Stella, it's six at night. When did he die?"

"Around ten."

"My father died *eight hours ago*? Why didn't you call? Do my aunts know? Does my mother know?"

"I know. You know."

"No one else knows? Is he…is he still…he's not in the apartment still, is he?"

"Yes, he's sitting in his rocking chair with the most glorious smile on his face," Stella told me.

"He's still in the rocking chair?"

"With the most glorious—"

"Okay, got it. I can't believe you left him sitting dead in a rocking chair for eight hours."

"I really don't like that word," Stella said. "His spirit has moved on." The dog barked, recognizing its name.

"What are you doing?" My question was answered with silence. "Stella, are you still there?"

"I'm here," she said.

"What are you doing? What have you been doing all day?"

"Painting the piano," she said.

Our hotel room overlooked the Grand Canal and came with a balcony large enough to comfortably seat four people at the wrought iron table. "Can I sleep out here?" Katie asked as soon as she saw it.

"Absolutely not," I replied. "You'll roll off the side."

"There's a four-foot railing," she reminded me, then shook it to show how sturdy it was. Pointing to the eight-inch tile lip,

Katie assured me, "I couldn't jump off this balcony, much less *roll* off it." In the end, she won me over with persistent reason.

The following morning, she giddily regaled me with reports of a cruise ship blowing its horn at seven in the morning and birds squawking overhead as if to beckon her to wake "up, up, up!"

As we went downstairs for breakfast, Katie and I passed the painted piano again. "You're not going to make me practice, are you?" Katie asked as she caught me looking at it a moment too long.

I smiled and assured her she had nothing to worry about. "I was just admiring the artist's work."

"Good," Katie said brightly. "Let's see what Italy has in store for us today."

Venice was the brightest city I'd ever been to, partly because the ever-present water reflected the sun all day. And partly because none of the buildings were taller than four stories so the blue sky spread above us like a circus tent. Venetians were experts at accenting the natural aquatic tones with cerulean tile and colorful Murano glass.

Katie suggested we buy a *vaporetto* pass and hop off and explore whenever something looked interesting. We led each other down the winding alleys of stone buildings punctuated by small piazzas with churches, galleries, and pastry shops.

Katie remained enamored with the Venetian mode of transit, but soon found something she adored even more:

birds. Birds were everywhere, especially in San Marco Square where, if people stood as still as a statue, pigeons would land on them.

Every day included a visit to San Marco Square because it was the focal point of the city. The large piazza was the site of the ancient, multi-domed basilica with a majestic blend of Byzantine, western European, and Islamic architecture. It was also the place to go to people-watch, grab a cup of coffee, or find an Internet café.

We attended free opera, the Peggy Guggenheim Museum, and blew through our arts pass until we had nothing left to do but hang out at the beach. While we floated in neck-high water at Lido Beach, dark clouds moved in quickly and rain became hail within minutes. We raced out of the water and toward our towels, and Katie gasped as coin-size snowballs hit her. "What the heck is this?"

"Cover your head," I warned as we continued running from the beach and toward the *vaporetto* stop. "It's called hail."

"Is it just in Italy?"

"No, we've got hail back home too," I told her as ice pelted us.

"It hurts," Katie said. I pulled her into a doorway, and we watched people running by us as if in an apocalyptic movie. Within a few minutes, our film transformed into a Fellini flick when an Italian man sauntered down the street singing that he had umbrellas for sale. People rushed past him, tossing money and grabbing their shields, yet the man remained unflappable, treating every transaction as if he were offering gelato to a toddler. He hadn't a care in the world, and everyone around him had gone mad.

I purchased two umbrellas and hail nailed me several times. "*Grazie, signora*," the man said, smiling broadly. "You have the most beautiful day."

"He seems happy," I said to Katie as the man walked away.

"What's not to be happy about?" Katie said with a shrug. "An umbrella salesman in a hailstorm. Life is good."

We made it to the *vaporetto* station a half hour later and squeezed on with other disappointed beach-goers on Lido Island. Passengers huddled inside the crowded waterbus as hail fell onto the deck like a meteor storm.

The hail stopped as abruptly as if someone had flipped a switch. Within a minute, the grey clouds pulled back like curtains and made way for a cluster of fresh white clouds backlit by sunshine. I'd never seen a sky that was both golden and gray, but the effect was magical. The cloud was rimmed in gold, and streams of light shot from behind it as if something otherworldly were occurring. A professional photographer could have snapped some great shots and sold them to Hallmark for religious greeting cards.

"Can we get hot chocolate?" Katie asked. "All I want to do is dry off, sit on our balcony, have a hot chocolate, and watch the boats go by."

After several failed attempts to find hot chocolate, some-one recommended we try the bar next to our hotel. It seemed odd that no restaurants offered this drink, but we figured, when in Venice, we would do as they said. Katie and I walked into the Cheers-style pub complete with a cast of characters much like the ones from the sitcom. Norm looked up from his station at the bar while Sam wiped down the countertops. "Have a seat," the bartender said.

"Thanks, we just want to get a hot chocolate to go, please."

Moments later, Sam appeared with a mug of hot chocolate and placed it on a table in front of Katie. I thanked him, but reminded him we'd asked for it to go.

"*To go?*"

"Carry out," I clarified. "You know, in a paper cup to take with us."

He seemed genuinely offended that I would treat his drink like a common coffee from Starbucks. "No, you sit and drink here."

"In a bar?" Katie said. "I'm eleven."

Glancing back at the bartender, I told him we wanted to take the hot chocolate with us.

He scoffed. "In a cup made of paper?"

"Or Styrofoam, whatever you've got."

"I only have real cups," he sniffed. "You sit."

I looked at Katie, soaked from seawater and rain, and knew she would quietly accept this bartender's demand. I also understood her heart was set on her original plan. On one hand, it is important for children to understand that they can't get everything they want. On the other, Katie was hardly at risk for becoming a spoiled teen. In fact, I sometimes worried she was so easy-going that she might not assert herself and advocate for her needs. The battle of the hot chocolate seemed so trivial and yet there was something compelling for each of us. For Katie, it was creating the perfect setting to enjoy her post-hailstorm drink. For me, it was showing my daughter that what she wanted was important, and that sometimes it is okay to push back a bit.

I mustered my courage and told Sam that I was going to take the hot chocolate to our hotel and return with his mug in an hour. "No, she drink here."

Katie watched, wide-eyed. I saw her open her mouth to tell me it was okay, she'd drink the hot chocolate at the bar. I placed my hand on her shoulder to interrupt. "No, we're going back to our hotel. We're at the hotel right there. I promise I'll come back with your cup."

"No, you never come back," he said walking towards us. "You steal my cup. Everybody steal, steal, steal from *taverna*."

Backing up toward the door, I assured him we would return his cup. "Let me restore your faith in humanity. I promise you I will be back in an hour. I didn't travel seven thousand miles to steal a mug."

"If you don't come back, you are thief!" He turned his head and peered at Katie. "You mama is thief if she don't come back!"

"I promise you will have this cup back within an hour," I said, slowly backing toward the door.

As the daylight hit us, Katie looked at me in shock. "I can't believe you did that."

"I'm going to return it to him as soon as you're finished. But don't rush. When we get upstairs, really enjoy the hot chocolate."

I knew that Americans have a reputation for having a sense of entitlement, and I struggled to stay on the right line while still making sure Katie and I had the best experience. Did she need to have her hot chocolate on the balcony? No. And had I made some missteps during our travels? Yes. Yet I could not imagine making another choice as I watched her sitting on the balcony against a backdrop of steel-colored clouds illuminated by the early evening sun. Katie closed her eyes and began sipping her hot chocolate. Birds squawked overhead and tourists chattered below. "Thank you, Mommy," Katie said. "I would've drunk it there, but it's better here."

"Do you think that guy is going to drop dead from shock when we actually return the mug?" I asked Katie.

"*Mama mia!*" Katie said, imitating Sam. "I cannot believe it, she no steal a my precious mug!"

I joined. "She even clean it for me! People, they are a good, after all."

Still sitting on our balcony, I asked Katie, "You know what the best part of Italy has been so far?" She peered over her drink, her brows rising to coax me to continue. "Watching you drink that hot chocolate."

"There's no greater pleasure than watching your child enjoying food that you provided," my father told me as we sat at Long John Silver's near Merrick. We had driven to Long Island for my Aunt Rita and Uncle Arnold's surprise anniversary party but were both too hungry to wait another two hours until dinner would be served.

"Yeah?" I asked, crunching a fried shrimp.

"You probably don't get it at thirteen, but one day you'll have a child and she'll eat a shrimp and you'll know exactly what I mean."

"I understand what you mean," I insisted, though it wasn't quite true.

"Figures you would," my father said, dragging a shrimp through tartar sauce. "You're the only person who really gets me."

I basked in my father's appreciation of his complexity but soon remembered I really had no idea what he meant. I was having trouble grasping basic algebra in school. My father's existential crisis was beyond me, but I dared not let on for fear of disappointing him. If the one person he thought truly understood him really didn't, where would that leave him?

"Is that why you and Mom got divorced?" I asked. "Because she didn't understand you?"

"What?"

"Aunt Rita and Uncle Arnold have been married twenty-five years. Is that because they understand each other and you and Mom don't?"

"Maybe," he said, sipping his Coke. He lit a smoke. "All marriages have a shelf life. Carol and I had six years of understanding each other well enough to be happy. Then we understood too much."

I nodded as if this made perfect sense, but my parents actually seemed to understand and accept each other just fine. It was tough to imagine why they had divorced, though it was more difficult to picture them married. Years earlier, I stumbled across their wedding album buried deep in my mother's closet. On the cover was a black-and-white photograph of the two holding hands, running down the steps of a church, their mouths agape in laughter. My mother's veil and hair were in motion; specs of rice blurred in flight. When my mother found me looking at the photograph, she sat next to me. "We look so young."

"You and Daddy were *married*?" I asked, the notion seeming absurd.

"You didn't know that?"

"I thought you were just friends."

"Now we're just friends," my mother explained. "But let me tell you, we wouldn't have been if we had stayed married one more day."

On the afternoon my father picked me up for my aunt and uncle's anniversary party, my mother asked if she could get a ride to a wedding she was attending at the Carlyle Hotel near Central Park. She wore a form-fitting silk and sequined burgundy cocktail dress with heels that would be featured in the following month's *Vanity Fair* magazine. My mother brought her dress to her favorite hat shop for a perfect topper. When the milliner could not find the pillbox he envisioned for the outfit, he made one.

"No problem, Carol," my father replied before asking for some Perrier water to pour in his car radiator. "That's some get-up you're wearing."

As we neared the Carlyle, my mother spotted an army of limousines parked in front of the five-star hotel. Bentleys and Rolls Royces outnumbered the black stretch limos, none of which looked as though they'd ever seen a prom night. "You can drop me off on the corner," my mother said.

"The corner?" my father asked.

"Yes, the corner will be fine," my mother said as her throat tightened.

"I'm your chauffeur, not your pimp. I'm not dropping you off on a street corner; I'll take you to the door," he replied.

My mother's voice shot up an octave as we passed the corner and neared the elegant entryway. "The corner is fine. I want to stretch my legs."

"Are you embarrassed of your limo, Princess Ragu?" my father asked. "Because I can class it up a bit for your new friends." He tipped his black newsboy cap, which could pass as a chauffeur hat.

"Just drive around the block. I want to stretch my legs before I go in," she said, laughing nervously because she knew my father was onto her.

"Not on your life," my father said, pulling his dilapidated ketchup-colored Pinto into the cluster of limousines. "Stay put." He got out of the car and walked to the passenger door to open it for her. My mother giggled then pressed down on the door lock. She smiled and shook her head to tell him she was not opening the door. My father signaled that she should roll down the window.

She opened it a crack. "Just take me to the corner," my mother said.

"If you don't unlock that door, it's going to get worse," my father threatened lightly. A long white car pulled behind my father's, and a short older gentleman, who bore an uncanny resemblance to the Monopoly guy, stepped out with a much younger, taller date. My mother sank into her seat and nodded emphatically.

"Don't say I didn't warn you," my father whispered into

the crack of the window. He then removed his leather jacket and laid it on the ground for my mother to walk across. "Madame," he said haughtily.

"Oh for God's sake," my mother huffed. Looking back at me, she unlocked the door and opened it. "Your father refuses to grow up." As the door opened, my father bowed deeply. My mother held out her hand and waited for my father to help her out of the car.

Popping another deep-fried shrimp into his mouth, my father laughed at his afternoon hijinks. "I think I taught your mother a very important lesson today," he said. "If you ask someone for a ride, you need to let them take you all the way to the door. You understand what I mean by that?"

"Of course," I replied, eating a few more shrimp than I cared to.

He inhaled another puff and promptly began hacking. "And when you have children, really watch them eat. Don't just flip it on autopilot, because before you know it," he said, swallowing, "they'll grow up and move on."

Trip Three
....

Spain
2011

8

MADRID

Katie and I left for Spain two days after her graduation from middle school, where she gave a commencement speech that offered classmates advice for starting high school given to her by the adults in her life. "Every time I tell grown-ups I'm going to start high school, they say they wish they could go back and do *so* many things over," she explained weeks earlier as she sat at her keyboard typing. "So I'm making a top ten tips list." Katie looked at me, her facial features now thin and delicate. "What would you tell kids my age?"

The question alone exhausted me. "I guess I would tell you to enjoy life, to embrace every moment and focus on the journey instead of the destination."

"Yeah, I'm looking for something a little pithier," Katie said.

"Fine, tell them that passion is fleeting, but the Internet is forever."

"That's good," she said, tapping the keys.

I thought about whether or not I was really embracing the moments in my own life. Some of them were easy, like dinner parties with William's great cooking and a houseful of laughter. I organized theater nights for our friends. And Katie was now a good enough piano player to do sing-along nights. Other moments were less embraceable. When the toilet backed up; buying a new phone plan; the time our roof sprang multiple leaks in a rainstorm and our home became an obstacle course of water-filled buckets. Even with the drudgery, though, life was relatively smooth, which in some ways made me more afraid of dying. *This is too good*, I would think, lying awake in bed. *It can't last. The other shoe will soon drop and it'll be a fatal blow to my head.*

William warned me that one day we really are going to get old and die. "Why waste energy worrying about the inevitable?" he asked.

I looked at him incredulously. "You are not Jewish, are you?"

I was amazed at how fast Katie and I could run down the crowded streets of Madrid. Being chased by bulls didn't hurt. The ground beneath us rumbled as thousands of human feet—and hundreds of hooves—pounded through the winding streets of the Spanish capital. From the corner of my eye, I saw an angry bull gore a man then leave him bloody for others to trample. I turned back, but Katie grabbed my hand. "Keep moving forward or they'll kill you," she shouted. We flew through the narrow, dusty streets until something reached out from a doorway and pulled us in. My back slammed into the stone wall, which was surprisingly cushioned.

Katie was already in the doorway with a cigarette dangling from her mouth. My father reached to light it for her.

"I knew you weren't really dead!" I said, gasping at the sight of him.

"You say that every time," he replied, laughing. It was so good to hear his voice again. He sported a vintage Nathan's T-shirt, well-worn jeans, and leather clogs; his hair was thick with long sideburns.

I grabbed his hand before it lit Katie's cigarette. "Don't let her smoke," I scolded. "How did you get here?"

"Same way as usual."

"Are you staying?" I asked.

"It's just a quick visit to say hello," my father said. "Let me be the first to wish you a good morning and welcome you to Madrid where the local time is now seven o'clock."

"Am I dreaming?" I asked. He nodded to confirm. "Why do you only visit in my dreams?"

"You couldn't handle knowing I'm real, but if I come to you in dreams, you'll always have doubt." He paused. "The captain has now turned off the seat-belt sign." He shook my shoulder and told me to wake up. Then again.

"Wake up, Mommy. We're here." I opened my eyes to see Katie tilting her head down to look at me.

"I slept on a plane?" I said in amazement.

"You took an Ambien and passed out a half hour after we left New York," Katie informed me.

"That explains a lot," I said, standing.

"Another freaky Ambien dream?" Katie asked. I nodded. "You should try counting sheep or something non-hallucinogenic."

I told her she was right, but that was my third time taking Ambien and the third time in my life I had fallen asleep without a struggle. "How do you feel, Katie?"

"Good," she chirped as we exited the plane.

"So do I," I said, amazed. "I totally accept that it's morning."

"Me too," Katie shared. "Is it possible we beat jet lag?"

"I think we did."

We decided to save the taxi fare and try our hand at navigating Madrid's subway system. At fourteen years old, Katie was like a giraffe as she towered over me with her long skinny legs, knobby knees, and a head quizzically tilted. Katie walked toward the city map near the subway entrance and plotted our course.

"Aren't you little Miss Christopher Columbus!" I said.

"Let's hope not."

We checked our bags at our hotel near Plaza Mayor and walked toward Retiro Park with a few pastries and coffee we'd picked up along the way for a breakfast picnic. Katie and I soon discovered that sitting on early morning grass sounded charming but was actually just wet, so we relocated to a wooden bench under the canopy of a tree and watched rowboats make their way about a small pond rimmed with stone columns and statues.

An hour later, we were walking through the cool halls of the Reina Sofia Museum, admiring one of Europe's largest art collections. "Isn't it funny that the San Diego Museum of Art is doing a huge exhibition of Spanish art, and some of the pieces are on loan from Madrid?" Katie said.

"You worried we're missing out?" I asked.

Katie snorted. "Mom, we're in Spain. I'd hardly call this missing out."

"Yeah, and the exhibit will be in San Diego for a month after we get back," I thought aloud.

"You're not exactly a Zen master, are you?" Katie teased.

We went on for hours, giggling as we renamed paintings. We replaced our old game of imitating pretentious art critics with pretending we were master painters in psychotherapy.

"Tell me, Pablo," Katie began in her best Freud accent. "Vhy all ze bulls everyvhere? Bull, horns, horns, bulls. I zink ve have some issues."

Putting on my syrupy compassionate voice, I added, "Tell the bull how you feel. Now what does the bull say back to you, Pablo? Be the bull."

Katie giggled. "That sounds like Daddy." She was right. Nothing pleased William more than when one of us came to the breakfast table with reports of an odd dream. His eyes lit up over his morning coffee as he offered a session of his chair therapy/dream analysis. Why he is an attorney and not a therapist is a mystery to me.

After lunch, Katie turned to me and said she wasn't well. It felt as through the ground were sloshing beneath her, she said. "I need sleep."

We returned to the Hotel Regina and I suggested that Katie rest for two hours, but no longer. "Let's make sure you don't get a full night's sleep right before bedtime, okay?" She agreed.

When Katie rose at five that evening, she asked if we could get some breakfast.

"Um, okay," I replied.

"What are we going to do this morning?" she asked.

"Katie, it's evening. We arrived earlier today."

"That's weird," she said with a shrug. "So what are we going to do this evening?"

I explained that, while she was napping, I looked in our guidebook and realized that *Guernica*, Picasso's oversized black-and-white mural, was housed at the Sofia Reina Museum. We were baffled at how we'd missed it.

When Katie and I were planning our trip, we agreed *Guernica* was a must-see. We loved that when Picasso painted the anti-war piece, he brought international attention to the Spanish Civil War. It was a great reminder that art really could instigate political change. And on pure visual appeal, with its more than fifty shades of gray, *Guernica* was a cubist masterpiece.

"We missed *Guernica*?" Katie asked, astounded that we overlooked the enormous canvas.

"It must be off in a special area," I explained.

"Let's go back and see it!"

"Now?" I asked.

"Why not? What time do they open?"

"It's evening, remember?"

"Oh, right," Katie said, putting on her shoes. "What time do they close?"

"Not for another few hours."

"Let's check it out," she said.

I grabbed my purse.

Later, we stood before the painting, which stretched twenty-five feet across and reached eleven feet high. It was not, in fact, hidden in a remote part of the museum. It was in plain view where we had walked right past it at least a half-dozen times earlier that day.

"I can't believe we missed this," I said with a laugh.

Katie shook her head in disbelief. "That whole thing about us beating jet lag…" She trailed off.

"It's called denial, my dear."

I was home for the summer after my first year at college, and my father was spending some time with Rita and Arnold while he underwent a round of chemotherapy. Their lush backyard burst with colorful roses that they had planted and pruned together. In the corner was a great weeping willow that arched dramatically, creating a curtain of delicate green strands. A wooden bench faced a narrow canal where ducks visited daily, knowing they could count on my uncle for generous portions of deli bread.

"You know I was the captain of my soccer team at Brooklyn College, right?" my father said, fidgeting with his fingernail cuticles, a habit he'd taken up since he was forced to quit smoking. Well, cut back on his smoking.

"There was one game when I fouled a player and the other team went nuts. They started shouting, 'Get him!' For God's sake, it was an accident. I even gave the guy the peace sign, like 'Sorry 'bout that, man,' but these people were out for blood. So a guy finally knocks me down, and while I'm on the ground, he kicks me in the face and his cleat splits my lip wide open."

"That's crazy."

"Blood is everywhere so the coach pulls me out and tells me I need stitches for my lip."

My aunt came out to the backyard, holding a pitcher of lemonade. A hummingbird hovered as if it were listening to my father's story.

He continued. "I realize that if I leave the game, I'd be giving those guys exactly what they want. They would've taken me out."

"Are you telling your bleeding lip story again, Shelly?" My aunt placed down glasses.

"It's a metaphor, Rita," he said, turning to me. "You know what a metaphor is, Jennifer?"

"I'm eighteen," I reminded him, rolling my eyes.

"Right. Anyway, I took a sock and put it on my lip. I bit down real hard to hold everything in place."

"Very unsanitary," Aunt Rita added.

"I told you it was a clean sock, a spare from my bag," he snapped. "So after I put the sock on my lip, I ran out onto the field and you know what? I scored a goal. The winning goal." He paused to see if I understood the subtext. I did not. My aunt disappeared back into the house, and my father sighed and continued. "That's how I feel about this cancer. I don't want it to take me out of the game. I want for us to just stick a sock in it and keep going."

"Stick a sock in your cancer?"

My father paused. "What I'm asking is if we can pretend everything's normal?"

He had just been complaining that the only thing

209

people wanted to talk about with him anymore was his cancer. My father said no one asked him about politics or music or even the weather anymore. He called himself the all-cancer channel.

On the bench, my father shifted his diminishing weight. "You've been staring at my knees for the last half hour. If you're distracted by this skeleton, just tell me to put on long pants so you don't have to look."

"It's so hot," I said. "Aren't you more comfortable in shorts?"

"I'd be more comfortable if you would look me in the eye and talk to me about anything other than cancer."

Like a soldier receiving orders, I stiffened. "I can do that. No problem," I lied.

I wondered what the rules of engagement were though. I knew I couldn't talk about his illness. And I knew that I should carefully avoid looking at the parts of his body that were ravaged, like his jaw and collarbone. Or his knees and elbows as they became more pronounced with his weight loss.

Was I enough of an actress to play the role of the self-contained daughter enjoying a normal summer day with her father though? All of my teachers at acting school said that in order to be convincing in a role, one must truly become the character. I could hear them advising me to fully embody the part, to craft my blinders so skillfully and edit my language so masterfully that, in time, I would lose myself and become the part. They told me that during my time on stage,

I should no longer be the real Jennifer, but the character as written by the playwright.

Still, I needed a script.

"Does this mean I can never ask how you're feeling?"

"I feel like shit. I'm a dying man, which means I am always going to feel like shit, so I'd rather you didn't ask because neither of us is going to like the answer."

Don't cry, do not cry, I urged silently. *He has the hard part of the dying. The least you can do is be strong.*

My father sighed, hoping his fuse hadn't been too short. "Look, radiation feels like someone is putting out cigarettes all over my arms. Chemo makes me feel like the time I took off my gas mask in boot camp. Then I come home and vomit blood. One day soon, all of this will kill me. I am never going to see you graduate college, I'll never walk you down the aisle, and I'll never know your children, so asking how I feel isn't really a conversation I want to get into." He looked at me to gauge my reaction, which I quickly switched from horror to neutral. He lightened his delivery. "It would give me great pleasure to spend my remaining time with you talking about all the beautiful things in life. Cancer is boring the shit out of me."

A long silence hung in the air. I realized I wasn't one of those emotionally sturdy people who could hold it together during the tough spots, then go home and fall apart. There was no stepping on and off stage. Compartmentalization was a gift I did not possess. I was going to have to shut down completely so I could give my father what he needed.

I could practically hear the heavy creaking of each series of stage lights turning off, until the theater was completely dark.

"What sports season is this?" I managed.

"That's my girl," he said.

Aunt Rita returned, this time with a plate of macaroons, my father's favorite.

"It's baseball season, and I think the Brooklyn Dodgers have a real shot at the World Series this year," he said.

"They left us in 1960, Shelly," my aunt reminded him.

"It was fifty-seven and I'm making a point. You didn't hear the first part of the conversation, so you don't know what we're talking about."

She softened, remembering his condition. "I'm sorry, what was your point?"

If my father were healthy, his sister would have shot something back. With cancer, she pitied him and backed off.

"My point is that sometimes the real story sucks and you need to stick with the version that's going to make you happy."

Katie and I explored the museums and historic sites of Madrid, always gravitating back to Plaza Mayor to watch its street performers in the evening. The central plaza in the city, the courtyard walls were the color of sun-baked brick and eggnog. One wall was adorned with painted angels positioned between windows. At the center stood a bronze statue of King Philip III on his horse.

A chubby man played Beatles songs on the vibraphone, fluidly moving across the keys with two mallets in each hand. In another corner of the plaza, a guitar trio strummed fiery Flamenco tunes. Our favorite performer, however, was the baby panhandler. The character was half human, half doll, created by a man cutting a hole through a baby stroller and poking his head through it. His face was painted mime-white, and he wore a frilly pink baby bonnet. He fashioned an infant body from a doll and placed it under his real head. What defined his persona, however, was the kazoo-like gadget placed in his throat, which made him sound like he had a voice box used by larynx cancer patients. In perfect English, the baby whined, "Give me money. I need money." Katie raised her eyebrows with horrified curiosity.

"Should we give it money?" she asked.

Encouraged by Katie's inquiry, the baby began wailing, "Give me the money! Give it to me now. Whaaaaaa!"

"I feel like I'm being mugged by a munchkin," I whispered.

The baby apparently had bionic hearing and began whining, "Stick 'em up and give me your money." When Katie dropped a euro in the tip jar, the baby began singing that he liked money to the tune of Reel to Real's "I Like to Move It."

"This is so freaky I can't stop watching," Katie whispered, though not softly enough. The baby's next verse was about how he is so freaky, freaky.

We ventured out of Madrid on a half-hour train ride for a visit to see the rolling hills of Toledo that inspired El Greco in the late sixteenth century. Katie and I had seen some of his stormy landscape series at the Metropolitan Museum of Art in New York and online, but after seeing the actual town, we concluded that the Spanish artist either painted exclusively during the rainy season or was severely depressed. In our eyes, Toledo was charming and bright. As we walked through the precariously slender streets, Katie and I imagined El Greco stepping across the cobblestones, down the path to his studio nestled at the bottom of a hill. This site was now converted to an El Greco museum, which housed Biblical scenes, self-portraits, and Toledo landscapes. Our museum guide mentioned that the artist sometimes inserted himself into the paintings, which sparked Katie's interest in playing the El Greco version of Where's Waldo.

We ambled down the streets of what was once the capital of Spain, noticing the unique blend of Arab, Jewish, Christian, and Roman architectural and artistic detail. It was the living embodiment of the bumper sticker that spells "Coexist" using symbols like the crescent and star of Islam,

Star of David, and Christian cross. In El Greco's day, Toledo seemed to have been a town of hippies with high-necked, frilly collars.

When we climbed to the top of the Alcázar to see the view of Toledo, Katie noted that the city resembled a pastel drawing with its dry, muted colors of nature. The hills varied in shades of hay, some fresh, some weathered. Gentle mounds were dotted with small bushes and trees, lining the pale river.

The following day, we hopped on a bus to see the ancient (but still functioning) Roman aqueduct, an enormous multi-level bridge of stone arches that stretches across the small city of Segovia.

Walking down a side street in Segovia, I stopped dead in my tracks at the sight of a young accordion player, the spitting image of my father at twenty. He sat in front of a building that was painted royal blue on one side, white on the other. What made the image even more jarring was the fact that my father began his music career on the grinder, never having had any training in piano. The musician tipped his white straw hat as I dropped a euro in his case. As we continued walking, I heard the opening three notes of one of my father's songs before it quickly transitioned to a different tune altogether. "Wonderful days, happy hours," I said in amazement.

"I'm having a good time too," Katie said.

"No, I mean that's the song I thought that guy started to

play," I explained. "It was one of my father's songs, his least favorite, but he used to quote it a lot when he was dying to remind us to focus on the good times."

"How does it go?" Katie asked with a skip, then pointed to an ice cream shop to request a cone.

Most of my father's songs were ballads with a folksy seventies vibe, but this had a distinctly sixties pop feel. I sang the chorus, then got to my father's final wish. "When I'm gone, don't bring me flowers. Just remember the better times—the wonderful days, the happy hours."

Katie clapped. "I think you do that," she said.

"Do I?"

I wanted to tell Katie that I wasn't sure this was a good thing. It was just a silly lyric my father wrote in his youth, but a philosophy he clung to until the end. And I wasn't sure I completely agreed with it any longer. I think we should remember the better times. I believe we should reminisce about the wonderful days and happy hours. But I also don't think it's healthy to ban flowers, symbolic or otherwise.

Asking someone to forgo mourning and accentuate the positive sounds noble. Doing so took its toll on me though. During my father's illness, I did not shed a single tear, even when I was alone. In place of grieving, I developed trichotillomania, an obsessive-compulsive disorder similar to cutting. I pushed the lashes from the corner of my right eye into the eyeball, creating the slightest but most satisfying stabbing pain. Both psychotherapists I consulted told me I did this because there was something I didn't want to see. Each said that the mutilation of one's eyes was indicative of an unwillingness to look at something painful. They called it Oedipal, referring to the final scene of *Oedipus Rex* when he gouges out his eyes. I called to cancel future appointments with them.

Even at my father's funeral, I did not cry. Preparing that morning, my mother stepped lightly around our apartment searching for the right words. I carefully applied makeup and asked if I could borrow one of her fur hats because it went perfectly with my winter white ensemble. At the funeral home, I overheard someone whisper that my color choice was inappropriate for a funeral, and I wished I could muster up some feeling to respond. I desperately wanted to feel something, anything: hurt feelings, righteous indignation.

When I delivered my father's eulogy, my voice never cracked. I comforted acquaintances as if it were my profession. While my Aunt Rita prepared her home for the seven-day *shiva* period of mourning, I informed the family that I would be hopping on a plane the following day and meeting my friends for spring break in Fort Lauderdale. There, I drank brightly colored drinks and tanned until my skin blistered and peeled.

In Segovia, Katie praised my ability to remember the wonderful days and happy hours, but I wanted to tell her that the day my father died, I lit a joint like it was a memorial candle and kept it burning for ten years straight, until the day I got pregnant with her.

There was a day I wrapped myself in a sleeping bag and snuck outside of my mother's house during an ice storm so I could get high. I struggled to keep a flame lit in the fierce wind. For a moment, I wondered if I might have a drug problem. Then my lighter produced a steady torch and I took it as a sign that everything was fine. Years later, in San Diego, my friend and I dialed our connection who supplied us with pot every Friday night after work. He said he wouldn't have anything for us until Sunday afternoon. Devastated at the idea of going through a weekend without the benefit of being high, my friend and I began calling everyone we knew, everyone we'd ever met, every long shot. In the end, we drove three hours to Los Angeles, arriving just shy of midnight. Had we made it minutes later, it would have been my first drug-free day in five years. Even on my wedding day, I snuck out during the reception and snuck a puff with a bridesmaid who kindly held back my veil so it wouldn't catch ablaze.

I wanted to tell Katie that when my father died, I bought his brand of cigarettes at the airport before I flew home for his funeral. For three years, I smoked the cigarettes he couldn't, then closed my eyes and smelled my fingers to remember him.

I wanted to tell Katie that I moved from New York to California so I wouldn't have to see old haunts I had shared with my father, and yet he regularly visited me in my dreams. I wanted to tell her that there really was no way to escape pain, only ways to divert it.

One day, when she was old enough to process the information, I would share that my sole motivation for kicking my pot-smoking habit was the intense desire to do right by her, the baby growing inside me. The day I learned I was pregnant with her, I knew I had to kick my habit. More than I needed to tune out, I needed to tune in to motherhood. It was time to retire my bong and replace it with prenatal vitamins. Katie took pride in her achievements and would have likely felt satisfaction knowing she was a catalyst for change even before she was born. But I didn't want her to feel she was responsible for saving me, then or ever. That was too heavy a responsibility for a child to carry.

Plus, we were spending a beautiful, sunny day in Segovia. Katie was enjoying a bubble-gum-flavored ice cream cone. When she smiled at me, it was with a set of metal braces. This was not the moment.

My friend Nancy sent me a message on Facebook with a reminder that I must locate the convent near Plaza Mayor where cloistered nuns bake and sell cookies. In an effort to find the place, I approached store owners, communicating in broken Spanish and charades. Like a nun, I knelt and made the cross on my forehead and chest the way Grandma Aggie had done at church. I reached into an imaginary oven, smelled my delicious cookies, and popped one in my mouth, exclaiming, "*Muy bien*! *Deliciosa*!" No one had any idea what I was trying to say. The best I got was directions to a bakery. One kind shop owner thought I was praying for cookies and brought us into the back of his store to share his personal stash.

Katie used her middle school Spanish, asking people where the Catholic Sisters of Jesus lived. The merchants around Plaza Mayor looked at her as if she was insane and me worse for standing beside her nodding affirmatively.

Finally Katie told me she Googled it and found that we were looking for the Convento del Corpus Cristi. "Some guy blogged about it, follow me," she said, leading me to the Mercado San Miguel, adjacent to the Plaza Mayor. "Facing the market, take the street running along the right side," she advised as we walked. "Then after a half block, you will see a small plaza on the right called Plazuela del Conde de Miranda." We looked to the right and sure enough, there it was. "Cross through the plaza and you will see a number three, then a wooden door to the right of it," Katie said looking up. "There it is! And on the door, it should say '*Dulces*.'"

Katie and I scurried to the oversized carved wooden door, where there was an intercom with a button to ring for *Dulces*.

We pressed the small white button on the brass plate and waited. Finally the intercom started crackling and an elderly woman's voice greeted us in quick Spanish.

I had expected the cloistered cookie-baking nun to have a warm and inviting resonance, as if she were delighted by our arrival. Although I did not understand her words, it was clear this was not the case.

"*Dulces, por favor*," Katie said. The woman groaned and rang the buzzer.

As we entered, we looked around the empty foyer. Katie noticed a paper sign with an arrow leading to the area where cookies were sold. Though the building was not air conditioned, the air was crisp and cold. Its thick stone walls were painted the color of mint toothpaste with small votives burning above parchment prints of Jesus and Mary. We walked down a corridor, then another. A sign directed us down yet another hallway and through a courtyard. I hoped I could remember my way out.

Finally we reached a dimly lit room with a sign that promised we had arrived. Inside was nothing but a lazy Susan with a chain that was thick enough to shackle King Kong. I felt like we were scoring drugs, albeit from nuns.

There was the voice that had buzzed us in, asking a question in Spanish. "She wants to know what kind of cookies we want," Katie informed me, noticing a menu of treats taped to the wall.

"I don't know what any of this means," I told Katie.

"I can order," she told me before carefully requesting chocolate cookies.

The nun barked at us for nearly thirty seconds as Katie's brow knit in confusion.

"I'm pretty sure that meant no," Katie said.

"Ask her what they have available."

The color drained from Katie's face. "I'm not asking her anything else," she replied.

"Just ask—" I began before Katie quickly interrupted.

"I am not talking to that lady."

We heard another sigh, this one more exaggerated than the last.

Struggling with my Spanish, I asked the nun what Katie later told me translated to "What cookies are my most good?" The nun began strumming her fingers. "All cookies are good cookies," I managed to say in Spanish.

Katie whispered, "Say *cualquier dulces*. Tell her we'll take anything and just put money in the hole."

I placed eight euro on the lazy Susan and pulled the chain to rotate the table. Katie and I looked at each other and held back a laugh as the nun took the money and started muttering angrily in Spanish. We heard a thud of a box being dropped carelessly and the pull of the chain. This was quickly followed by the nun's heavy footsteps and the slam of a door.

Katie opened the small door of the lazy Susan and found a box of orange-flavored shortbread cookies.

"They should call these nuns the Sisters of Perpetual Impatience," I said, looking for the exit.

"Let's sit in the plaza and eat them," Katie suggested, clutching her prize.

A half hour later, Katie's chin was dusty with crumbs. Crafty sparrows hopped about the stairs where we sat, picking up cookie crumbs that escaped from our mouths as we chatted. Two barrel-shaped older women in orthopedic shoes passed by. One looked at us and told the other, "*Turistas estupidas.*" We can never be certain, but the voice sounded awfully familiar.

That evening, our last of six nights in Madrid, Katie seemed distracted as she ate her dinner. "What are you thinking about?" I asked.

"Home," she said. *Uh oh.* "Cross-country practice started last week and I'm going to be really out of shape when we get back."

"Do you want to try and find a place to run when we get to Seville?" I asked.

Katie shook her head. "I miss home."

I nodded, trying not to panic. I told myself that trying to convince Katie she shouldn't be homesick would have the opposite effect. On the other hand, I wondered if homesickness wasn't like spilled milk—the longer you leave it unattended, the worse it got.

"I miss Windmill Farms," Katie said.

Windmill Farms? "The grocery store?" I asked.

"And the Del Cerro Pool," she said, her eyes filling with tears.

I was lost. One part of me wanted to remind her that our pool membership was the biggest waste of money in our family budget because Katie had to be begged, cajoled, and dragged there every summer. And whenever we visited Windmill Farms, she asked if she could sit in the car while I went inside and shopped.

"And Daddy, I miss Daddy," she said, bursting into tears. "I want to go home and see Daddy."

I hugged her as she sobbed into my shoulder and repeated that she wanted to go home and see her father. "It's hard," I told her. "I miss Daddy too. But you seem to be having such a good time."

"I hate Spain."

"You hate Spain?" Katie shook her head to confirm.

"It's freezing," Katie replied. "And I have a headache."

"Freezing?" The temperature broke a hundred degrees every day. I felt her forehead. "Katie, you have a fever. Let's get you back to the hotel."

After Katie took a cool bath, I tucked her into bed, wondering what I would do if she still had a high temperature in the morning. I went downstairs to the lobby to ask if we could extend our stay an extra day if we needed. "Of course, *señora*," the manager told me. I phoned William from downstairs and asked him to call our room to talk to Katie, explaining that I needed to run down the block to buy some Tylenol.

When I returned, she was sleepily agreeing with him about something. Then she laughed and asked if he could tell her a story. With droopy lids, she smiled and accepted the glass of water and Tylenol I offered. She listened contentedly while William regaled her until she dropped off.

"You're a miracle worker," I told him, picking up the receiver. "What did you tell her?"

"I told her that Windmill Farms and the pool will be waiting for her when she gets home, and I am always a phone call away," he said. "I told her it sounded like she needs a good night's sleep and Spain would probably look a whole lot better in the morning." There was a long silence. "Jen, are you still there?"

Now it was me who was crying. "William, I'm out of my league here. I think maybe we should come home."

"You've done this before, you know what you're doing, you've just hit a wall. Are you sick too?"

"I don't know," I said, dolling out a few Tylenol for myself just in case. "Maybe. Will you come meet us in Seville? We miss you."

"Meet you in Seville?" William said with a laugh.

"It's not funny. I need you."

"Get a good night's rest and if you're still feeling shaky, I'll do some rescheduling and catch up with you in Barcelona."

"You will?"

"Of course, but please only ask if you really need it. I've got a lot scheduled and I can't afford the time or the money right now."

"But you *would*?"

"I would," he assured me.

With that promise, my heart untangled. "Okay, I think that's all I needed to hear. I'll call you tomorrow and let you know if we're still in Madrid or went on to Seville as planned."

In the morning, I woke without an alarm clock and felt better than I had all week. Katie remained sleeping, so I felt her forehead and found that her fever had broken. I quietly packed our suitcases and hoped Katie would wake up without any sentimentality about our grocery store or community pool. I had packed everything except Katie's toothbrush and a change of clothes, so I decided to go downstairs and buy her coffee and a muffin from the bakery at the corner.

As the doors to the hotel opened, Madrid looked more alive and beautiful than I had ever seen. The colors were brighter; the noise of traffic sounded like music. I felt like a better version of myself, immediately filled with an overwhelming sense of joy.

When I returned to the hotel, I floated up the stairs. "Katie," I whispered, setting her breakfast down beside her. "It's time to wake up." She opened her eyes, looking like a newly hatched baby bird.

"What time is it?" she asked.

"Almost eleven," I said.

She sprang up. "I need to pack."

"I packed for you," I said, appraising her condition. "And here's some breakfast. All you have to do is eat, brush your teeth, and change your clothes and we'll go to Seville."

Katie tilted her head and looked at me as though I had done something utterly amazing. "That was *so* nice of you," she said. Then placing a hand on mine, "Thank you, Mommy."

What the heck was in those cookies?

I smiled. "How are you feeling this morning, Katie?"

"I feel great," she said, last night's drama completely forgotten. "How do you feel?"

"Quite well," I said. "I'm going to go drop Daddy a quick email and give the front desk our key."

Eating her chocolate muffin, Katie waved. "Tell him I said hi."

Downstairs, I sat at the computer terminal in the lobby and let William know that all was back to normal with us and that we were off to Seville. "Our daughter has inherited either your strength or my denial," I typed. "The jury is still out, but my money is on her resilience."

Handing in my keycard, the manager nodded. "You don't need the extra night?" I confirmed. He tapped on his keyboard a few times and looked up. "You are checking out early?"

I gulped. Had it really been nearly thirty years since I'd heard that expression?

"No, not checking out early," I said, slightly shaken. "Staying on schedule."

"Would you forgive me if I check out early?" my father asked me a week before I left for my sophomore year in college. We were sitting on the outdoor patio of Spumoni Gardens in Bensonhurst, eating our multicolored ice cream while my friend Matt was in the restroom. Christmas bulbs were strung from the trees despite the fact that it was a scorching night in August.

"Do you want to go home?" I asked, realizing it had been unfair to drag him out in his current state.

"I don't mean tonight," my father said.

I placed my hand over his, noticing how the skin hung loosely over his bones and muttered a few words.

"So, if I need to OD on something, it won't change how you feel about me?"

"No, Daddy, nothing would change."

Matt returned to our table, his eyes nervously darting about the surroundings. My father smiled at Matt and switched gears. "This your first time in Brooklyn?"

He replied with an emphatic nod of the head.

Silence hung as people around us laughed uproariously,

enjoying the final nights of summer. At the next table, men with names like Vinny and Paulie spoke loudly about their "sangwiches" and "busting chops" while my father had just asked for permission to kill himself.

I told him I could never hate him and there was nothing to forgive.

Matt was my best friend in high school, the chubby kid who never got in trouble despite his constant disruptions. In tenth grade, my mother enrolled me in a private school on the Upper East Side after I couldn't hack the three-train commute to the performing arts school in Harlem I'd started just three days earlier. She finagled a partial scholarship and drained her saving account so I could attend the tiny prep school with well-heeled, sheltered kids like Matt.

A few feet away, two men started arguing. "Let's take dis outside," one said. The other quickly reminded his adversary that they were already outside. With that, the two started laughing and patting each other's backs, affectionately calling each other stupid motherfuckers.

My father looked at Matt and asked, "Scared?"

"Terrified," Matt replied.

My father laughed. "This is like a field trip for you, isn't it?" he asked without bitterness.

"Sort of," Matt replied.

A few hours earlier, Matt and I had been sitting on the balcony of his parents' luxury high-rise with no plans and a full tank of gas in the family Mercedes. I suggested we drive out to Brooklyn to see my father. Matt shrugged in agreement, and before long, we were crossing the bridge. Thirty minutes later, we rang my father's intercom. He buzzed without asking who was there. When Matt and I arrived at my father's apartment, the door was ajar. We knocked and an unfamiliar male voice invited us in.

My father and his friend stared at us, dazed. Finally, one spoke. "You guys cops?" the young man asked, placing a bottle behind his back.

"That's my daughter," my father said, as though he'd just figured it out. "JJ, what are you doing here?"

"You remember Matt, right? We thought we'd come and visit. Is this a bad time?"

My father's friend quickly got up and grabbed his hoodie, patting the pockets a few times to make sure the contents were secure. "I need to get going, Shelly, I'll catch you later."

"What were you guys doing?" I asked.

"I was sharing some of my cough medicine with Manny," my father replied.

"Your cancer medicine?!" I asked. "Don't you need that?"

"I can always get more."

"Does that guy have cancer?" Matt asked.

My father laughed. "Manny's a drunk; he ran out of booze so I hooked him up with some of my cough syrup. It is some potent shit, I'll tell you that." The buzzer from downstairs rang. My father slowly lifted himself from his rocking chair and made his way over to the intercom. He told a woman named Jag that she should come back another time. "Tonight's no good," he said. She persisted, saying she could make it quick. My father told her to come back tomorrow, that his kid was there.

As my father and Jag negotiated a new time to visit, Matt turned to me and whispered, "Is this normal?"

"Define normal."

"I'm serious, Jennie, I think your dad's dealing cancer medicine."

"*Dealing?*" I said, appalled. "My father is sharing. Just because he's not a Wall Street yuppie doesn't make him a drug dealer, Matt. Don't be so judgmental."

Matt held up his hands in surrender. "If you say so."

My father turned to us, unsteady on his feet. "Okay kids, we need to get out of here. Where should we go?"

"Let's go to Spumoni Gardens and get some ice cream," I suggested.

"Ever had spumoni, Matt?" my father asked.

"Can't say I have," my friend replied.

My father nodded; a decision had been made. His hands shook as he struggled to lock the door with his keys. "This place in Bensonhurst has the best in the world. You're gonna love it."

The descent of the elevator startled my father, who gripped the handrail for balance.

Matt looked at me nervously. "I'll drive," he said.

As we walked outside, my father gave a snort of a laugh. "Nice car," he said to Matt.

"It's my parents'."

"I hope so," my father said, linking arms with me as we walked across the street.

With a mix of kindness and cluelessness, Matt helped my father into the car and fumbled for something to say. "How are you feeling, Shelly? I mean, are you…" he drifted off.

"I feel terrific, Matt. I think I'm going to beat this thing." The car door slammed shut.

9

SEVILLE

K atie's post-fever bounce lasted through our two-and-a-half-hour trip from Madrid to Seville. As we began our journey south to the Andalusia region of Spain, my daughter burst into laughter when the waiter on the train informed us that one of our choices for lunch was bull. I've always found the upside of having a short illness is that once I recover, I am euphoric with gratitude over the absence of discomfort. The unremarkable is suddenly the sublime. Apparently I passed along this trait to Katie.

"Every time you take a bite of your lunch, I'm going to tell you that you're full of bull," she informed me, laughing. A half hour later, we watched *Burlesque*, a movie we had dismissed as a fun dance musical when we saw it months ago in San Diego. Now we were captivated and wondered why Christina Aguilera hadn't won an Oscar for her performance.

Our spirits escalated even higher when we reached the hotel, Las Casas de la Judería, a sprawling sixteenth-century palace in the historic Santa Cruz district. Seville was hot as a sauna; nonetheless Katie and I fell in love with it for its quaintness. The city was straight out of a storybook: labyrinthine cobblestone roads leading to a cathedral that was, according to our tour book, the largest Gothic building in the world and the third largest church in Europe. Each little shop looked as though it might have a secret room within, complete with a princess toiling away on a spinning wheel. Not far from our hotel was a river dotted with small turrets flying regal flags.

A concierge from the hotel showed us to our room, through two courtyards, past an uneven staircase and a broken column, and across an alley. The room looked as if it had been lifted off the set of a Harry Potter movie. Katie squealed with joy when she saw where we would be sleeping for the next four nights. She ran to the four-poster bed and lifted the burgundy quilt. Looking under the bed, she said, "I feel like there should be a book of Latin spells hidden in this room!" She then ran to the cushioned picture-box window and claimed it as her reading nook. The room was beyond charming with hardwood floors, an armoire, and black desk. The lamp was covered by a heavy beaded shade; its bulb was no more than thirty watts. The only part of the room that looked as if were designed in the current century was the bathroom, which belonged in a spa. I ran my hand across the marble surfaces and smiled at the sight of a shower large enough to wash a baby elephant.

Our first evening, Katie and I returned from a brief walking tour of the city and sat at an outdoor café across the street from the hotel. A man wearing an apron introduced himself as David and took our drink orders, water for me and chocolate milk for Katie. When he returned with our drinks, he asked if he could sit down. I agreed. I always love when waiters kneel beside the table as if they are about to share some intimate secrets of the kitchen, but sitting at the table was even cozier. David began asking what kind of meal we were in the mood for and offered a few recommendations. Katie and I were surprised to see him flag down one of his coworkers and give him the order. I hoped he intended to share the tip because he was the laziest waiter I'd ever seen.

"Where you from in America?"

"San Diego," I answered, thinking nothing of the idle chatter. He told us about the Corpus Christi Festival happening later in the week, how bells from the Giralda Tower would fill the city and all of the townspeople would march through the streets, many carrying six-foot crosses on their backs. Men would sport three-piece suits and the women would wear dresses and pantyhose despite the heat. Some would carry giant flames of incense.

"Not me," he said, lighting a cigarette. "I am no martyr.

Get it?" He laughed at his joke. Twenty minutes later, he hadn't moved from his seat.

When our food arrived, David thanked the waiter and ordered a glass of wine for himself. Katie and I shot each other a look of confusion. "Aren't *you* our waiter?" I asked.

David laughed as if the suggestion were absurd. "I'm friends with the owner. I help a little by greeting guests," he explained. "What hotel do you stay with?"

Immediately my mind raced back to my mother's persistent warnings about Katie and I being kidnapped. Flashing before my eyes was a ten-second clip of the movie *Taken* I'd accidentally absorbed while channel flipping a few weeks earlier. Liam Neeson sat across a table from his daughter's kidnapper, desperately begging, "Let her go!"

"I cannot do that," the smarmy man replied. "It is not how my business works." Liam cried out in agonizing pain. I switched the channel.

Back in reality, I grabbed my shrimp fork, ready to kill David and dip him in cocktail sauce if he looked at Katie the wrong way. "I don't know where we're staying," I said coldly.

"Would you like help finding a hotel?"

"No," I returned with a tight jaw.

Throughout Europe, people had been friendly to Katie and me: feeding us, striking up conversations, and sharing local tips. But there was something off about David. He had a definite creep factor.

"Why are you angry, Jennifer?" David asked. "I know *Sevilla* and can get you a good price at a hotel. Tomorrow, you come to my house and we will have a traditional Spanish breakfast."

"We are not coming to your house," I told David.

He was taken aback. "Why no?"

I was silent. Katie followed my lead and ate her dinner quietly as David asked us a series of probing questions.

"What is this about?" I said bluntly.

"I do not understand."

"What's your angle?"

"I am just being friends. You are too suspicious," David told me.

"My husband will be down to meet us in a few minutes and he's a very jealous man, so you should probably go," I said.

"He's at the hotel cleaning his gun," Katie added.

"'Cause he's a police officer," I said.

David smoothly replied that he would like to meet William. "He will enjoy my mama's *tortilla* at breakfast tomorrow. Of course he is invited too."

"Oh," I said, deflated.

"But I thought you have not yet found a hotel," David said with a smile.

"We need to go," I said. Then, dumbly, I asked David if he could get our check.

"Don't use your credit card," Katie whispered when David left the table. "Now he only knows our first names."

After we left, David perched himself on a stool on the sidewalk in front of the restaurant, which was problematic because our hotel was located directly across the street. We circled the block several times until we saw that he'd found another tourist to chat with. Heads down, Katie and I scurried into our hotel where we relayed the events of the evening to our concierge. "Is this normal?" I asked. "Do people just sit down at your table and join you for dinner here?"

"No, this is not at all customary," the hotel clerk said, shaking his head with concern. "This is very strange behavior."

"If anyone comes around looking for us, please tell them we are not at this hotel," I asked.

"Absolutely, *Señora*."

"You've never heard of us."

The concierge nodded. He said he had also seen *Taken* and assured me that he would safeguard us. He buzzed for a bellboy to escort us back to our room.

Katie looked worried. "Remember how you always tell me that I shouldn't leave my drink unattended?" I confirmed. "David brought my chocolate milk to the table. What if he put a roofie in it?!"

This was crazy. He had served Katie her chocolate milk more than an hour ago and she didn't seem even the slightest bit sleepy. I assured her she had nothing to worry about. We sat on our bed in silence for a minute. "Maybe I should drink some water, just to be safe," Katie suggested.

"Maybe you should," I shot back too quickly. Before long, Katie had consumed a gallon of water. She slammed her glass on the bedside table and pronounced herself flushed.

I realized I should call William and let him know we had arrived in Seville safely. He heard my voice and sighed audibly with relief. "Where are you? Did you change hotels? I've been so worried."

"Worried, why?" I asked, wondering if he telepathically sensed my panic over David.

"I called the hotel and when I asked for you, the guy said no one by that name had checked in and hung up on me. I called back and he said he's never heard of you."

The following morning, I asked Katie if she remembered our bizarre dinner guest. "Too Friendly David?" she asked. I was relieved that she had total recall. Her fears of her chocolate milk being drugged were unfounded. "Let's get some breakfast."

The dining room of Las Casas de la Judería was like a greenhouse, light pouring in from every angle. Breakfast was fresh fruit, assorted meats and cheeses, pastries, breads, lox, wine, juice, and champagne. We agreed that this hotel was now the gold standard by which all others would be compared.

The hotel's status was cemented when we were shown the tidy rooftop swimming pool where we decided to lounge until the temperature dipped below a hundred degrees. As it turned out, this never happened.

When the clock near the cathedral struck noon, the pool was filled with fellow guests lazily floating in the cool water, the streets below us barren. No one actually swam. We simply stood, steam practically rising from our bodies as we submerged ourselves.

Katie parked herself in the shallow end with a book and a bottle of chilled water. The pool deck was made of long planks of light wood that supported white canvas lounge chairs. In a shaded area, shelves displayed fluffy white towels; a cooler offered a variety of complimentary drinks. I got out of the pool and pretended to sleep on a lounger while quietly observing an Italian cougar wearing a gold bikini. She lay on her stomach reading a magazine while her twentysomething boy toy spread oil across her back. The two cuddled close on a single lounge chair, which proved difficult because of the wide rim of her hat. She laughed and planted a red lipstick print near her playmate's lips. Part of my fascination with the woman was that she was the spitting image of one of the moms from our neighborhood back home. Lauren was certainly no prude, but it was bizarre to see her doppelganger

canoodling with a man half her age, the two smoking cigarettes and becoming increasingly physical. It was the same
jarring sensation I have every Halloween when I realize that
the Grim Reaper is actually the peewee soccer coach. An hour
later, the Italian couple was asleep in each other's arms as
Katie approached my chair to reapply sunscreen. I pointed at
the woman and whispered, "Doesn't that look like Bradley's
mom?" Katie's eyes popped with recognition.

"Is it?" Katie leaned in for a closer look.

"I certainly hope not, or her husband is going to be
pretty upset."

Katie knit her brow. "It can't be her," she said squinting.
"Unless they have a long-lost son that no one knows about."

"Long-lost…?" I trailed off, realizing Katie's take on
the situation.

A blustering Frenchman jumped into the small pool like
a cannonball, much to the chagrin of the Englishwomen in
sunhats clustered in the corner. Cannonball's wife scolded him
in French; his response was to pick her up and throw her in.

"I do hope this *idjit* will tire soon," a Margaret Thatcher-
esque woman told her cohorts. Hats nodded in agreement.

The Prime Minister of the pool got her wish; the man
lifted himself out of the pool, glancing to see if anyone was
watching his sinewy arms flexing. He promptly poured himself a generous glass of red wine, drank it, then fell asleep.

At eight that evening, a clerk from the hotel told everyone

the pool was closing. Sighs of disappointment and muttering in different languages filled the thick air.

Katie and I dried off and walked to the Guadalquivir River where we passed several off-duty horse-drawn carriages, their drivers asleep, the horses lethargic from the heat.

The pink sky scrolled past us on an hour-long boat ride down the river. I stood at the front of the boat and held out my arms to feel the breeze. All I needed was William to stand behind me like Leonardo DiCaprio did for Kate Winslet and we could have been the middle-aged version of *Titanic*. Remembering the ending of that cruise, superstitiously, I lowered my arms and stopped humming the Céline Dion song.

At ten, the city was blanketed in gentle periwinkle, the evening air finally cooling. We found a restaurant and sat outside for dinner.

Katie and I returned to the hotel at midnight, disappointed that we had missed the lobby's resident pianist. The lounge was an eclectic blend of cozy chairs in disparate patterns. Set against Spanish tile was an assortment of lamps ranging from *Little House on the Prairie* to *Best Little Whorehouse in Texas*. A black grand piano sat in the corner.

"I'm going to play," Katie informed me.

She sat on the bench, gave me a little smile, then filled the room with a jazz improvisation. Six years of lessons had paid off.

A woman in a flapper dress and her husband stopped to listen as they walked through the lobby of the hotel. I peeked up from my novel and winked at her. The couple sat beside the piano, never glancing at the player to notice her age. They drank brandy and chatted until they stood to leave twenty minutes later. The gentleman dropped a euro coin on the piano and jolted at the sight of my fresh-faced child. He laughed and said something in Spanish to his wife. The two smiled at Katie and gestured applause before they exited.

Katie nodded her head politely, professionally. When the couple was out of sight, Katie looked at me with wide-eyed excitement. She gestured to the coin with a chin-nod to ask if I'd seen her tip. I winked to confirm. My daughter continued playing, now with a straightened back and new air of confidence.

Our bus pulled into Cordova in the mid-afternoon—just as every tourist attraction was closing. Katie and I trekked to the Alcázar, creating a brick-colored dust cloud with every step we took, until we made it to the front gate where a woman posted a sign that the last tour had already left. Before I could express my disappointment, Katie sighed with relief. I raised my eyebrows to inquire about her expression. She shrugged. "You've seen one Alcázar, you've kind of seen them all."

I smiled. "You do appreciate how lucky you are to be bored with the fortresses of Spain, don't you?"

"I do," she assured me. "But we've been to three Alcázars in ten days. I get it. War, cannons, glory to Spain."

The woman at the Alcázar ticket booth told us that all of the historic sites were closing early that day and we would be well-served to return the next. "The only thing to do today is walk around town," she said.

"That sounds perfect!" Katie said, looking toward the nearly dry river and dirt track surrounding it.

The woman grinned at Katie's youthful enthusiasm.

After the first lap around the river, our feet were covered in red dirt. I told her about my ten summers at Camp St. Regis.

An hour later, Katie grabbed my hand. "I really do get that it's a privilege to be burnt out on Alcázars, but I am enjoying this much more. It's really nice just to have time."

"I'm so glad you appreciate that, Katie. This really is a luxury."

"Time? Or the whole Alcázar burnout thing?" Katie asked.

"Both."

She nodded. "Yeah, you're right."

It was bittersweet to see that my daughter had learned the lesson my father shared with me so many years ago.

My father lay on my bed, wiping away tears. "I don't want to die."

The room was so quiet I could hear my own breath. I could hear the footsteps and the voices of pedestrians walking on the street six stories beneath us and envied the ease of their chatter. I had no idea what to say to my own father.

He continued. "I know that any time we get on earth is a gift, but I'm not ready to go yet. I want to see what happens next. I feel like I'm about to make it big."

It was the first time I had ever seen him express sadness over his death, and I groped aimlessly for the right words, for any words. I knew I wasn't supposed to ask about his illness, but what were the rules about responding when he brought it up?

I thought it was probably okay to talk about his death when he broached the subject. Or was switching topics the kinder course of action, the one he specifically requested just weeks earlier?

My heart beat with the cadence of a stopwatch as I struggled for the right words to say. "I know," I said lamely. But I was painfully aware that I knew nothing. How could I possibly understand what it felt like to know my days were numbered, to feel the life drain from me?

There were so many questions I wanted to ask him. I wanted to hear about his favorite memory of our time together. I wanted to hear about his favorite girlfriend. I wanted him to repeat old stories about how, early in their marriage, my mother accidentally spilled Ajax in their beef stroganoff, then decided to stir it in, hoping he wouldn't notice. But having him go through such an accounting was selfish and cruel. I wanted to fill my scrapbook of memories, but asking him to relive the memories of his short life would have been torture.

I thought about hugging my father, but I knew it would make him feel weak. He comforted *me* with hugs, not the other way around. As I sat by his side, I was overwhelmed by my inability to make a move, then felt instantly guilty because he was far more overwhelmed by the knowledge that this was his final summer. If I despised my helplessness, I could only imagine how much he loathed his own vulnerability.

It was noon and although he said he had woken up with a burst of energy, my father was now ready for a nap. We had just returned from the post office where we had gone to mail a box of clothes and shoes to my dorm room. My father's car was in the shop so he had taken the subway into Manhattan, saying he wanted one more visit before I shipped off for my second year of college.

We hailed a taxi. My frail but energetic father helped the driver lift the box into the trunk and hopped into the back seat.

"Where to, mon?" the driver asked.

The driver's voice excited my father as Caribbean and

European accents always did. He asked the same question as always: "Ever heard the song 'Only a Fool'?"

"Never heard it," the driver said. "Where to?"

"The post office on Twenty-Third Street," I said.

"I'm driving you six blocks?" He muttered something more, then adjusted his brightly colored knit cap. I wondered why someone with thick dreadlocks would also wear a hat in the August humidity.

"You never heard it?" my father asked, incredulous. "That song was a huge hit on the islands. Where are you from?"

"Jamaica," the driver said. "Why you hail a taxi for six blocks? I can't make a living with no six-block fares."

"We can't carry the box," I explained.

"I'm surprised you've never heard my song," my father said, then began humming the opening notes and sang, "Why do I keep fooling myself, when I know you love someone else, only a fool breaks his own heart." He looked at the driver expectantly. "Sound familiar?"

The man muttered and turned on his radio. "Six fucking blocks." He began to speed down First Avenue, turning sharply at the corner.

My father grabbed onto the armrest and inhaled deeply. "Take it easy, brother. My daughter gets car sick," he said.

"She not gonna get sick driving no six blocks, mon. And I'm not your brother."

I looked out the window, a trick I always found helpful

in battling motion sickness. And partly because I knew my father was mortified at my seeing him steady himself during the rough ride. As I watched the Duane Reade and Dunkin Donuts zip by, I realized that my looking away was not only for his benefit.

"Can you slow down?" my father replied.

The driver ignored the request and stepped on the gas.

Trying to lighten the moment, I whispered to my father that I'd never seen such an uptight Rastafarian. My father smiled, then leaned forward, one hand gripping the armrest, the other pressed against the Lucite partition between driver and passengers. Five minutes later, the taxi screeched to an abrupt halt in front of the post office, slamming my father and I against the back of the seat.

"Better than Coney Island," I said, turning to my father, whose eyes were closed, his breathing labored.

The driver scurried toward the back of the car. "Let's go, mon. Help me with this box."

"I'll get it," I told my father.

He shook his head. "Give me a second to get it together."

"I haven't got all day," the driver shouted, now standing at his open car trunk.

My father got out of the taxi and walked to the trunk. The two lifted the box, which my father promptly dropped.

"What the fuck is wrong with you, mon?!"

"What the fuck is wrong with *you*, asshole?"

"Asshole? Asshole? I will kick your fucking asshole, mon."
He lifted his fist.

"Stop it!" I screamed at the driver. "Can't you see he
has…" I drifted off.

"I've got a bad back," my father explained.

"Don't be hailing no taxi to drive six blocks, mon. I need
to make money."

My father gathered every ounce of energy he had and stood
straight. "And I need to get my daughter to the post office."

The two stood facing each other in silence, fists balled.

"I know your fucking song and I hate it, mon."

My father's eyes lit up. "You *have* heard it."

"That's what I said. I know the song and it sucks."

The taxi pulled away, leaving us on the street with my
package. "That driver was crazed," my father said. "But you
heard him, he knows the song. I knew he was full of it, everyone knows that song. It's a standard in the Caribbean."

He lifted the box effortlessly and carried it into the post
office. My father remained high for the next half hour as
we sent my package to Michigan and walked back to my
mother's apartment.

Then he crashed. "I need to sit," he said, walking over to
my bed. On second thought, he said, he needed to lie down.

I felt crushing guilt that I was about to leave for Michigan,
with its vibrant autumn foliage and football Saturdays. In
Ann Arbor, everyone was young and healthy. Campus was

a place where we all had fresh slates and a world of possibilities before us. I looked at my father and felt even a heavier guilt that I was looking forward to returning to my uncomplicated life.

"I'm running out of time," he cried, his tears running onto my pillow. I held his hand, struggling to respond.

I had never seen my father express fear, much less cry before. He was always the one who could calm my anxiety and tell me that everything was going to work out. Now he was doing the exact opposite. It felt as though I were standing at the edge of an endless open field and the person who had always led the way suddenly evaporated. Some people die in phases; this was his first step.

A few nights earlier, although he was flying high on cough syrup, my father had the presence of mind to ask for my forgiveness if he needed to check out early. I was stone cold sober and didn't think to ask the same of him. I had checked out emotionally, shut down to save myself, and I wondered if he could ever forgive my detachment. It was a question that haunted me still.

Finally, after my inane comment that I knew he didn't want to die, I mustered a trite platitude. "The time we've had has been great. Not everyone gets that."

His eyelids began to grow heavy. "I've always said that the spirit is everlasting and the soul is eternal, but when you're facing death, you wonder if maybe that's all bullshit."

After a long pause, I told him I wasn't sure either. "Do you...do you want a glass of water?"

He squeezed my hand and nodded. "I'm glad we got this extra day." He closed his eyes. "Time is a luxury. Some of us just get more of it than others."

10

GRANADA

We arrived in Seville on a twenty-first-century
Eurostar train and left on something akin to
a wagon train. The train to Granada was small
and black and looked as though men in striped overalls
should be shoveling coal into it. It was all quite charming
until an hour into the journey, when we started rounding
bends and reaching higher elevations. I tapped Katie, whose
nose was buried in a book. "How are you feeling?" I asked.

"Great, how are—" Katie replied, lifting her head. "Whoa,
you look terrible."

"I never get sick on trains," I told her.

"Well, this is more of a stagecoach," she said. "Let me get
you a Dramamine. We have two more hours." Katie rifled
through my backpack and handed me a bottle of water and
a bitter pill for motion sickness. "Water and sleep, Mommy.

That's the best medicine." I smiled at her parroting the advice I always gave her. I quickly fell asleep to the image of Katie, my father, and I holding hands walking down a yellow brick road. I saw only our backs, but I was certain it was us: three generations with me in the middle, staggering, struggling to find my footing.

When I opened my eyes, I was struck by the sight of a mother and her twentysomething daughter sitting across the aisle in our compartment. Both of the women wore hiking boots and sported long black hair. The mother looked content; she smiled, weathered lines marking her skin. Her daughter donned a ribbed white tank top with a lacy purple bra peeking through. The mother patted her lap, a signal to her daughter to rest her head there, then began combing through her child's mess of braids. I don't know why I found them so compelling, but I was unable to keep my eyes off of them. The daughter sat up for a moment and reached toward her backpack, tossed on the seat across from them. She rummaged around a side compartment and pulled out a single bottle of water and fruit roll-up. The young woman tore off a piece of the flattened apricot sheet and placed it in her mother's mouth. She then fed herself a slice, rested her head back down, and resumed her appointment at the makeshift railway salon.

Noticing my gaze, the mother looked at me, glanced at Katie, and smiled. She continued combing her daughter's hair. In that brief moment of connection, I felt I was glimpsing my future with Katie and wondered if the mother, likewise, felt a sense of melancholy for her daughter's childhood.

Still woozy, I closed my eyes again, but smiled internally at the recognition that this was the first time I'd dared imagine myself with Katie as an adult.

When we arrived in Granada, my motion sickness hadn't passed. Two American college students at a coffee shop advised me I might be suffering from altitude sickness since we were now in the Sierra Nevadas. They said the elevation was actually quite low, but some newcomers felt queasy on their first day in Granada.

At the start of our downhill walk to town, Katie and I were awestruck by the panoramic view of snowcapped mountains, an odd backdrop considering it was well over a hundred degrees outside. "Talk about things looking one way and feeling another," a red-faced Katie said, wiping sweat from her brow.

We continued downhill, passing several businesses named for Washington Irving, and I confessed to Katie that I hadn't really done my homework for this two-day visit to Granada. "We have reservations to see the Alhambra tomorrow, but to be perfectly honest, I have no idea what it is. A church? An Alcázar? I'm really not sure. And I don't know how Washington Irving fits in."

"Really?" Katie said coyly. "You don't have a map with color-coded stickers?"

"Nope," I swatted her playfully.

"I am liking this unprepared Mommy," Katie said, whipping out her phone. "Let me see here. Alhambra. Granada. Spain."

She's never going to get reception up—

"Boom! Okay, it says here that the Alhambra was originally designed as a military area then later became the residence of royalty and of the court of Granada in the middle of the thirteenth century." She continued reading from the Alhambra website. "Throughout the thirteenth, fourteenth, and fifteenth centuries, the fortress became a citadel, with high ramparts and defensive towers, that housed two main areas: the military area, or Alcazaba, the barracks of the royal guard, and the funky cold medina."

"Funky cold medina?"

"Just checking to make sure you're still paying attention. It just says Medina, which is the court city, the location of the famous Nasrid Palaces and the remains of the houses of noblemen and plebeians who lived there."

She pushed a few more buttons. "So it was a Moorish fortress, and it says on another site that the Alhambra was the seat of government for the ruling Moors until they were exiled in 1492. Then it was the home to Catholic kings. Blah, blah, blah, oh, this is cool: the architecture is a mixture of the earlier Arabic style and the later Christian modifications, making the Alhambra a microcosm of Spanish history."

"And how does—"

"Washington Irving wrote the book *Tales from the Alhambra* which was inspired by his stay here," Katie said.

We continued walking in the unfiltered heat. Despite our sunhats and glasses, we were baking as we made our way down the unshaded sidewalk. Katie pointed out a grove where we could stop and cool off—a good idea, I thought. Until I realized it was a graveyard.

"Why don't we walk a little further and see if we can find a restaurant where we can sit down and have a drink?" I suggested.

"I've got a bottle of water we can share. Let's just sit for a few minutes," Katie said, looking exhausted.

"I hate graveyards," I said. I looked again at Katie. "Okay, we'll cool off and then hit the road again in a few minutes, no longer."

"I wasn't asking to stay forever," Katie quipped.

Moments later, I found myself passing through the gates of a graveyard for the first time since the unveiling of my father's tombstone, a year after his death.

I have always found the rituals around death awkward, especially when they related to my untraditional father. Ritual was so antithetical to who my father was that it felt forced to observe the Jewish tradition of unveiling a tombstone. Loved ones gather around the cemetery plot on the one-year anniversary of their departed's death and uncover the stone as if unveiling a masterpiece.

I resented the fanfare. After all, when he was dying, my father told me he wanted to be wrapped in an Oriental rug and dumped in the East River. At the time, I laughed, but his point was taken: he didn't want to follow any religious traditions in death that he hadn't subscribed to in life. Of course we weren't going to dump his body in the river, but having an unveiling at the Jewish cemetery was like having a Latin Mass for Timothy Leary.

At the time, I didn't appreciate that such traditions were to comfort the survivors, so I had a bit of a chip on my shoulder about having to go back to the cemetery in the dead of winter to see the Dead Shelly Show, a term he had coined for his inevitable funeral and unveiling. He turned up his nose at convention, and I felt that by doing the same, I was keeping his memory alive.

When the veil was lifted from the stone, a cold slap of wind hit me as I read his full name: Sheldon Donald Coburn. I crossed my arms.

Sheldon. No one ever called him Sheldon.

My anger dissolved as I read a line beneath, the date of his death.

Aunt Rita asked if anyone would like to say a few words. With her thick New York accent, she said that I had done such a nice job with the eulogy at the memorial service and urged me to share a few thoughts.

"Okay," I said. The dozen or so close family members looked at me, expecting a touching story or perhaps a poem by Kahlil Gibran. "He died in February. The stone says January." A collective gasp was followed by my aunt's quick assurances that the mistake would be fixed immediately.

I heard my father's voice as clearly as if he were standing next to me. "They killed me off a month early," he said with a hearty laugh. "That's perfect! What a perfect ending—a tombstone with a typo." I knew with absolute certainty he would love it.

After weeks of negotiation, Aunt Rita agreed to leave the tombstone as is: boldly, unapologetically imperfect. Now I felt as if the true essence of my father's memory was chiseled in stone.

Though I have serious doubts about the existence of an afterlife, it gives me comfort to hold out hope there might be a spiritual plane beyond our human existence. Whenever I hear stories of the deceased visiting their friends on Earth, I have three thoughts about my own dad. One: thank God

I will see him again. Two: we'll have a great laugh over the tombstone typo and the painting of the piano. Three: why hasn't he shown up? If there are visitation privileges, why hasn't he come to see me?

Sometimes I wonder if he is angry with me for not being a better daughter. I wonder if he wasn't able to forgive my early emotional checkout. I had left him to die alone in a rocking chair with a benevolent madwoman caring for him.

When I have these thoughts, my more pragmatic side makes a convincing case that if the spirit does evolve, it can fully understand human limitations. My father loved and accepted the shell I had become in our last few months together. Why would he change his position in a state of elevated consciousness?

On a purely emotional level, though, I'd always felt alone and forgotten. Where were my pennies from heaven? Where were my signs that he broke on through to the other side and everything was cool?

Knowing that I yearned for some kind of beyond-the-grave connection with my father, my cousin Kathy referred me to a medium. "Lana is the real deal," she assured me. Kathy wanted to connect with her sister, Diane, who had been in Miami at the time of their father's murder. The older of the sisters, Diane was nineteen and had been spending time with Ernie in Florida.

Diane cut short her trip very suddenly and showed up

on her mother's doorstep in New Jersey without explanation. Ten days later, Ernie's body was discovered in his home, decomposed beyond recognition. When my mother went to Florida, she approached her brother's house and was struck by the odor that finally alerted the neighbors that there was a body inside. A police officer held out his arm to block my mother from going any further. "There is nothing inside that you should see," he warned her. Ernie's remains had been removed, but the house was a crime scene where a man had been fatally beaten and strangled.

After Grandma Aggie died, information started slowly leaking that Ernie's death was not a heart attack after all. No one thought Diane was involved in the crime, but it was clear that she either discovered the body shortly after the murder or fled the scene as it was happening. Whenever my mother pleaded with Diane to give her information, her niece teared up and said she couldn't talk about it. She soon began buying wine by the gallon and drowned her memories every day, until she died of cirrhosis of the liver at forty-four, the same age Ernie was when he was killed.

Kathy told me that Lana the medium makes all of her appointments for the upcoming year on one day in December. She begins accepting phone calls at nine in the morning and by noon is booked for the next twelve months.

On the given day, I dialed Lana's phone number as soon as the clock struck nine on the East Coast. Busy. I hit the redial button another dozen times, all with the same result. I waited a few minutes then hit redial again, then again, then again. Busy, busy, busy.

Later that night, Kathy called to ask if I'd reached Lana.

"No, I called for an hour and couldn't get through."

"Well, I did," Kathy said. "I am going to see her in October and I booked a phone consultation for you the following week."

"Really?" I said, trying to tame my excitement at the thought of speaking to my father after twenty-five years.

I just had to wait eleven months for my appointment.

The day after Kathy's appointment with Lana, I called to get the details. "She was frighteningly accurate," Kathy said. There was no doubt in her mind that she had made a connection to the other side. "I didn't get through to Diane though," Kathy told me. She explained that her sister was not available, but she spoke with her father-in-law.

My heart sank. As much as I missed other relatives, I had closure with them. I hoped they were doing well but didn't have any pressing questions to ask. If Grandma Aggie wanted to pop in at the end to share a quick story, that would be fine, but I was dialing in for my father.

Kathy began. "Lana asked if I knew of anyone who

was in the military because she saw a man in a uniform." My cousin informed me her maternal grandfather was in the Army. Lana told Kathy her grandfather wanted her to know that everything was good on the other side and that he was at peace. "Then she saw a little girl twirling like a ballerina," Kathy said. "Diane and I had a music box in our room with a ballerina that spun on the lid. And then she said she saw lemons and asked if I knew anyone who liked lemons. I told her that Grandma loved lemon meringue pie and she said she saw an old woman giving her a thumbs up."

"Grandma Aggie?" I asked.

Kathy confirmed.

"A thumbs up?" Aggie was a hefty Italian woman who wore rayon floral pattern dresses with a Kleenex tucked into her sleeve. She wore a bra that could only be described as bulletproof and thought the television show *The Flying Nun* was disrespectful to the church. I couldn't imagine she had transformed into the Fonz in heaven.

"That doesn't sound right."

"Well it was," Kathy assured me. "She gave me details that she couldn't possibly have known." Then she told me the lengthy but vague message her father-in-law asked my cousin to relay to her husband.

When I told William about Lana, he warned me not to get my hopes up. "What is it you want to hear from this medium anyway?" He tapped away at his computer as I unloaded the dishwasher.

"I'll know she's legitimate if my father says, 'JJ, are you *crazed*? Of course I forgive you. Everyone was doing the best they could at the time, and I made mistakes too. You have nothing to feel guilty about.' I need him to use the word crazed because he always said that instead of crazy. That's how I'll know it's really him."

My husband walked over to the sink, turned off the running water, and sat me down. "Jennifer," he said, "I guarantee you that your father was not mad at you. The forgiveness needs to come from you." He shifted uncomfortably, clearly editing himself.

"Go on, say it," I encouraged.

"I don't want you to be disappointed," he said softly. "There is no afterlife, so your father can't absolve you of your transgressions, perceived or otherwise. Only you can do that, and I don't want to see some charlatan break your heart."

I bit my lip hard, hating what he was saying, but loving his protective instinct. "So you know with absolute certainty that there is no afterlife?" I asked.

"As sure as anyone can be," William said. "But I *am* certain there are scam artists who exploit people who desperately want to believe there's something more out there."

"But you admit there is a *possibility* of a life beyond what we know?" I asked.

"It's highly improbable."

"But possible?"

"I suppose anything is possible, but it's—"

I interrupted. "I know, highly improbable. But I'm going to give it a shot. What if all these years he's wanted to get in touch, but I haven't known how to answer the call?"

"How much does she charge?" William asked.

"It's free," I returned quickly.

"The price is right."

"But she accepts donations," I said, sheepish.

"Do what you need to do, Jen, but don't get your heart set on this."

But it was too late for such advice. As much as I knew William made sense, I wasn't able to curb my intense desire to phone in to heaven and hear that my father was not disappointed in me.

On the appointed day, I called Lana for our phone session, which began with Lana telling the story of how she discovered her gift. "I was born with a rare congenital disorder," she began. I breathed deeply, practicing patience. Maybe she thought her bio would give me a broader understanding of the process.

Two and a half hours later, my face was buried in my

hands as I silently begged her to stop talking about herself and connect with the other side.

"Are you ready to begin, Jennifer?"

Finally!

"I see a ballerina twirling around," she said. "Is that you, Jennifer? Did you take ballet lessons when you were a little girl?"

I did, in fact, take ballet lessons at the Joffrey, but much to my mother's disappointment, never showed a teaspoon of talent or interest in dance. I was more of the class clown, something the elegant swans at the ballet school did not appreciate. What I hated even more than the boredom of class was the clear disdain the teachers showed for my clunky form and absence of coordination. I begged to quit, from my first lesson all the way to my final class two years later.

"You were so happy then, Jennifer," Lana said lightly, as if she were seeing a vision of me as a child. "You were so carefree and joyful when you were dancing."

She paused dramatically. "Oh, something very strong is coming through now."

My heart leapt.

"Your father is before me now and he's in a uniform. Was he in the military?"

"Um, very briefly," I replied.

My father was in the U.S. Army only a few days, but never did well with discipline, the cornerstone of success in the military. After an incident in which my father and his friends got high and wandered off base to a strip joint, the Army politely told him and the other hippies that they were released from duty. There was no war, nor was there any other urgent need for soldiers, his sergeant explained before removing their dog tags and sending them home.

"Yes, I see him very clearly saluting," the medium said. "Was he killed in the war?"

"No."

"No, but he was proud. I see him and he is very proud to wear the uniform. He earned a medal, didn't he?"

"Nope, there were no medals," I said, beginning to deflate.

"Oh yes, I see now. That's a dog tag. He's wearing a dog tag under his shirt."

My eyes stung with tears forming in my eyes. Still, I clung onto hope. "Does he have anything he wants to tell me?"

"Did he like lemons?" She heard a sniffle escape from me. "It's okay, dear, he says it's okay to cry."

I said nothing, trying to stifle tears. "He loved his lemons, didn't he?" Lana asked.

"I never saw him eat lemons," I said. "I mean, I guess on fish or whatever, but lemons weren't a favorite or anything."

Why did this medium always mention lemons? Why not a sure bet like pizza or ice cream?

"Lemon pie? Lemonade?" the medium proposed.

I fell onto my bed with the weight of someone who had

just caught a boulder. My father is really truly dead, I realized. There is no great beyond. My father is not on a cloud doing bong hits with Jimi Hendrix. Somehow I had to make it through the final minutes of this phone call.

"Well, everyone likes lemon pie," I said. "And who hasn't had lemonade?"

"I see him eating fish."

Maybe because I just said it.

"And he worked with his hands," Lana said with a spark.

Yes! Oh my God, it's true, he did work with his hands. Just like most everyone else in the world—who has hands! Like computer programmers, musicians, ditch diggers, and doctors.

I looked at the clock and realized I had ten minutes left. Lana continued. "He wants you to know that he is safe and happy and that he is very proud of you."

"Anything else?"

"Do you have children?"

"I have a daughter, Katie."

"Only one?" Lana asked. "He says he wishes he was there to spend more time with Katie, but that he is her guardian angel."

More time with Katie? How about any *time.* I found myself feeling angry at both Lana and my father. At Lana, because she was playing a cruel game; my father, because he hadn't been around to meet William, much less Katie. I understand that people with addictions don't sit down with a pad of paper and carefully weigh the risks and benefits of their indulgences. They are not big on long-range planning—like meeting their grandchildren. Still, there was a part of me that felt marginalized knowing that, on some level, he chose getting high over sticking around.

"Your father has another message for you," Lana said. "You will soon become pregnant again so Katie will have a little playmate."

This really was amazing news. I'd had a hysterectomy a year earlier so I wasn't sure where this pregnancy would be housed. And Katie would be leaving for college right around the time my conjured baby was entering kindergarten, so it was hard to imagine them as playmates.

"Okay, thank you for the reading," I was able to muster.

"Your father says he loves you very much and it's okay to let him go."

I gulped and hung up the phone. Immediately, I called William, sobbing. "My father is dead," I said when he answered. "You were right, the medium was a fraud. I feel so gullible for even thinking this could happen."

"Why?" William said. "You didn't believe her; you weren't at all gullible."

"But I wanted to so badly," I said, gasping for breath. "I went in completely wanting to believe this woman—this ridiculous woman who told me my father liked lemonade and that he had hands."

"Sweetheart, I love that you are open to things," William said. "I know this was a disappointment, but look at all of the things you try that work out well. Sometimes you're open to things that don't pan out, but that's part of the package."

"I hate myself right now."

"I can't believe I'm saying this, because I think all of this magical thinking is a bunch of horseshit, but just because this woman was a fake doesn't completely rule out the possibility of an afterlife. It just means she is a really bad medium."

"You think I should try a different medium?" I asked.

"No, I think you should try a good therapist who can help you work through some of these issues with your father," William suggested. "I think you need to stop looking toward the great beyond and explore the great within."

At the entry gate of the Alhambra, I purchased two audio tours for Katie and me and began walking in the direction the haughty voice instructed. The guide had the same upper crust accent as Thurston Howell III. We walked through a forest path to reach the impeccably manicured grounds where the Alhambra stood. We continued to a walled courtyard with a green pond in its center. Arabic prayers were chiseled in painfully intricate detail across every inch of sand-colored wall. The audio guide voice implored us, "Pause for a moment and imagine what it was like when I was here oh-so-many years ago with the king and queen and their royal court."

"Who is this?" Katie asked.

I shrugged.

We continued following his lead through the grounds, gasping at the dramatic effect of blue skies framed by Moorish arched windows and sliced by the intricate ironwork.

The voice asked, "Is this splendor not a veritable feast for the senses?" Katie and I began laughing so hard we had to sit on a bench. People knit their brows, likely wondering what we found so amusing. How could they *not* be cracking up at this pretentious wanker? Perhaps they weren't listening to the English language version.

"'Twas so many years ago, but I recall seeing the ladies of the court brushing their lovely hair as they prepared themselves for the royal feast. The flowing silk of their gowns made them look as though they were angels delivered to us from heaven. I do confess that I once caught a glimpse of the queen, her beauty so fair, it brought pleasure to my innermost senses."

Katie's eyes popped. She took her earpiece away and whispered, "Did this guy just say he…?"

"It kind of sounds that way, Katie, but maybe he just meant he thought she looked really pretty."

Katie shook her head with disgust. "Who is this guy supposed to be, anyway?"

"I have no idea."

We pressed the button to resume his commentary. "Oh, the ladies with their lovely gowns and quiet beauty," he waxed on.

"This guy is gay," Katie said. "Who goes on and on about ladies and their clothes and how much he loves them except a super-repressed gay guy?"

Snooty Pants continued. "I believe there is nothing that captures the loveliness of the natural setting of the Alhambra more than a room filled with the divine magnificence of the female form."

Katie looked at me with one eyebrow arched. "We definitely have a case of the gentleman doth protest too much."

The voice continued to guide us. "As I walked about the grounds, I swelled with inspiration as I viewed the stiff and bold tower penetrating the clouds above," the voice said.

Katie's head whipped toward mine with a swish. I held my hands over my mouth as we laughed. "See!" Katie said. "What straight guy carries on this way about how much he loves the ladies?"

"It is a bit much," I conceded.

"And, you know what he's talking about with those big hard towers, right?" Katie asked.

"I grew up in Greenwich Village, kid. I got it."

"Who is this guy anyway? He keeps talking about himself like we should know who he is."

272

As if on cue, the voice continued. "During my stay here, I penned *Tales from the Alhambra* as I sat on the fallen tree trunk you see to your left."

"Washington Irving!" we said in unison.

"He's so…dramatic about everything, isn't he?" Katie said. "Let's say Washington Irving as our new way of describing someone when they're being over-the-top."

When we stopped to look at the endless fields of yellow flowers, we found ourselves surrounded by school children and other tour groups like Teen Tours and Roads Scholars. They set in like fog. But an hour into our tour, we mastered the game "dodge the tour group." When we saw a group approaching, we'd cry, in our best Washington Irving accent, "Run, run like the wind!"

The gardens, with their explosive colors and scents and endless views, proved too distracting for us. Suddenly we were in the midst of a dozen elderly Koreans, taking photographs and making rough sketches of the Arabic arches of the Alhambra.

A four-and-a-half foot tall woman with a salt-and-pepper pixie haircut smiled and said hello in English. Katie said hello, then was quickly hypnotized by the view ahead of her.

"Hello," I said to the Korean woman and her friend, who was about an inch taller. Never before had I felt so statuesque.

"Where is your home?" the woman asked in halting English.

Slowly, I answered, "We are from America. California."

A man turned to join the conversation. "I wish they are all the California girls."

"Where are you from?" I asked.

"Ah, Korea," the taller woman said, nodding her head.

I nodded as if this was very meaningful to me. "Ah, Korea," I said nodding back as I thought about what to say next.

Obviously nothing about Kim Jong Il.

Sharing that I survived on Korean barbecue in college seemed ditsy.

While I groped for something to add about Korea, I could only think about the girl I met in 1976, new to our fifth grade class, fresh from Korea. Jimi Lieu did not speak a word of English yet somehow our teacher persuaded the soft-spoken newcomer to stand before the class and sing a Korean folk song. Since Jimi did not have the words to decline the invitation, she stood in front of the chalkboard in a brown corduroy skirt and oxford shirt. She smiled shyly and began singing. "Chap-pudda cha-anida, do-do-di-do-di-do," she sang, moving her hands and swaying every time the song returned to the "do-do-di-do-di-do," part, which was frequent.

Standing in the garden of the Alhambra, I nodded at my two new friends. "Ah, Korea," I said and began singing Jimi Lieu's song. The women's eyes popped, and a man beside them was agape.

"How you know Chap-pudda song?" the man gasped.

The shorter woman barked at the rest of her group, and they rushed over. Although I don't understand a word of Korean, I am sure she said something like, "Come listen. The giant yellow-haired woman knows the Chap-pudda song!"

Soon I was in a line with eight women singing the song, complete with hand motions. Men held cell phones over their heads recording this strange sight. After more than three decades, I could only remember the opening line and tune so I hummed most of it.

Katie's attention returned to me with a laugh. "What's going on?"

"We are rocking the Alhambra, that's what's going on."

"Can you teach me?" Katie asked me, then looked to the Korean women.

"Yes, we sing song together," she said.

I placed Katie next to me and whispered the first line for her. The group began again, now with Katie.

When we finished, the group applauded and someone asked, "How you know Chap-pudda? It very old song."

"My classmate Jimi Lieu sang this song for our class, like every day in fifth grade," I explained, wondering what the teacher had in mind, bringing this child up before us every day and forcing her to sing.

The short woman held my hands and she said that we were meant to meet to share this moment. She looked at Katie adoringly, then at me with a smile. "You are from

275

America. We are from Korea, but here are we. Same garden at Spain at same minutes."

"Yes, quite a coincidence, wasn't it?"

She knit her brow, not understanding the word.

"Lucky, lucky," I tried again.

"No lucky, lucky," she said, nodding her head emphatically. She pointed to the sky. "We must meet and sing song together."

"But why?" I asked.

"Mystery," she chirped. "But meant to happen."

After we said good-bye to our Korean friends, Katie laughed again. "One minute I was looking at the view and the next thing I see you singing with a bunch of Korean ladies." I smiled. "Aren't you glad you remembered that song?"

"I am," I replied.

Katie tilted her head philosophically the same way my father used to before sharing a thought. "Now I know what you mean when you say music is one of the few things in life that can connect people no matter where they're from."

I smiled as I heard my father's voice. *Music is about universal connection*, he told me hundreds of times.

"I think today has been my favorite one in Spain so far," I said, grabbing Katie's hands and continuing to walk down the path of the Alhambra gardens.

"Yeah, singing with those ladies was fun," Katie said.

Years after my experience with the bogus medium, I still

maintained very serious doubt about the existence of an afterlife. But that day at the Alhambra, I was certain that my father could be very much with me—and by extension, with Katie—long after his death.

11

Barcelona

Katie and I flew from Granada to Barcelona on my forty-fifth birthday and checked into a monolithic hotel with a marble and gold lobby designed to impress. A carpeted double staircase reached down like the arms of a welcoming hostess. Above us hung a sparkling chandelier the size of a Volkswagen. But the Avenida Palace was all style and no substance.

A bellboy showed us to our room as if he were being escorted to his own execution. His shoulders were slumped; each step he took was leaden. As the door to our room closed, Katie and I heard the sound of cannon fire. Within minutes, we heard another boom from down the hall. Then another.

After we unpacked, Katie noticed rumbling beneath us. "Are we having an earthquake?" I wondered aloud. We went downstairs and told the concierge, who shrugged and said I must be mistaken; there was no rattling, he insisted.

"Today is my birthday. Can you recommend a nice place to celebrate?" I asked.

"*Señora*, this is Barcelona," he said with a heavy sigh. "Every place to eat is nice."

The natives we met in flight and on our shuttle from the airport were quick to tell us that Barcelona was part of the Catalonia region of Spain, which was, in their estimation, far superior to the rest of the country. Their claim seemed like a promise while the hotel worker's remark sounded dismissive.

As Katie and I made our way out the front door, a hotel clerk called out to us. "Hey, you leave your room key at front desk and pick up when you return," he demanded. Many European hotels used this system, so the request didn't bother me. But his delivery was so gruff it was as though he was accusing me of walking off with an armload of towels.

Wanting to conserve our spending to get the best experience possible, I suggested we save my birthday celebration until our final evening in Barcelona. "Let's just walk around, explore, and grab a quick bite tonight," I said.

"Sounds like a plan," Katie said.

I handed in our key, and Katie and I headed out for our first evening in Barcelona. As my eyes moved from my map to the street sign, Katie checked out our new surroundings. We reached the street corner and noticed a subway station.

"That's why our room shakes, Mommy." She turned her head quickly to check behind us. "Look down the street," she said. I squinted to read the sign on the second subway station. Katie enlightened me. "It's a different exit to the same station. Our hotel is over a subway line."

Remembering the clerk who looked at me as though I was crazy when I complained about the room shaking, I shook my head with annoyance. Quickly, I reprimanded myself internally.

So what if there's a little shaking in our luxury hotel. You are forty-five years old today, in good health, and in Barcelona. These are First World problems, so shut up and enjoy life.

We approached the Plaça de Catalunya, and I stopped a man to ask where to find a supermarket. He pointed at a tower a few blocks away that looked like a hotel.

"*Eso es un supermercado?*" I said, scrunching my face.

"*Si,*" he said, pointing down.

I asked again, incredulous. "*El Corte Inglés es un supermercado?*"

He nodded to affirm and continued pointing down emphatically.

We continued walking toward the plaza, a landmark that reflected the city's seamless blending of the historic with the contemporary. Around its periphery were buildings ranging from old world confections to modern businesses. At the center of the plaza were fountains and sculptures, neoclassic to avant-garde. A large monument to Francesc Macià, former president of the Catalan government, punctuated the main fountain. The ruler was no more than a bust set on a stiff pedestal, but behind Macià was what looked like a misshapen pyramid topped with a fallen staircase.

"This looks like an earthquake hit Giza," I said to Katie. "How is this a tribute to Francesc Macià?"

Katie gave me a Euro-shrug and said, "Spain."

Macià stood guard over the fountain; a nude goddess hunched thoughtfully in green water. It was almost Rodinesque in its stature, but featured a doughy woman rather than the buff Thinker.

Students and couples dotted the plaza while clusters of demonstrators marched with cardboard signs and set up tents and shanties to protest Spain's economic crisis. A papier-mâché corpse in a coffin lay with the word "*España*" on its forehead.

Katie and I walked a block to El Corte Inglés. I gasped when I saw the man sitting beside the entrance. The accordion player we had seen in Segovia—the one who looked like my father—was sitting on the sidewalk playing for tips. He sported the same white straw hat he wore when we first spotted him two weeks ago, 325 miles away. Katie squealed, "Segovia!" She pointed at him and said, "We saw you in Segovia." He smiled and nodded as he continued playing "Lady of Spain."

At the end of his song, I dropped a coin in his tip jar and asked, "How did you get here?" It took me a moment to realize that was the same phrase I always used when I dreamt my father returned for a visit.

He replied, "My car."

Thankfully, Katie spoke because I could not. I had been desperately hoping for a cryptic message, one I could interpret as a wink from the other side.

"That's so cool," Katie said. "So you just drive all over Spain and play music?"

"Yes, I drive wherever I wish. Barcelona, Paris, whatever look nice."

"Awesome," Katie said.

I looked at him a moment longer, hoping he would whip out a lemon. Instead, he pressed out another song on his grinder and looked away.

"Come on, Mommy," Katie said, grabbing my hand. "I'm hungry."

I waited another moment, taking in the image of the street musician. "Okay," I said. "Let's move on."

Katie and I walked into the lobby of El Corte Inglés, which looked a lot like Macy's. The main floor was packed with mannequins, handbags, perfumes, and shoes. "My Spanish must be really bad. This isn't a supermarket," I said to Katie. She pointed to an escalator heading down.

This subterranean grocery store was probably nothing special for the locals, but for us it was a culinary playground with its colorful packaging and new and familiar products. We saw Mr. Clean on a bottle of *Don Limpio Baño*. And Tony the Spanish Tiger was pitching *Zucaritas*, growling that they're *Grrriquisimas!*

The canned fish aisle was like nothing I'd ever seen before. I am accustomed to a humble American selection of tuna, sardines, salmon, and clams, but El Corte Inglés devoted an entire double-sided aisle to canned octopus, squid, cockles, oysters, mussels, and sea urchin. Shoppers could select from up to a dozen brands of octopus, each offering a variety of seasonings ranging from salted olive oil to spicy tomato.

I purchased a can of octopus and a thick roll of bread. Katie grabbed a cheese sandwich at the deli, and we headed to the Cathedral Plaza for our five-euro picnic dinner.

The Cathedral of Santa Eulalia was the focal point of the plaza, surrounded by cafés, small shops, and hotels. Across from the enormous Victorian and Gothic cathedral stood an architectural college. Across its lower roofline was a whimsical Picasso frieze of primitive-looking stick figures.

While Katie and I sat on the steps of the cathedral eating our dinner, the sky grew darker and the college switched on a set of purple lights to illuminate the Picasso wall painting.

A man appeared on the roof, about two stories high, and began walking toward the edge.

Oh no, he's going to jump! I cried internally.

Then he removed a violin from a small case and began playing. "Look, a fiddler on the roof!" Katie said. The man began playing slowly then grew more intense. Minutes later, he was playing classical music so furiously and passionately, his bow arm blurred.

"Wanna get dessert?" Katie nodded her head toward the small waffle shop about thirty yards away where we could have ice cream, chocolate, sprinkles, butterscotch—or all of the above—atop a doughy grid, fresh from the waffle iron. Katie placed an imaginary candle at the center and pretended to light a match and connect it with the wick. As I blew out my invisible birthday candle, Katie asked what I wished for.

"You know the rules," I told her. "It's a secret."

The truth was that I never made birthday wishes. Twelve years earlier, I had spent the night with Katie in an oversized hospital crib with my eyes squeezed shut and promised that if my one wish were granted and she was okay, I would never ask for anything again.

Katie was thirteen months old when she had her first seizure. At a *Sesame Street Live* show, I noticed her holding out her arms and shaking. "Look how excited she is," I said to William. "Seeing all of these characters must be really intense."

Then she did it again during intermission.

"That's weird, she keeps shaking," I said to William, who turned to look at our daughter in better light. He watched her and furrowed his brow. "Let's call her doctor," he said.

We answered a flurry of questions, shot rapid-fire, and ten minutes later, were racing from the arena toward the hospital. From the corner of my eye, I saw Big Bird return to the stage as the *Sesame Street* theme song piped in for the second act.

That night, a team of doctors watched Katie experience several series of brief seizures. Her arms splayed, her neck stiffened, and her jaw locked as her upper body shook.

She's teething, I assured myself silently.

"Is she running a fever?" one of the doctors asked us.

"Yes," I blurted, then corrected myself. "No, sorry, she isn't. I don't know why I said that." But we all knew exactly why I'd instinctively offered up this lie. I needed an answer, a reason this was happening.

The following day, we visited a pediatric neurologist in a pale blue office trimmed with wallpaper of baby ducks following their mother. His waiting room was filled with children who had a range of neurological conditions. A preteen boy sat at a table that had a roller coaster of wire and wooden beads attached to its top. The boy's fingers were tense as he struggled to move a bead. Another child emptied a plastic crate of Legos onto the floor and howled with what could have been agony or delight. One sat in a wheelchair, staring ahead, devoid of expression.

The neurologist performed a series of tests, like watching Katie's eyes follow a light from one end of the room to the other. He observed her walk, and as I watched him, my fists curled like a gambler's, rooting for his racehorse. When the doctor tapped Katie's knee, I cried with excitement when her reflexes were normal.

A half hour later, the doctor dispassionately informed us that there were three possible outcomes: Katie would outgrow her seizures, develop mental disabilities, or die. Only time would tell.

Did this man just tell us that only time would tell if our daughter would live or die?

There was a ride at Coney Island called the Hell Hole where people stood upright in a cylindrical chamber, then spun so fast that centrifugal force pinned them to the wall. I went on this ride exactly once. I remember feeling the skin from my face melting into my skull and my stomach threatening rebellion. Just as I thought the nausea could not get any worse, the floor dropped from the bottom of the Hell Hole and I was suspended in midair, stuck in a spinning wheel with the head of Satan cackling.

The pediatric neurology office was the Hell Hole without the promise that the ride would ever end.

On the drive home, William and I were silent for a half hour before I told him I was absolutely certain that Katie was going to be fine.

William's fingers curled tensely around the steering wheel. "No offense, but you're kind of the queen of denial," he said.

"Maybe, but I have a very strong feeling about this. She's going to be fine."

"I hope you're right," he said, choking back tears.

"I am. I'm definitely right about this," I insisted too loudly.

In the following weeks, William logged nearly a hundred hours at the medical library at the University of California San Diego. He recorded Katie's episodes on video and graphed them on a chart. Every waking hour that he wasn't at work was spent trying to make sense of Katie's condition. I took Katie to the playground with missionary zeal, as if trying to appease the gods by showing how grateful she was for life. We both groped for control of a situation quickly spiraling out of our hands.

"Did I ever tell you I was born dead?" my father asked, his eyes closed as he soaked in the sunshine in my Aunt Rita's backyard. He had, in fact, shared this with me many times, but now that he had cancer, it was one of his greatest hits. "Yom Kippur, 1936," he began. "The doctors were walking me down to the morgue when I started crying. They looked down and I wasn't blue anymore. Everyone said it was a miracle."

Rita sat beside him and smiled. "Mama said he rose from the dead, which is probably why she always treated him like the Messiah."

My father put his hand over Rita's and squeezed it. "I figure I got a pretty good deal for someone who wasn't supposed to live a single day. I really have nothing to complain about."

Nothing to complain about? I thought silently. I realized that my father was trying to keep a positive attitude, but the comment jabbed nonetheless. I had plenty to complain about in losing my father. I smiled tightly, ignoring the mix of emotions linked with knowing my father chose a short life with his addiction over a longer one with me.

"Your father has the most wonderful outlook, doesn't he, JJ?" Aunt Rita waited for a response then asked again. "Doesn't he?

"Yeah," I responded. "It's really amazing."

Our lies became my father's palliative care.

Eighteen months, six doctors, and countless tests passed before Katie started predicting her seizures, or *seashores* as she pronounced them.

"Before she has them?" her neurologist yelped. "That's not supposed to happen."

"She's two-and-a-half years old, Doctor. None of this is supposed to happen," I said.

He suggested one more round of tests in which he would glue electrodes to Katie's head and attach the wires to a machine that would monitor her brain activity. We had done this test before, but only in three-hour stints. This time, the doctor wanted to keep Katie overnight at the hospital and videotape her for twelve hours.

The nurses at the hospital were surprised when I climbed into the five-foot crib with Katie but didn't argue. I watched Katie sleep with a turban of gauze bandages wrapped around her head and searched for words as I prayed awkwardly. Being agnostic is the worst. My Grandma Aggie was absolutely positive that when she died, she would be with Jesus. She had no doubt. William is equally sure that once he dies, that's the end of the road. I yearned for the comfort of certainty.

In the hospital crib, I watched Katie sleeping beside me. Her toddler cheeks were chubby, and her eyes delicate slits. Katie's little gumdrop mouth moved rhythmically as if she were nursing. Her little toes looked like rows of corn kernels.

"Let Katie be healthy and I will never, ever wish for another thing as long as I live," I whispered.

The next morning, Katie told me she wanted to watch her *seashore*, so we agreed that the next time she felt one coming, she'd let me know and I'd take her to a mirror. When she sounded the alarm, I raced to get her to a full-length mirror just in the nick of time. She had her usual series of a half-dozen short seizures, all the while standing upright and watching herself in the mirror.

When she finished, she looked at me and said plainly, "I done with *seashores*." And she was.

Three neurologists agreed that Katie was absolutely experiencing seizures, yet they defied many of the typical characteristics like loss of consciousness. Her primary pediatric neurologist had never seen a patient predict her own seizures, though it was undeniable that her body involuntarily stiffened and shook during these episodes. The doctor's final diagnosis was that this case was "really weird."

Days later, I told William I made a deal with God at the hospital. I'd woken up in the middle of the night to the humming of medical equipment. Drunk on grief and sleep-deprived, I begged to exchange fates with my daughter and die in her place. "So I'm definitely going young now," I told William.

"You've been saying that since we met," he reminded me.

"But now I've sealed the deal," I said. "I want Katie to be okay, but I'm going to miss you guys so much," I said, tears rolling down my face.

"Don't you think every parent who's had a sick child tried to make the exact same deal?" William said softly. "If there was a God, would he really choose *us* for a miracle? No, he'd pick true believers so they could spread the good word." He placed his arm around me. "There's no deal. This is very old baggage you're carrying around."

I blew my nose. "Promise?"

"Listen, if you ever make another bargain like this, offer up my life, will you?"

"You are such a good person, William."

"It has nothing to do with being good," he said. "Offer me up, and I won't give it a second thought. You can rest easy."

I smiled.

William said gently, "Be thankful, we got lucky."

After a loud first night in Barcelona—doors slamming, shouting voices—I decided to let Katie sleep in. Thankfully, she was able to snooze through the morning cannon fire.

I went downstairs to the breakfast buffet and smuggled a few pastries for Katie. I left them on her night table with a note letting her know I'd return in an hour, certain she wouldn't be disappointed about missing my trip to the Laundromat.

With my map in hand, I walked through the Cathedral Plaza on my way to the Laundromat near the water-front. A four-man band played "Maple Leaf Rag" near the church steps. I stopped, breathing in the freedom of having no pressing plans for the morning. On a whim, I could decide to sit on my laundry sack, grab a waffle, and listen to piano music that made me feel as if I were in a silent movie.

I sat across from the cathedral and watched people pass through the plaza. College students with heavy backpacks trekked by. Couples ambled hand-in-hand past the church, gazing at its perfectly symmetrical spires and arches pointing toward the heavens. A woman holding a small Union Jack flag overhead herded a tour group of a dozen middle-aged women.

Soon, street vendors began setting up tents and displaying their treasures. As the ragtime band continued playing, I fingered through faded Spanish comic books, loose chandelier pieces, and vinyl records. An older woman sold dishes and teacups; a man with a barber handle mustache displayed a glass case filled with vintage jewelry. A father and son stood behind a table offering sports memorabilia from European teams who played in the sixties and seventies.

When I arrived at the Laundromat, the attendant asked if she should separate my whites from colors or just toss everything in together. I smiled, remembering William and my early days together. "*Solo uno*," I said. "Let's see what happens."

William and I started playing house very quickly in our relationship. I was twenty-four and he was thirty. I was done with the club scene and William had never started it. Spending a Saturday night doing laundry and watching a video sounded positively romantic. He cooked dinner and I washed the dishes. All the while, we never ran out of things to talk about.

On that first night of domesticity, William took note of the fact that I was tossing all of my laundry into one machine. "Don't you separate your whites?"

"Meh," I said. "Seems like a hassle."

"A hassle?" he said, looking at me as though I told him I never bothered brushing my teeth. "How do you keep the colors from running?"

"I don't care, they can run," I replied. "Life is short; let the colors run if they want."

He tilted his head. "But your underwear…" he said, drifting off. "And your socks. They're going to turn blue if you toss in that Michigan sweatshirt."

"William, I think you should know right now, I have many neuroses, but this is not one of them. I don't care if my panties turn blue, and if you do, maybe you'll have to be that amazing husband who's in charge of laundry."

Oh my God, did I just say that aloud? I thought. *Who talks about marriage four weeks into a relationship?*

But he was the one and I knew it almost immediately. My father once advised me to marry a man like his sister

Rita's husband, Arnold. He said, "I'm a good father, but a shitty husband." I laughed silently because this was exactly the same advice my mother gave me, almost word for word.

William was a modern version of Uncle Arnold. He possessed a nice blend of integrity and acceptance. I needed both empathy and understanding and he had it in spades.

I poured a bit too much Tide into the washing machine to avoid looking up at William.

"Looks like I'll have to be," he said. "You're using a gallon of detergent there." He paused for a moment. *Here it comes: the part where he tells me that it's been really fun doing our laundry, but he's really not looking for a commitment.*

"I hate to ask you this, Jen," he began tentatively.

Here we go.

He scrunched his face. "Have you ever done laundry before?"

In the weeks that followed, I discovered that William was unusually insightful. He came from a family of anthropologists and was a source of boundless information about other cultures. Nothing struck him as weird; it was simply the custom of a people he had not yet studied. This would come in handy when I introduced him to my family.

We started house-hunting one week after our first batch of laundry and closed escrow on our tiny cottage on our eight-week anniversary. We moved in to our new home on Thanksgiving Day and, after a full day of hauling furniture from truck to house, shared the turkey special at a diner. William wiped a bit of gravy from his mouth. "I know I'll meet your mother when she comes to San Diego for Christmas, but when do I meet your father?"

I felt as though I dropped my fork, but when I looked at my hand, I was still holding it. "What?" I asked.

"When do I get to meet the famous Shelly Coburn?"

It was as though our waitress set down a huge platter of uncomfortable silence. "Why would you say something like that?" I finally asked.

"Because I want to meet him and, you know, talk to him about you and me," William said.

"My father is dead."

William looked shocked, wide-eyed and slack-jawed. "When did he die?"

"Five years ago."

"Five *years* ago? I thought…" he drifted. "You always talk about him in the present tense. I had no idea."

"No, I don't. I talk about him in the past tense."

"You don't. My sister asked when I was going to meet him," William said. "She told me I'd better make a good impression because he was obviously very important to you. You talk about Shelly as if he's alive."

"Well, he's not," I said, looking intently at the sliced carrots on my plate. "You're never going to meet him." My eyes welled so I bit my lip, my trigger to stop tears.

I liked that William wasn't uncomfortable with my pain.

He didn't frantically tell me it was okay because he understood that it was not. He didn't slather on the platitudes like so many other well-meaning people did. I knew they were trying to be kind when people told me that my father was in a better place or that I was lucky to have him while I did, but it always felt like a conversational pivot, a desperate attempt to change the topic to anything other than death.

I blew my nose in the paper napkin. "I'm not supposed to cry."

"Why not?"

"I should remember the better days," I sniffed.

"Can't you do both?" William asked.

As his words sank in, I shed my first tears over my father's death. "Why now?" William asked with the curiosity of a therapist.

"I don't know," I replied, hearing the clanking of silverware at another table. "I just never could until now."

Returning from the Laundromat in Barcelona, I decided to walk down to the waterfront, which was marked with a large, colorful ceramic sculpture by Roy Lichtenstein. The piece had the same comic book style as his well-known lithographs of kissing couples and tearful women. But the Barcelona Face was abstract, difficult to decipher. With red polka dots covering most of the surface, the sculpture is all primary colors, a splash of blue and a stroke of red that perhaps represent eyes and a mouth. Bright yellow caps the piece; the same sunny shade curves beneath the face.

Heading back to the hotel, I explored the winding stone streets of the Gothic Quarter. Elegantly chiseled historic buildings housed soap shops; chocolate boutiques lined the narrow streets. An itinerant musician played his flute in a small doorway.

In love with Barcelona, I floated through the streets, emerging into the bright plaza, then back to the hotel where Katie was still asleep.

I went downstairs to the lobby to access their Wi-Fi and noticed a man sitting in his chair, his eyes darting from the elevators to the stairs. A teen girl trotted down to him.

"Finally!" he huffed in an American accent.

"Mom said she still needs to dry her hair and Missy hasn't showered yet," the girl told him.

"How much longer?"

"About an hour," she said.

"An hour?" he barked. "We're in Barcelona. I don't want to sit in a hotel lobby all day; I want to see the goddamn city."

His daughter shrugged and told him not to shoot the messenger then disappeared back upstairs.

I wanted to whisper to him the secret that I had just discovered: he can leave. I wanted to tell him that a block away was a place where he could sit at a table on the sidewalk and drink muddy hot chocolate with a sugary churro stick. In my fantasy life, I lean in and share this with the fellow traveler. In reality, though, he was a stern dad, the one who could break up a good time just by entering the room, so I kept my nose down and checked Facebook.

That afternoon, Katie and I stood in line to enter Sagrada Familia, the unfinished sandcastle church designed by Spanish architect Antoni Gaudí. Our necks bent back like Pez dispensers as we looked at the structure, the quirkiest cathedral I had ever seen. It looked as though a child dripped soaking wet sand to create something that was at once elegant and spooky.

The outside of Sagrada Familia was adorned with multiple sides of meticulously sculpted Biblical characters. The inside was a study in mastering the use of natural light. Windows were perfectly placed to create the sense that God himself was reaching down from heaven through the ceiling of this church. Long streaks of light broke through the ceiling windows and spread like spotlights on a stage.

Part of the ceiling looked like taffy being pulled from the center. The stained glass windows were like Jolly Rancher candy. Even the crucifix at Sagrada Familia had a playful vibe. Instead of looking as though he were suffering on the cross, Jesus looked like he was parachuting in from heaven. The cross was unusually high and suspended in midair with a canopy that looked like the top of a carousel.

It was the first time I'd ever thought of Catholicism as whimsical.

Katie shrieked with delight as she recognized grids with Fibonacci numbers repeated in the church basement. She explained the math concept she had learned that year in school as I looked at her blankly. "Zero plus one is one, one plus one is two, two plus one is three, three plus two is five, five plus three is eight, and so on," she said, pointing to the numbers.

"Um, so what?"

"Now look at how the line is encircling the numbers and forming a snail shape," Katie continued. "The Fibonacci sequence is found in nature a lot, like sunflowers, pinecones." A boy about her age overheard her and the two gleefully chatted about math for a few minutes as I exchanged confused looks with his parents.

At our appointed time, Katie and I climbed to the top of the thirty-story tower. Sagrada Familia offered panoramic views of Barcelona from the modest apartment buildings just below us to the cruise ships pulling into the sparkling blue port. The view was mostly whitewash and clay tile rooftops, with a sprinkling of modern and historic buildings. Piercing the skyline was Agbar Tower, a mirrored skyscraper that is usually mentioned as one of the world's most phallic buildings. Washington Irving would have loved it.

As we explored every thrilling nook of the church, Katie

and I agreed that Gaudí was our new favorite artist. The following day, we planned to visit his house in Park Güell. But first there was an evening of dinner, waffles for dessert, and musical entertainment in Cathedral Plaza.

Before Katie and I left for Spain, my friend Kersten had given me a list of her favorite places in Barcelona, where she had spent a year during college. We finally found one of her dinner spots where the waitress told us "Bugs Bunny" was the daily special.

"*Quiero Bugs Bunny, por favor,*" Katie said.

"Really, you want to eat Bugs Bunny?" I asked.

Katie winked at me and whispered, "It's not *really* Bugs Bunny, Mommy."

"Very funny, but still, it's a rabbit."

"You just ordered chicken," she said.

The following day, we took the subway to Park Güell, stopping along the way at a bakery that mercilessly tempted passersby by displaying giant meringue puffs in the window.

The entrance to Park Güell was marked by two of Gaudí's designs, small homes that looked like iced gingerbread houses. Two long white staircases led to an enormous gazebo-like structure. But before visitors made the climb, a mosaic tile lizard at the base of the steps greeted them. On one side of the stairs was a dirt lot where vendors sold necklaces, fans, and souvenirs. On the other was a multi-level park with flowery gardens and cavernous, open pathways. At every turn was colorful tile mosaic work either inlaid into supporting walls or freestanding as sculptures.

The elevation offered a spectacular view of Barcelona. As we stepped into the seashell-pink Gaudí house, I immediately wanted to return with my mother. I would love watching her head snap from one direction to the next as she took in the artist's funky furniture design. I could easily see Gaudí's olive-and-purple velvet love seat in my mother's apartment. The wooden chairs were rustic and slightly misshapen, yet polished until they shone like glass. The pieces that would make her gasp aloud were Gaudí's light fixtures. I could not stop snapping photos of the elongated emerald-colored and bejeweled chandelier. Some lamps were stark and modern; others looked like a glass bouquet of flowers hanging from the ceiling. A few looked like lava lamps without the glass encasing, amorphous colorful blobs floating freely. The home was like a Victorian acid trip.

I saw a photo of Antoni Gaudí and smiled at the thought of him and my mother walking through Greenwich Village with their arms linked. They could have been best friends, stopping at every moving sale, playfully fighting each other for the artful castoffs of gay guys redecorating.

Days before Katie and I left for Spain, we met a couple who told us we should hop on a train and take a day trip to Montserrat, about an hour from Barcelona. They said we would see the most gorgeous views from the mountain-top and be able to visit a monastery that housed one of the famous Black Madonna sculptures.

With less than a minute to spare, we jumped on a train from Barcelona to Montserrat. Katie whipped out her Kindle and began reading as I eavesdropped on a dozen English-speaking young travelers. None was older than twenty.

There were four punk rock Australians, a mix of clean-cut Europeans, a young man from India, and one from the United States. They had connected at a youth hostel in Barcelona and decided to spend the day together. Four were seated on the floor. They tried to engage two young girls from Florida, who were polite but clearly not interested in tagging along with the group once the train stopped in Montserrat.

"What hostel are you staying at?" the Indian boy asked.

With a southern twang, the brunette Floridian said she once accidentally spent a night at a hostel thinking it was a regular hotel, but soon realized she would have to share a bathroom with other residents, and there was not enough room for her hot rollers. The blond sweetly added, "I need a place that has enough space for all of my shoes." Two European girls exchanged amused looks. If anything, they felt sorry for their American counterparts for missing out on the fun of hostel life. "You meet a lot of people our age," a girl with a German accent said. My heart sank. *Their age. I would never again be their age.* I didn't particularly want to stay in a youth hostel, but the reality that I was disqualified was jarring.

I gave Katie a gentle nudge and whispered, "This will be you in a few years."

She looked up. "Huh?"

"These kids," I said, gesturing discreetly. "One day, you'll be able to travel with friends and stay in youth hostels and meet people from around the world. People your age."

"Right," she said, completely disinterested.

A hard-edged Aussie girl tried to shock the southern belles with a story about how she left for her trip, simply telling her family, "Fuck all of you, ay." The Floridian with pageant-ready hair looked down at her perfectly manicured hands. Sunlight glistened from the gold cross around her neck.

Soon the group was earnestly debating the ethics of vegetarianism. They were passionate in their views, completely convinced that anyone who held a different opinion was a fascist.

Katie kept her nose buried in her book. It was impossible for her to feel reminiscent about a life that was still ahead of her, but I was amazed that these older, independent kids didn't intrigue her in the least.

"Katie," I whispered discreetly. "You should listen to this. This is your future."

She looked up. "This book is really good," Katie said. "Plus I don't care about a bunch of grown-ups talking about meat."

We arrived at Montserrat and took a tram up mountains that resembled jagged saws. As far as the eye could see were sweeping views of mountaintops and trees beneath us, all veiled by a thin sheet of atmosphere.

At the site of the monastery was a stone structure that looked like nature's surrealist take on Mount Rushmore. Inside was a statue of Black Madonna sitting on a golden throne holding Baby Jesus, who gave viewers a peace sign. "Don't you think it's kind of stupid that they call her *Black* Madonna, assuming she must've been white?" Katie pondered.

Outside there was little to do other than hike and take in the scenery. William is an avid hiker and would have loved spending the day in Montserrat. I like walking on paved ground; I need the security of knowing that when I step down, everything is where it's supposed to be. The only one who seemed less excited about the terrain was the Asian woman sporting kitten heels with striped knee socks.

As Katie and I hiked the trail, we came to an area that was so completely devoid of sound, I worried for a moment I might have lost my hearing. Then I heard the delicate trickle of a waterfall, so small it would fit in a therapist's office or a backyard Zen garden. We sat on a boulder that looked like an oversized bread roll and watched the water flowing.

"I want to show you a little pocket of sanity in New York," my father told me when I was six years old and we were driving to the Cloisters. "Whenever life gets to be too much, I come to the woods up here, have a smoke, and everything is cool again."

The Cloisters is the home of the lesser-known Metropolitan Museum of Art in Washington Heights. The site is surrounded by gardens, walking paths, and a few wooded areas. My father liked to call our adventures mountain climbing, though looking back, the drops were fairly shallow. Back then, it was serious business. Once, my father pretended he was falling off the side of our mountain. "Help me, JJ!" he cried. "You need to save me."

I remember looking down at my red Keds sneakers, terrified that I was going to lose my father. I leapt to the edge of the ravine and reached down to grab a thick chunk of roots to secure myself. Then I leaned over the side and extended my free hand toward him. He was on his stomach looking like my neighbor's G. I. Joe doll, crawling through a warzone.

"Grab my hand, Daddy," I called.

He reached for my hand and missed by inches. "I'm not going to make it," he said with great dramatic flair.

My heart pounded with the thought that my father was going to die falling off the side of a mountain because I wasn't able to help him. I couldn't save him. "Stay there, I'll get help," I said.

"No, you can do it," he said, suddenly inching his way up until our fingertips touched. Moments later, our hands were intertwined and my suddenly supernatural strength pulled him back to me.

"You did it, JJ. You saved my life," he said, hugging me tight.

It never occurred to me that this was a game because nothing about it was fun. Even after I was dubbed a hero, I was horrified at how close I had come to losing him. "You rescued me." He kissed my head. "It's a lucky man who has a daughter strong enough to save his life."

12

THE DALÍ TRIANGLE

Located a few hours outside of Barcelona, the Salvador Dalí Triangle is formed by three cities, all with Dalí museums. A massive collection of his art is housed in a traditional museum in Figueres; his summer home in the seaside village of Port Lligat is a testament to his architectural genius; and his wife Gala's castle in Púbol reveals that of all of Dalí's surreal creations, his marriage was the most bizarre.

We first heard about the Dalí Triangle three years earlier when William, Katie, and I were visiting Aunt Bernice in Florida, the summer before Katie began sixth grade.

The centerpiece of Aunt Bernice's living room is an original Dalí sculpture with three golden prongs that look like tree branches reaching five feet from the floor. In its center rests a clear stone.

As a child, I always thought the piece looked like an

engagement ring the ogre from "Jack and the Beanstalk" might present to his beloved. Bernice got the sculpture for a song when she was a young woman because of a misunderstanding with the gallery owner in Manhattan. He had originally quoted her for the piece sitting next to the Dalí, then two weeks later told her of his blunder when she came to pick up her new sculpture. Bernice told the man that she had already rented a moving truck and made several costly changes to her living room in preparation for the new sculpture. She told him it would be most ungentlemanly of him to renege on their agreement. "I've scheduled a party for its homecoming," Bernice explained. A half hour later, the man was packaging the piece for her.

Recalling the story from an era of pin curls and soda fountains, my eighty-four-year-old aunt sighed and lamented that she was no longer able to drive to see her favorite artist's work at the Dalí Museum in St. Petersburg, five hours away. "I'm lucky to get to the Winn Dixie on my own anymore," she said before taking a bite of her ham sandwich.

William shot me a look that asked if we should take an impromptu road trip. I smiled and nodded.

En route to our bed and breakfast in St. Petersburg, we stopped at Thomas Edison's winter home in Fort Myers where Bernice said she felt very comfortable because she could understand the technology on display and the banyan trees in the garden had more visible veins than her legs. As we crossed the Everglades, my aunt casually dropped the fact that we were crossing Alligator Alley as rain came down like a carwash. The last thing we saw clearly was a yellow road sign, warning "Crocodile Crossing." William looked in the rearview mirror to ask a question before noticing that Katie and Bernice had fallen asleep in the back seat, their heads leaning into each other's, fitting perfectly like puzzle pieces.

The following day at the museum, standing in front of Dalí's enormous canvas, *The Hallucinogenic Toreador*, the tour guide told us the museum housed the largest collection of Dalí's work in the United States and the second largest in the world.

"Where's the largest?" Katie and I asked in unison. I waited for her to dub this moment "a personal jinx" and say that I owed her a soda. Silence. I wondered when that had ended.

The guide told us about the Dalí Triangle, where we could not only see the artist's paintings, sculptures, and jewels, but his birthplace and burial ground too.

Getting from Barcelona to Figueres was easy. We hopped on a train and two and a half hours later, followed the throng of tourists for a half-mile trek through the dusty streets. We passed modest apartment buildings, bargain clothing shops, and an oversized bodega. A group of boys walked down the sidewalk kicking a soccer ball.

In the distance stood a white museum with a row of giant eggs lining the roof. Rimming the structure were several Oscar-like golden statues and sculptures of women balancing baguettes on their heads. "This must be the place," a young woman said to her friend a few paces ahead of us.

In front of the museum was a sculpture of a sitting man with an egg head tilted to the side. In its womb was a bust of Catalan philosopher Francesc Pujols. *Yes, this was definitely the place.*

Once a theater, the Dalí museum was created by the artist with the support of the local government in the seventies. The museum site held sentimental value for Dalí because it was where he held his first art show at age fourteen. He died in an apartment attached to the museum and is buried beneath it.

Inside, a dizzying array of Dalí paintings and sculptures competed for attention. A giant mural he designed for the opera *Labyrinth* and the photographic oil *Gala Nude Looking at the Sea Which at 18 Metres Appears the President Lincoln* were displayed under a glass geodesic dome. Nearby stood a brick niche where a rhinoceros head, rust octopus, and cubist angel hovered over a statue of Moses. An enormous glass window opened to a courtyard with a centerpiece sculpture of a rotund Queen Esther mounted onto the back of the car where, suspended above, there was an overturned rowboat dripping faux water droplets. For one euro, visitors could prompt a downpour inside Dalí's *Rainy Taxi*, which was occupied by a life-sized model chauffeur and manne-quin passenger.

As we looked at a sculpture of a woman wearing a corn-on-the-cob scarf and baguette hat, a woman turned her head quizzically and asked her husband if he thought Dalí was on LSD. "He says no," the husband replied, looking at a guide-book to the museum. "He says, 'I *am* the drug.'"

"He *is* the drug?" the woman.

"Yes," the husband said, taking in the details of the piece, like the ants crawling across the bust. "We're tripping on Dalí right now. It's a nonchemical high."

Across the street from the train station in Figueres was the Sarfa bus terminal with coaches leaving for Cadaqués every few hours. The seaside village bordered Port Lligat where the only tourist attraction was the home of Salvador and Gala Dalí, another corner of the Triangle. The villages are located on the northern tip of the Costa Brava, a stone's throw from France.

Although the bus was clearly marked "Cadaqués," I ner-vously asked the driver if he was, indeed, going there.

He returned the question with a sharp glare and corrected my pronunciation.

I tried again, mimicking his inflection.

He barked at me again, rolled his eyes, and waved us onto the bus. We were leaving the safe environs of Barcelona and Figueres, where American tourists were everywhere. Katie and I were headed to a part of Spain I wasn't quite sure I would be able to manage. I hadn't felt such a lack of confidence in my travel skills since we first landed in Paris when Katie was eight. Thankfully, at fourteen, she was still unable to detect my uncertainty. I was equally grateful for the fact that she had maintained her sunny spin on the cultural differences that terrified me.

As Katie and I sat at the front of the bus, she whispered that it was really cool how the driver didn't give us a scripted customer service rap thanking us for choosing the Sarfa bus line.

The journey took one hour, two Dramamine, and seven prayers to Saint Christopher, just in case he was listening. The bus wrapped around a narrow road that clung to the edge of a mountain. I dug my fingernails into my palms as Katie read her book. When we began our descent, the view opened up to an expanse of bay connecting to the Balearic Sea, which connects with the Mediterranean further south. Enormous rocks erupted from the water, obstacles for dozens of white fishing boats.

Katie and I got off the bus and went to the ticket booth to ask where we could catch a taxi. My daughter had a huge smile on her face because the driver had just snapped at her when she thanked him for the ride. "It's just so…real," she told me.

A woman at the bus station laughed bitterly at my inquiry about taxis. Of course she had no map for us either. I stood paralyzed, wondering if everyone in Cadaqués was going to treat us with contempt.

"Look at that road, Mommy," Katie said, pointing to a path where people were coming and going dressed in swimsuits. "Let's follow them." I had no better idea so I let Katie lead. As we made it down the path, the seaside came into view. Suddenly Cadaqués was alive, its main street a smooth stone path that was filled with small hotels and restaurant tables on one side; the seaside was dotted with tourists swimming and scuba diving.

All of the homes along the hillside were white, a contrast with the steely evening sky and mountain backdrop. As streetlights began to flicker on, the village took on an ethereal glow. Katie noticed a small blue sign listing nearby hotels. "Look, keep walking this way for our hotel!" We continued on the stone path, listening to the soundtrack of playful chatter, sangria glasses clinking, and seagulls squawking overhead. The soft evening breeze washed over us, and I could feel my stress leaving with it. We had entered a different world.

Ten minutes later, a clumsy young man looked up from the reception desk at the hotel and welcomed us to Cadaqués. He showed us to our room overlooking the hotel pool and a quiet patch of shoreline.

The following morning, a redheaded pixie at a smoothie shop mixed our breakfast drinks in her blender. I thought about calling William to suggest we move here and enroll Katie in the local high school. We could work at the smoothie shop, or perhaps the art gallery next door. Outside, a man emptied a bucket of water onto the patio of his restaurant and began sweeping. *I could do that*, I thought. *I could get a job at a restaurant and clean the patio at eleven in the morning.* The man noticed me staring and asked Katie and I where we were from. When we told him, he sighed, "Ah, California," undoubtedly romanticizing the life we led in San Diego.

Katie and I walked up a dirt hill, horseshoeing around to make our way back down to Port Lligat. Through treetops, we spotted two silver alien heads perched on the roof of a home. Katie raised her eyebrows and led the way down the rocky path to the house on the bay. The first thing we saw was a rowboat pierced by a tree in Dalí's front yard. The second was the water that surrounded three sides of the home.

The artist bought the property in 1930 when it was a tiny fisherman's hut and added onto the whitewash home for the next forty years until it was a sprawling, multilevel estate. The Dalí house-museum had very few neighbors: a hole-in-the-wall deli and an unoccupied gallery across the narrow dirt road, a bait shop on the dock. There was room for little else.

A small group stood at the Dalí house doorway, people shifting their weight as they waited for their appointed tour. Since Katie and I arrived a full hour before our scheduled time, we grabbed lunch at the deli. Seagulls flew in the cloudless blue sky, occasionally plummeting down to bob for fish.

A man playing Spanish guitar music sat a few yards away, plucking something that was at once sultry and sentimental. I took a bite of my anchovy and tomato sandwich and watched as Katie read a book, eating sliced fried potatoes. *I don't need to be this happy at once*, I thought. *Can't I save some for later?*

A better part of me admonished that I should enjoy the experience now and stop searching for life's doggie bags. "Katie," I whispered. She looked up. "Do you want some dessert?"

She sat up and nodded emphatically. "They've got Chipwiches in the freezer," Katie told me. I handed her a five-euro bill.

"Chipwiches!" I exclaimed. "Are you kidding me?"

Katie nodded. "Grab one for me too."

That evening, Katie and I went to dinner at a tiny restaurant, a beach house chiseled into a hillside. A woman showed us upstairs to a converted bedroom that could only fit three small tables. She opened the shutters to reveal flowerboxes and a bay view and offered us wine. A half hour later, a heavy man with the air of a restaurant owner came upstairs and told us what he was cooking. This evening, he was playing chef and waiter, yet he didn't seem in the least bit harried. When I ordered two appetizers and two main courses, the man began to shake his head. "Too much food for little girls," he said. "I cook big meals. You share the paella, then if you still hungry, we get you more to eat."

"Really?" I said, impressed with his down-sell.

"Yes, *señora*. We have all night."

We do?

We did. After the man brought our food, he checked back an hour later to see if we wanted more food, but he had been right; his serving of paella looked more like a catering tray than a meal for one or two. He returned forty minutes after that with an ice cream cake that tasted like frozen Snickers.

"What was your favorite part of the Dalí house?" I asked Katie as we sat at the table.

"I liked the pool with all those stuffed snakes coiled around the cabana."

"And the Michelin Man standing in as lifeguard," I added. "That was crazy. What do you think that was about?"

"What's any of it *about*?" Katie said, the Euro-shrug now one of her natural gestures. "What did you like best?"

"I loved how sunlight pours into all of the windows of the house." Katie nodded in agreement. "I guess what I enjoyed seeing most was his unfinished painting."

"On the plywood?" Katie asked.

"It looks like he was starting to paint an angel. But you know Salvador Dalí would never paint *just* an angel. He must have had some crazy plan for it, but no one will ever know what it was."

Our tour guide told us that the project was interrupted when Gala became deathly ill, and then the artist never had the heart to finish it.

"I loved it when that French lady started crying on our tour," Katie said, rolling her eyes. "So French."

In San Diego, when I was planning our visit to the Dalí Triangle, I wondered if two nights in Cadaqués would leave us with too little to do. As it turned out, both Katie and I agreed we could easily spend a month in the village. There were scenic walks to be taken, scuba diving to try, and endless street performers to watch. Plus the cafés and restaurants were always filled with people looking as if they were in no hurry to go anywhere at all.

We arrived in Flaça by train and took a taxi to the castle Dalí created for Gala as her private getaway in Púbol. To say he bought her a medieval castle would be just half the story. Dalí refurbished it to Gala's every specification, regardless of how difficult. When she said she wanted a throne suspended in midair, he asked how high. He created art for her walls inside and landscaped her garden with a fountain made from twenty-seven busts of the German composer, Richard Wagner. As thanks, Gala told her husband that he was only allowed to visit her if he had received a written invitation because she might be entertaining one of her young lovers. Dalí didn't mind though. He said he took masochistic delight in Gala's request.

We were the only ones at the castle who weren't part of an American tour group of seniors. Each was decked out in U.S. flag T-shirts and red-white-and-blue sequined sun visors to commemorate Independence Day back home. Together we looked at Gala's dresses, furniture, and personal effects, but the most riveting part of the tour was listening to our guide, an art historian, share the love story of Salvador and Gala. "The French poet Paul Éluard, his wife Gala, and their daughter Cécile visited Dalí at his home in Cadaqués one summer, and by September, Gala had taken up with Salvador," she said with an Eastern European accent.

"Really?" a matronly American woman asked, appalled.

Our guide smirked. "Yes, but Éluard was no stranger to Gala's sexual proclivities. He had spent several years living in Paris with Gala and the surrealist Max Ernst in a *ménage à trois*."

"Lord have mercy," the woman gasped.

"Did Eduardo kick his butt?" an older man asked our tour guide.

Our tour guide raised her brows. "Did Éluard…?"

"Kick his butt for stealin' his wife?" the man asked with a protective arm on his wife's back.

"No, no, they all remained friends," the guide replied, failing to hide her glee in scandalizing her audience. "It was a surprise to their friends, though, because Dalí's only love until then had been a man."

"Sweet baby Jesus," a woman muttered. "I thought we were going to see melting clocks."

"What became of Cécile?" I asked. "Did she stay in Cadaqués with Gala and Dalí?"

"No," the tour guide replied without a smile. "Gala was, how you say, not a good mother."

"So Gala left her husband *and* her daughter?"

"Yes," the guide said, moving the group along to the crypt where Gala's body was buried.

As we walked downstairs, I asked the guide how old Cécile was when her mother left her. "She was eleven," the tour guide replied dismissively. Turning back to the group, she continued. "There is Gala's leopard purse still sitting in their car. She died in Cadaqués, but Dalí knew she wanted to spend her last moments in Púbol so he put her body in the car and drove her here to her final resting spot."

Back at the hotel in Barcelona that evening, I Googled Cécile Éluard and found a black-and-white photo of her as a little girl with a giant bow in her hair, looking down, unaware that her mother would leave her a few years later. Another website included reflections about her childhood home outside Paris, where murals by Max Ernst were later discovered beneath wallpaper. Cécile said she hated the house. On the outside, the home appeared normal, but inside it was a very different story with its surreal paintings of birds and other creatures.

"What happened to you, Cécile Éluard?" I asked the screen.

"Are we going to the Magic Fountain show?" Katie asked, pulling me back into reality.

Twenty minutes later, Katie and I joined hundreds of people on the steps leading to the Palau Nacional, the national museum, in Montjuïc Park and waited for the sky to dim from lavender to grape. We squeezed shoulder to shoulder, each step filled with tourists eagerly awaiting the show of lit fountains changing color to music. Finally, sprays of pink water pulsed into the sky as we listened to the music progress. Katie's eyes lit up as she recognized the tune "Circle of Life" from *The Lion King*.

On the return trip from Spain, Katie and I spent a week with my mother in New York. We decided to see Stella, who was a live-in caretaker for an elderly woman in the building where my father died. I watched the familiar elevator door close and floors pass through the small glass window and wondered what had happened to Stella's paintings on the walls of their Brooklyn Heights apartment. Had her mural been covered with wallpaper? Would anyone care if it were discovered?

Stella greeted us at the door wearing a sundress she fashioned by slitting open the bottom of a pillowcase and creating straps from fishing wire. She had always been a thin woman but now weighed less than ninety pounds. Religious music hummed from a small cassette player, and the smell of boiling vegetables filled the air. Her charge was sleeping in the bedroom, freshly showered and diapered.

Stella was on duty twenty-four hours a day and slept on a cot in the kitchen, where she tried to cozy the space with black-and-white photos of my father in the final stages of cancer. His arms are crossed over his chest as he stares into the camera, looking annoyed to be photographed.

"Was my father angry at me before he died?" I asked Stella.

"He was angry at everyone," she said.

"So…yes?" I looked at the floor and noticed Stella had painted it white. "How do I get past that?"

"How do you pass Go?" Stella replied. "How do you collect $200?"

That evening, back at my mother's apartment, I resumed my online search for Cécile Éluard. My mother popped her head in the door of the guest bedroom and scolded me for being on her computer. "Turn that thing off and put the cover over it before we all die from radiation sickness," she demanded.

"Do you think Daddy was angry at me before he died?" I asked.

My mother sighed, having answered the question several times already over the years. "I think that is an easier question than the one you really want to ask," she replied.

"And what question do I *really* want to ask, Dr. Freud?"

"Whether or not you're angry at your father for abandoning you," she said.

"*Abandoning* me?!" I snapped. "He died. It's not like he left to join the circus. You can't get angry with someone for dying."

"Why not?" my mother asked.

"Because that would make me a complete jerk," I said.

"It's normal to feel abandoned," she said.

"Will you stop using that word?! There's a big difference between someone leaving and dying."

"What's the difference?" my mother asked.

"One is a choice and the other is just a raw deal," I said.

"I meant what's the difference to you, Jennifer?" my mother asked. "Regardless of how it happened, your father is no longer there for you, and I think it's entirely reasonable for you to feel angry about that."

Katie joined my mother in the doorway. Holding her phone up, she said she had found Gala's daughter online.

"Cécile Éluard?" I asked eagerly.

"Yeah, there are lots of people online who also want to know what happened to her."

"Do we know her?" my mother asked.

"No, she's just…" I trailed off. "She's Salvador Dalí's stepdaughter. I'm just curious about how her life turned out."

"I didn't know he had children," my mother said.

"And?" I asked Katie, sounding a bit more panicked than I meant to.

"She did great. It says she was an art dealer and a book dealer. She married a poet, and there's a picture of her hanging out with Picasso and all of these big writers in Paris, and she looks really happy."

My shoulders dropped with relief. Cécile's rejection hadn't ruined her, as I had feared. "Can you show me the picture, Katie?"

Katie began tapping as my mother and I flanked her, leaning in to get a look. "There she is," Katie said, pointing to Cécile.

My mother gasped. "Look at that other woman in the middle. What a fabulous hat!"

"She's smiling," I said, squinting to see Cécile. *She's all right.*

Trip Four

Amsterdam and Paris

2013

13

AMSTERDAM

Six months after Katie and I returned from Spain, I told William I wanted to take another European adventure before our daughter left for college.

"She just started high school," he reminded me.

"It's going so fast, isn't it?" I said. "We're going to turn around and she'll be gone." My sadness over Katie's inevitable flight from the nest now rivaled my fear of dying.

"So where will you two be off to next?" William asked.

"I was thinking Amsterdam," I told him. "Then back to Paris."

"When do you want to go?"

"Tomorrow," I shot. "But it'll take about two years to save for a trip, so I figure we could take off right after her sophomore year."

William nodded thoughtfully. "I've been waiting for you

to tell me Amsterdam was on the itinerary. That's going to be…" he drifted, unsure of the right words.

"A mixed bag," I finished. My father loved Amsterdam, but it would be hard visiting and knowing I would never swap stories with him. Though he had been dead nearly thirty years, I still occasionally reached for the telephone to call him before realizing it was impossible.

New York was my father's permanent address, but Amsterdam was where he felt most at home in the world. He had told me the city was so mellow that even the dogs didn't bark. He also enjoyed the freedom to openly smoke pot. And he fondly recalled eating "space cakes" and listening to undiscovered bands at the Melkweg, a concert venue that had once been an abandoned dairy barn. What he loved most, however, was that the Dutch had embraced his song "Only a Fool" and catapulted it to the top of the music charts. Amsterdam was where my father felt most complete because his music career was a booming success. In the United States, he was a struggling musician with a few hits and more misses throughout the years. In Amsterdam, he had made it. It was a small pocket of the world where his dream had been realized.

As much as I wanted to see Amsterdam through my father's eyes, I was also terrified. What if the city had changed entirely and lost its chill vibe? What if the Melkweg had been leveled to make way for a Walmart? Most frightening, what if too much time had passed and no one remembered my father's music anymore? To be forgotten in Amsterdam would have been unbearable to him. I wasn't sure I could withstand witnessing the death of his legacy.

In December of 1978, when I was twelve years old, my father had recently returned from Amsterdam after having spent several weeks on an unusual mission. That fall, his writing partner Norman had been leafing through *Cash Box* magazine and noticed that "Only a Fool" was a huge hit in Holland. Not only had their song been a success for much of the year, it looked like it was on track to be one of the top sellers of the decade. But there was a problem. Neither Norman nor my father was given a writing credit. The performer, the Mighty Sparrow, was listed as the writer and composer, and my father and his friend were out in the cold. They didn't know who made the mistake and didn't really care, as long as the error was corrected. The bottom line was that there were royalties to claim. And the recognition would be validating for my father, whose confidence needed the boost even more than his bank account.

The pair scraped together the money to get my dad on a plane to set the record straight. He promised to return from Amsterdam with corrected paperwork, back payment, and two gold records: one for Norman, the other for himself.

Days after his return from Holland, my father and I were sitting in his car after our annual Cousins Club Chanukah party. He had picked up a new sweater overseas which was made from knotty wool and had leather patches on the elbows. My father also sported new hand-knit socks under his clogs. The awkward stitch told me a girlfriend made them.

My dad reached under the car seat and handed me a package wrapped in a brown grocery bag. This was his typical presentation of gifts from overseas, like European board games and exotic foods. He also frequently returned with albums by bands that were wildly popular in Finland or Norway. Inside this bag, however, was a gold record of "Only a Fool" encased in glass, listing my father and Norman as the lyricist and composer. My eyes popped.

"You got it!" I squealed.

Showing me the record, my father had a wide smile. "Merry Christmas. Happy Chanukah. Happy life," he said, handing it to me.

"For me?"

"My two greatest gifts should be together," he said.

"Are you sure you want to give this away? You worked so hard for it."

He laughed. "You got that right. I don't know what was tougher, writing the song or dealing with the music industry. This business is a motherfucker."

I nodded knowingly. "Is it real gold?" I asked.

"Of course."

"Is this the actual record? If we unframe it, would it play your song?"

"Are you crazed, JJ?!" he shouted. "Give it back to me. You can't have it." He grabbed the record from my hands.

"I didn't say I was going to do it, I was just asking," I cried.

"This is my life, do you understand?" he said. "You can't take someone's life and crack it open like a walnut."

"I didn't say I was going to," I said, defending myself.

He looked at me appraisingly for a few seconds.

"I was just asking a question," I pleaded.

"Okay, maybe I overreacted, but you have to promise me that if I give this to you, you're never going to unframe it. It's not the actual record; it's just symbolic."

"Okay, that's all I wanted to know!"

"You'll never take this apart, right?" he asked, eyebrows raised.

"Never," I promised.

"Okay," he said, handing back the record. "It's yours. Take good care of it."

Katie and I arrived in Amsterdam and immediately agreed it was the most beautiful place we had ever seen. Canals ringed and sliced through the city like the threads of a spider web. Lining the waterways were rows of narrow, two- and three-story homes with funky gables and brightly painted window frames. A few buildings had an art deco look, smooth stone inlaid thoughtfully into their façade. One brick townhome sported a giant marble bow.

The collection of bridges was equally eclectic. Some were classic stone arches. Another was a large white wooden bridge that looked as if it belonged in Nantucket. A bright orange, modern design was a cross between a sculpture and jungle gym. I couldn't take pictures quickly enough to capture the charm of Amsterdam.

The city also had its own distinctive scent. "I'm not going to get a contact high, am I?" Katie joked, seeing a backpacker strolling by with a joint casually pinched between his fingers. Katie had always been like William—and never had I been more grateful than during her teen years. She knew how to have fun, but always kept her eyes on the prize of getting good grades and running well for her high school cross-country team. Getting high, by contact or otherwise, was not on the agenda.

"Sorry, you're going to get totally baked from this," I said.

She raised her eyebrows. "Wait, really?"

"No, not really," I assured her.

"Look, I don't have any problem with other people smoking, I just don't want their choices to affect my lungs or brain or anything," Katie explained.

"Reasonable," I said, smiling at just how much she reminded me of her father. "I promise you will not get a contact high here."

What I could not guarantee, however, was that a bike wouldn't hit us if we didn't stop accidentally drifting into the cyclists' lane of the sidewalk. The ringing of tin bike bells was the soundtrack of Amsterdam, with more people riding bicycles than I'd ever seen. Businessmen in suits pedaled by. Hipsters with shorts and wool hats rode bikes. We even saw a woman, who looked as if she was pushing ninety years old, riding a cruiser with a basket filled with fruits and vegetables.

It began to rain just as Katie and I found the Melkweg and ducked in for a drink in its café, the gateway to the concert venue. The space was like an unpretentious diner with black-and-white checkered floors and a long counter. A young woman with the look of a woodland fairy flitted over to our table with glass mugs, one filled with steeping mint leaves, the other with hot chocolate. She also placed down packets of small cookies that tasted like shortbread soaked in caramel. When Katie told the waitress the cookies were the best she'd ever eaten, the pixie brought a few more. For the next half hour, Katie unwrapped cookies and dipped them in her drink as raindrops tapped the window. Every so often, someone opened the door to the concert area and we were hit by a blast of music. "My father used to listen to bands in there," I told Katie.

"I know," she said. "Maybe he sat at this table beforehand and hung out with that guy." Katie pointed to the manager wiping down the counter. "Are you going to ask if he's heard of your dad's song?"

"I don't know," I replied, my breath caught in my throat.

The manager noticed us staring and said hello in a

Midwestern American accent. We chatted for a bit and I mentioned that the Melkweg was one of my father's favorite spots to visit in Amsterdam.

The manager smiled politely. Katie looked at me expectantly.

"Do you know—" I began. "Do you know how we can get some more of these cookies?"

Katie knit her brows with confusion.

"You want more cookies?" the man asked.

I nodded.

"I guess we could sell you a package," he said, walking toward the kitchen. Returning with a sleeve of a hundred cookies, he asked if four euros sounded fair.

"More than fair," I replied, reaching for my wallet.

"I don't get it," Katie whispered when the manager was out of earshot. "Why didn't you ask if he knows the song?"

"I'm not sure," I told her. "I guess I was afraid he would say no. Amsterdam is perfect right now. I don't want anything to change that."

"Okay," Katie returned. "Thanks for the cookies."

A black man with a full, seventies-style afro entered carrying a guitar case plastered with stickers of bands from around the world. "Hey man," he said to another worker in the café. "I'm playing tonight." He nodded his chin toward the door.

"Right on," the guy replied, leading him to the concert space.

Amsterdam felt like a magical place where there had never been anything but peace, love, and harmony. But the next day we would be given a heavy dose of reality, a reminder of the evil that had a stranglehold on Europe during World War II.

We visited the Anne Frank House, climbing the steep stairs that led to the secret annex where eight people hid from the Nazis for two years. Katie and I looked at the young girl's diary, its cover the pattern of a tablecloth. Seeing her handwriting on the yellowed pages was painfully surreal. Bells from the church beside the house rang just as Anne Frank had described in her journal. I looked out the window at the homes across the canal and wondered who betrayed the people inside.

Video of Otto Frank, Anne's father, the only survivor of the annex, played on television screens throughout the stark space. He spoke about how he first read his daughter's journal after he returned from Auschwitz, and how stunned he was by the depth of her feelings and faith.

I glanced at Katie, who was now older than Anne Frank at the time she perished at Bergen-Belsen. I fought back tears thinking about all this child had endured before she ultimately succumbed to typhoid at the concentration camp. In her fifteen years, she spent two in a secret annex, then another two in concentration camps. In different circumstances, she would have had a very similar life to Katie's, one filled with friends and school and travel.

With that realization, my head snapped back to the television monitor featuring Otto Frank talking about losing his family. As heartbroken as I felt, I couldn't begin to imagine his pain.

A chaser of self-loathing quickly followed.

Why have you wasted so much time and energy senselessly worrying about death? I thought. *Look at what millions of people—Jews, minorities, gays, political dissenters, and the disabled—endured without the luxury of anxiety. These people had real problems. Harboring imaginary demons is ridiculously self-indulgent.*

Then a kinder voice of reason chimed in. *Stop. Just let go and enjoy life.*

Katie's words returned me to the moment. "Anne Frank wrote in her diary that, despite everything, she never lost faith that people were basically good," she shared. "That's kinda beautiful," Katie said.

"It is," I replied.

I looked at the photo of Anne Frank with her full wedge of hair and impish grin, then took a mental snapshot of Katie in her sloppy bun and cut-off shorts.

"Are you ready to get going?" Katie asked.

"Sure," I said, acutely aware that we had the freedom to make that choice. As we walked outside, I stopped for a moment to take in the feeling of the summer breeze on my face.

Soon, Katie and I were sitting at an outdoor café eating cheese-covered pancakes and listening to a musician play accordion while he floated down the canal in a one-man boat.

That evening, Katie and I were reading in Vondelpark when an absolutely baked Rastafarian stopped a police officer to ask for directions to the Red Light District, though he couldn't remember the name of the area where prostitutes stood on display in store windows.

Katie looked up from her book to watch the interaction.

"A lady friend for the night," Rasta John asked, snapping his fingers to jog his memory. The officer smiled and pointed the man in the right direction.

"Is *anything* illegal here?" Katie asked, laughing.

The following afternoon, after visiting the Rijksmuseum, an enormous fairy-tale castle filled with artwork, we headed toward the Van Gogh Museum. Between the two sites was an enormous reflecting pool; at its base, orange and white letters stretched nearly eighty feet spelling "I amsterdam." In the pool were sculptures that looked like oversized construction nails covered in colorful aluminum foil. Pink nails intertwined then rounded to look like wedding rings; green ones stood erect, wrapped around one another. Musicians and acrobats performed in front of the Amsterdam sign.

Vincent Van Gogh had been my favorite artist for as long as I can remember, so the half-hour wait huddled under our umbrella was well worth it for me. Katie, who has loved rainy days since she was a toddler, had only one complaint: I made her dress for the weather.

The multistory Van Gogh Museum was filled with two hundred of the artist's paintings, including his thickly coated swirls of evening sky. As expected, we saw paintings of purple lilies and yellow sunflowers. The permanent exhibit included Van Gogh self-portraits and landscapes with rolling hills. Though I always loved his paintings, I quickly learned that I knew very little about Van Gogh's work. I hadn't known how influenced he had been by Japanese art and what an impressive collection of prints he created. Many of his pieces had a distinctly Asian feel, like his wood bridge in the rain and almond tree blossoms. He told his brother Theo that he felt happier when he envisioned himself in Japan, a sentiment he expressed best in a self-portrait where he is Asian and surrounded by Japanese imagery.

Before Katie and I had left for Amsterdam, my friend Jonathan told me he saw a documentary suggesting Van Gogh didn't commit suicide but was accidentally shot by a boy from the village. In order to protect the child from prosecution, Van Gogh used his final moments of life to set the stage to appear as if he killed himself. I asked one of the docents if there was any validity to this claim.

"All claims have validity," he replied in perfect English. "If someone believes something, there is truth to it regardless of whether or not the facts support it." Katie and I glanced at each other, trying not to giggle. "The noble Vincent cover-up is a good story, but there is no way for me to confirm it personally because I was not there," he said. As he looked away, Katie pinched her index finger and thumb together and held an imaginary joint to her lips. She mouthed, *stoned*.

The following day was a drizzly one. Katie and I trekked to the Rembrandt House where we shamefully admitted to one another that we were much more interested in the flea market outside. "Let's go inside and give this a fair shake, then we can reward ourselves with a walk around the merchant tents," I suggested.

"Okay, it's pretty small," Katie said, craning her neck to look at the Dutch master's home. "On the way here, we passed a thrift shop called Out of the Closet. Can we go there too?"

"The place that does free HIV testing?"

"They had some really cool stuff in the window."

I shrugged. "Okay."

Katie smiled. "I've never done anything as hipster as thrifting in Amsterdam. I probably won't ever again."

"You peaked at sixteen years old. That's harsh."

After our breeze through the Rembrandt House, we walked through rows of vendors, a few who were selling pot lollipops, teabags, and accessories. "I've got to take a picture of this," Katie said.

"No Instagram," I said, reminding her that my liberal view of pot smoking wasn't widely shared and that most of her friends' parents would not appreciate the ganja posts. When Katie began high school, I told her that, in my opinion, smoking pot and drinking alcohol were essentially the same, though neither was a good choice for someone her age.

At the cannabis booth, a mother with a stroller put space cakes in her basket and asked questions about their potency. "Eat half then wait about an hour," said the seller, who looked eerily similar to Doc Brown in *Back to the Future*. "If you don't feel anything, eat the other half," he advised. I listened with rapt attention, fascinated by the normalcy of their interaction.

"Are you going to try a space cake?" Katie asked.

"Absolutely not," I replied.

"Why not?" Katie asked. "It's Amsterdam." I laughed, dismissing the idea, and walked to the next booth. I bought a new wallet and a killer pair of pink suede boots. Soon, as if by gravitational pull, we had circled around back to the guy with the space cakes.

Maybe just a bite for dessert. I paid the man five euros and tucked the cake in my purse.

On our final day in Amsterdam, Katie and I spotted a used vinyl shop called Second Life Music, so cool they didn't open their doors until one in the afternoon. The small store looked like my Aunt Rita's attic with its unfinished wooden beams and weathered loft area. I was taken back to my childhood when my father regularly rifled through used record shops searching for his music. When he found an album featuring one of his songs, he pulled it out proudly and showed everyone in the shop.

Okay, I'm ready for this, I said silently, bracing myself. "Let's look for my dad's song," I suggested to Katie.

"Why don't we ask the guy who works here?"

"No," I answered too quickly. "Let's just search on our own."

"Should I check under 'C' for Coburn?" Katie asked.

"Look for the Mighty Sparrow," I told her, settling in for a long scavenger hunt like the ones in New York with my father.

"*This* Mighty Sparrow?" Katie asked, lifting an album that read *Sparrow Meets the Dragon*. A picture of the black singer wearing a gold tuxedo jacket was set against an orange background on the left side; Byron Lee, the leader of the Dragonaires, held an electric guitar in front of an aqua back-drop on the right half.

"Oh my God," I gasped, flipping the album cover to read the song list. "You found it, Katie!"

The shop owner turned his head.

Katie was as giddy as I. "It was right there in front," she exclaimed. "I didn't even have to look for it."

"Thank you, Katie!" I said, pulling her in for a tight hug.

"Can we play this?" she asked the record shop owner. "'Only a Fool.'"

"Why not?" he replied, switching on the turntable.

I laughed, realizing that my daughter had a much easier time with the same request I had made thirty-five years earlier.

I longed to have my father with us at Second Life, to hear his voice regaling the shop owner with the story behind the record. The two were of the same ilk, the storeowner only a few years younger than my father would have been. I could easily picture them reminiscing about music of the seventies and wondering when it had all turned to crap.

I could feel my heart beating through to my fingertips as I asked the man if he knew the song.

"Know the song?" he answered, somewhat incredulous. Setting the needle on the track, he snorted a laugh. "Everyone knows this song." A smile spread across my face.

After a few seconds of crackling, I heard the Mighty Sparrow's voice singing my father's lyric. The shop owner started singing along, not missing a word. His friend, who had been sitting at a small table outside, drifted in and joined.

Katie turned to me in amazement. It was one thing to see a gold record hanging on our wall at home, but an entirely different experience to hear strangers singing words my father had written.

They know it, Katie mouthed.

"Every single word," I whispered.

When the song ended, the shop owner lifted the record from the turntable and asked if I wanted to buy it.

"Absolutely," I said. "My father wrote this song."

He looked at the label. "Your father is the Mighty Sparrow?" he asked, skeptical because of our different skin tones.

"No, the Mighty Sparrow performed the song," I explained. "My father wrote the words."

The shop owner looked at the record label. "It says here the Mighty Sparrow wrote the music and lyrics."

"That was a problem," I said with a tight smile.

He reached for a thick white book and dropped it onto the counter.

"Is that, like, the music Bible?" Katie asked the man.

"Yes," he replied seriously, not looking up from the pages as he flipped through for what seemed an eternity. "Here it is. 'Only a Fool.' Is your father S. Coburn or N. Bergen?"

I hadn't realized I was holding my breath until that moment. I exhaled audibly. "S. Coburn."

"It's a very nice song," the man's friend said.

The shop owner nodded and placed the record in a plastic bag. "Tell your father that people in Holland still love his song."

An awkward silence hung between us. "I wish I could," I finally replied.

"Ah, he is dead?" his friend asked.

I nodded to confirm.

"That's too bad," the man said.

I looked at the bag with my father's record the same way a widow might view her beloved's ashes after cremation. *Is this all that's left?* I wondered. *Forty-nine years of life and all that remains is a vinyl record.* My inventory of my father now consisted of a few photos, a gold record, a silver ring, a hand-written letter, and now an album plucked from a record shop in Amsterdam.

As if reading my mind, the shop owner gave me a sympathetic smile. "Your father may be gone, but his song still fills people with happiness…love," he said. The man pointed to the words painted on his storefront window. "His music, it is a second life."

I smiled, imagining my father's reaction to the music shop owner's philosophy. If my dad were with us, he'd hold out a hand, the gimme-five gesture, and say, "Right on, man. I always told her music is eternal." I was sorry he wasn't with us. At the same time, my sadness was diminished by a sense that my father was very much with Katie and me. And always would be.

That night, we had two boxes to check: a canal tour of Amsterdam and washing our clothes. I voted to do laundry then reward ourselves with the boat ride, but Katie suggested that since we were already out, it would be more efficient to cruise the canals first.

The combination of rain falling on the glass top of the boat and the purring of its engine had a lulling effect on Katie, who fell asleep halfway through our tour. I sat in the back with her as our fellow passengers toasted Amsterdam with large plastic cups of Heineken. Looking at my watch, I realized we would be back in our hotel in about an hour and decided to have a few bites of the space cake in my purse. I figured it would be like having a glass of wine, something to give me a light buzz for a night of laundry and packing suitcases.

As the boat pulled into the dock, I felt zero effect from the space cake, so I took a few more bites and put the rest back in my purse. Katie opened her eyes, disappointed that she had missed the ride.

Suddenly, my lips felt very warm.

What are lips anyway? I pondered this deep thought. *They're just fleshy mouth gates that serve no real biological purpose.*

Uh oh.

I wasn't nervous because of my dopey musing about lips. I was concerned because it had been exactly one hour since I cautiously nibbled Doc Brown's organic baked goods. In another sixty minutes, I would be hit by a second wave of space cake—and that was a troubling thought.

As we walked back to the hotel, I took some comfort in the fact that I felt fairly grounded, though definitely a bit gigglier and more thirsty than usual.

In the laundry room of the hotel, however, it was an entirely different story. I stared at the washing machine and panicked at the realization that I had no idea how to use it. Worse, I was in no condition to figure it out.

Katie noticed my expression and began trying to decipher what the buttons meant. Thankfully, she figured it out fairly quickly, but not before I began feeling suffocated by the size of the room. "I'm getting claustrophobic, Katie. Let's get out of here."

She scrunched her mouth to the side. "Hang on and let me put the money in the machine."

"Let's just wait until we get to Paris to do laundry. This place is giving me the creeps."

"Are you okay, Mommy?"

Oh God, what kind of mother am I? This was so stupid.

"I'm fine, just fine. Why wouldn't I be fine?"

"I don't know," Katie said, pushing euro coins into the machine slot. "You just seem a little…I don't know, weird."

Act normal. Breathe deeply and act natural. "No, everything is fine. Perfect and fine. Let's get back to our room!"

When it was time for Katie and me to head downstairs to move the wash into the dryer, I was panicking inside but could still fake semi-normalcy. But a half hour later, when our clothes were dry, the full effect of the space cake kicked in, and I was experiencing something far different than I had ever felt before. It was a forceful current of anxiety that pulled me under and would not let go.

Katie looked at her watch. "Let's head downstairs. The laundry should be dry by now," Katie said.

I looked at her wide-eyed. "I am not going back down there," I said, sitting on the bed in our hotel room.

"Okay, I'll go grab it," she said with a shrug.

"Oh no, you will not! You are *not* going down to that place alone."

Katie raised her eyebrow. "So you want to just leave our clothes in Amsterdam?"

Why did I eat so much of that damned space cake?! Why did I have to be such a greedy, impatient American? Did I really need to supersize a drug trip?

Focus. Focus. Katie just asked a question.

"No, let's do this. We can handle this," I said with intensity, rubbing my hands together.

Katie raised an eyebrow. "Yeah, I know. That's what I've been telling you."

Ten minutes later, we were back upstairs folding clean laundry. I was on my fifth refill of water, but my thirst was unquenchable. "Are you okay?" Katie asked.

"I'm great!" I shot.

"You don't seem great."

There was no hiding it. "Look, Katie, I need to tell you something."

"Okay," she turned toward me, still folding clothes.

"I had a lapse in judgment," I said. Katie looked blank. "I ate the space cake. And now I am just a tiny bit baked in Amsterdam."

"Really?" She looked amused.

I nodded, then fled to the bathroom to refill my water bottle. "I want you to know that we are safe and everything is going to be okay. I am just going to be really stupid and thirsty tonight because I'm baked in Amsterdam."

"All right."

I sat on the bed with the full weight of my remorse. "This is not the kind of mother I want to be."

"Look, it's not a big deal," Katie assured me.

"It *is* a big deal. I'm baked in Amsterdam."

"You really don't need to keep saying *in Amsterdam*. I know where we are," Katie said. "Hey, are you making an origami swan with my jeans?"

"Pretty, right?" I began pacing around the room frantically.

"What are you doing?" Katie asked.

"I'm going to walk it off. Sometimes you've just gotta get a foot on it."

"You do?" she asked.

"I really regret this," I told her.

Katie set the last of the clothing aside and lay on the bed.

"Okay, so it was a one-time thing. If you think it was so terrible, then don't do it again."

"Don't do it again? Are you kidding me?! I will never, ever, *ever* do this again. Can you get me some more water please? I feel like someone is shoveling hot sand into my mouth."

"I've got to tell you," she said, turning on the water. "This doesn't seem like fun." Katie filled a glass and turned back toward the bed, doing a double take as I began pretending to swim across the mattress. Underwater bubble noises soon followed.

"Sometimes you just gotta swim through it," I explained.

"Look, I know you're having a rough night, so I'm trying not to laugh at you, but the truth is, this is kind of hilarious."

"Noooo!" I wailed. "That is not what I want you taking away from this. This is not funny. I am baked in Amsterdam!"

"Okay, let's try to be positive," Katie said. "If it makes you feel better, I now have absolutely no desire to ever try pot."

"That's good, that's good."

Katie smiled. "Ever heard the expression 'Show, don't tell'?"

"I am a walking 'Just say no to drugs' ad," I said, taking momentary solace. "Now let's order room service."

"What do you want?" Katie asked.

"Chocolate cake and a gallon of water," I told her. "Sometimes you just gotta eat your way through it."

"You got it."

I sat on the bed and told Katie that I was not leaving that

spot until morning. "This is my life raft," I told her. "Just tip the guy five euro and sign my name to the bill." Then I grabbed a pillow and hugged it like a teddy bear. "Sometimes, you just gotta snuggle up to it."

She picked up the phone to order our dinner. "Katie," I whispered loudly. "I'm a little bit baked in Amsterdam."

As Katie ordered room service, I mouthed, *Don't get the cake.*

She shrugged to ask why I had changed my mind.

"They'll know," I whispered.

"Okay, just the burgers," Katie said into the phone.

"Katie, where are those cookies from Melkweg?" I asked.

As we ate our dinner, I told Katie we needed to discuss our plans for the following day. "We are supposed to take a train to Paris tomorrow," I said despite the fact that she was well aware of our itinerary. "Can we do that? Can we just get on a train and go to Paris?"

"Yeah, we've taken trains dozens of times. We got this," Katie said.

"What if it's cloudy?" I asked.

She suppressed a laugh. "We go to the train station, buy a ticket, and get on the train."

"Okay, okay, that's good," I nodded. She seemed like she knew what she was doing. "But what if it's sunny?"

Katie tilted down her chin and looked at me, incredulous. "It's pretty much the same plan regardless of the weather."

"Okay, good, good, that makes sense."

"Keep drinking water," Katie suggested.

"Oh God, I'm awful. I can't believe you have to take care of me because I'm baked in Amsterdam. This is so unfair to you."

"The only thing that's unfair was that I had to fold pretty much all of the laundry," Katie said. "And you're eating all of my cookies."

"I hate myself for this."

"Mommy, you know what your problem is?"

"I'm completely baked in—"

"In Amsterdam," she finished. "Okay, you're baked in Amsterdam, this has been established. But you know what your real problem is?"

I took another swig of water. "What?"

"You have no idea how to forgive yourself."

14

PARIS

When Katie and I arrived in Paris, the sun was shining and my head was clear, two welcome changes. Our taxi pulled into the Marais neighborhood, and there was Hôtel du Petit Moulin looking exactly as I had remembered it from eight years earlier.

The same could not be said of us. Katie was now a five-foot-six runner with hair down to her waist. Her face no longer had the chubby cheeks of a little girl. As for me, my hairdresser had done a good job of hiding the gray swiftly taking over. And like my daughter, I'd grown a few inches as well, except it was all around the waist. Over the years, there were very few sweets I had shunned.

I could easily envision the little hotel in its original life as a bakery because of its huge display windows. The more obvious clue may have been that the word *Boulangerie* was still clearly painted on the outside. Through the hotel windows, I saw vases bursting with purple and white orchids and billowy velvet drapes dipping beneath the frame.

When we stepped inside the hotel lobby, my eyes were immediately drawn to a small beaded Victorian lamp sitting on the reception desk. Animal-print throw pillows sat on plush velvet chairs and black leather sofas. A nook of the lobby was wallpapered in a pattern of books on the shelves; another wall was papered in a vintage print.

Katie and I took a tiny elevator to the third floor, then walked up an uneven spiral staircase with polka dot carpeting.

When we opened the door to our room, Katie's mouth dropped. It looked like something from a dollhouse, complete with a sloped ceiling. Two windows were angled toward the sky. Another window was set behind a small wooden desk made from an old sewing machine. Lavender walls were accented by artistic blocks of wallpaper, some floral patterns, others of women from the turn of the last century. "This is like *Little House on the Prairie*," I said.

"This is much nicer," Katie quipped. "More like *Little House on La Paree*."

"Do you remember stopping by here last time?" I asked.

She shook her head. "It was half a lifetime ago. I remember the big things like the Eiffel Tower, but not this."

Katie's mention of the tower made me long to see it. Something about laying eyes on the landmark solidified the reality that we were, in fact, in Paris. During this visit though, the image would not evoke panic like last time, I promised myself. Yes, we were still clueless tourists. And yes, we would still get lost. But this time I would try to accept that uncertainty was part of the adventure.

Katie and I planned to walk along the river toward the Eiffel Tower, but wound up heading in the opposite direction along the Seine. We passed a small amphitheater with just enough room for the dozen couples who were dancing. Within minutes, we passed another inlet with a group of dancers. When we reached a third group, we decided to stop and watch.

A Latin couple in their twenties danced seductively to Spanish music, their muscular bodies intertwined effortlessly, their eyes locked. The woman's silky brown braid rested on her exposed back. Her arms were perfectly tanned and sinewy. *I have got to get back to the gym*, I thought. The guy was equally sexy despite the fact he wore a gauzy white blouse knotted at the bottom. With his shoulder length wavy hair and coal-black eyes, he belonged on the cover of a romance novel. "Those two are *really* into each other," Katie commented. Her eyes soon darted to watch an older couple. An Asian woman with the legs of a professional dancer glided across the floor in the arms of her partner, a dead ringer for Martin Scorsese, with bushy eyebrows and a wide smile. "Her husband looks so happy," Katie said.

"He was a widow," I said, beginning to draft the man's life story. "He lost his first wife seven years ago. He never thought he'd find love again."

Katie jumped in. "But then he met Lynn at a dance class, and she brought him back to life."

A middle-aged couple made their way past us. The woman's fuzzy white hair made us think she had recently completed chemotherapy. "He held her hand every week at the hospital," Katie said as a lump filled my throat.

I continued. "And he promised her that as soon as her treatment was done, he would take her to Paris and they would dance the tango on the River Seine."

Katie and I both became teary-eyed, but quickly burst into laughter at our sappiness. "We are ridiculous," Katie said, wiping her nose. "She's probably in a punk rock band. Next week her buzz cut will be green."

The music changed and the sexy young Latina switched dance partners. The two stood inches apart and gazed adoringly into each other's eyes. "Wow, she's really into him too," Katie said.

That evening, we made it to the Eiffel Tower, though not on foot as planned. We sat on a boat with hundreds of other tourists, quietly watching the sights of Paris pass by us. I was more at peace than ever before and thought Katie was about to tell me she was having the same reaction when she tapped my shoulder.

"I don't feel so great," she said instead.

"Are you seasick?" I asked, though this would be a first.

"I just feel *really* tired."

By sunset, Katie was tucked in bed and fast asleep, a first since her preschool days.

Early the next morning, she lay in bed whimpering in her sleep. Her face was tight like a fist, her skin burning. Sensing my gaze, Katie's eyes opened. "My head hurts," she said weakly.

"You have a fever," I told her as I started to fill the bathtub with tepid water. "Let's get you cooled off and hydrated," I suggested, removing a bottle of cold water from the minibar.

Once Katie had been in the bath for a while, I went downstairs and found that although the hotel had a first aid kit, it didn't include anything to bring down a fever. When I returned to the room, I asked if she would be okay on her own for a few minutes while I went out to buy Tylenol.

Why didn't I bring Tylenol? I scolded myself. *Always bring Tylenol!*

"I'll be fine," she replied.

"The concierge is a nice young woman, so call the front desk if you need anything. I'll be back in ten minutes." I placed a cold washcloth on her forehead and ventured out.

I walked onto the desolate streets of early morning Paris to find that the supermarket was closed. Nearby was a fruit stand whose owner sold me juice and snacks, then mentioned that the only place to buy medicine on a Sunday would be the Republic.

"The Republic?" I asked. "Is that a neighborhood? A store? A government office?"

"It is the Republic," he said, pointing toward the door. I couldn't tell whether he was giving me directions or just kicking me out.

I decided to check on Katie back at the hotel, where I could ask the concierge how to get to this place called the Republic. Katie's eyes were closed, though her facial muscles contracted and expanded with discomfort. I cooled the washcloth and placed it back on her forehead. Her face smoothed and she managed a weak smile.

"Katie," I whispered. "I need to go to the Republic to get medicine."

She nodded.

"I brought back orange juice," I told her, pouring some into a glass. "Are you going to be okay for a bit longer?"

Katie opened her eyes. "What's the Republic?" she asked softly. She was lethargic and miserable but lucid enough to be curious, an encouraging sign.

As it turned out, the Republic was the name of a small plaza nearby which had a pharmacy that was open twenty-four hours a day, seven days a week. Despite the early hour, the line snaked from the front counter to the back door, about twenty people deep. When it was finally my turn, I was able to fumble through enough French to let the clerk know I needed medicine, but had to charade the word fever by placing a hand on my forehead and making a sad face.

"*Fièvre?*" the clerk offered with an eye roll.

Katie's fever broke later that morning, but she didn't have the energy to leave our hotel room. I sat beside her in bed, watching the white cotton sheet rise and fall with each breath. I read an entire novel, then in the afternoon, sat at our little desk and wrote postcards to family and friends back home.

At night, I listened to people chatting and clanking their silverware at the restaurant below. I heard a woman's high heels clopping against the street as she yelled at her boyfriend. I took a ridiculously long bath and then experimented with hairstyles pictured in a French fashion magazine.

The following day, Katie assured me she was fully recovered but soon changed her mind. After a half hour of looking at modern art at the Pompidou Center, she asked if we could sit at the snack bar and take a rest. Sipping fruit juice, Katie leaned her head into her hands and yawned. "I think I've spent the last twenty out of twenty-four hours sleeping. I'm like a koala bear." She lay down on the cushioned bench and yawned again. "I think I'd like to be a koala. Then I could sleep most of the day and just be like, 'Hey, this is what I do. I'm a koala, don't judge.'"

"Katie, sweetheart, I think you're still sick," I said.

She said nothing.

"Katie?"

The only sound I heard was her light snoring.

Another day of resting, reading, and eating croissants in bed returned Katie to her usual self, though she felt bad that we missed some time sightseeing in Paris. "We lost two days," she said apologetically.

"We didn't lose anything," I assured her. "We still had the days. They just weren't what we had planned."

I smiled realizing that I actually meant it and wasn't just telling her what I thought she needed to hear. The truth was that some things on our to-do list would not get done. But while I sat in our hotel room caring for Katie, something else had been accomplished, something for which there was no box to check. I had enjoyed life at its most ordinary.

"Didn't you want to go to Moulin Rouge last night?" Katie asked.

"Nah," I said, swatting away the idea with my hand. "After you fell asleep, I looked out these crazy windows and stared at the stars for an hour. *French* stars, Katie," I said. "How often do I get to do that?"

"You do know we're seeing the same stars we would at home, right? We're in the same hemisphere."

"But how often do I look at them?" I asked. "Like I said, we didn't lose anything."

My cousin Richard—my aunt Rita and uncle Arnold's son—and his family were visiting Paris at the same time as we were so we connected for two days. Richard and his wife Lora have two children: Tom, who is six months younger than Katie, and Taite, who is eleven years old. Joining the family was Ivan, a new aide who helps care for Tom, who was born with cerebral palsy. Despite his physical limitations, Tom has always been buoyed by a penchant for mischief rivaled only by his sister's. When Tom's wheelchair isn't burning rubber down sidewalks, Taite is often balancing on the handles as if they were gymnastic beams.

Richard and Lora are like an upscale, gender-swapped version of William and me, Lora being the measured spouse, Richard the scattered one. It is easy to imagine her wearing a white coat in the hospital laboratory where she is the head of gynecological pathology. He is an inventor who is like a younger Larry David with thick salt-and-pepper hair.

On our first day together, we ventured outside Paris to the Palace of Versailles. The façade and entry gates of the Baroque chateau were so laden in gold I had to squint from the glare. Inside, the opulence was overwhelming: seven hundred rooms filled with fine furniture, paintings, and sculptures. The ceilings were painted as elaborately as the Sistine Chapel. Looking around, I wondered if the royal decorator ever dared tell the residing king and queen that it was all a little too much.

As we entered the Hall of Mirrors, a long corridor with multiple chandeliers and looking-glass panels, Richard gestured to the throng of people. "What do you think Louis XIV would think of all this?" Not waiting for a response, he shrugged dramatically. "Who are all of these commoners in my home? This place was supposed to be for my grandkids."

We spent the afternoon shuffling through the crowded palace, one room looking similar to the next. The sea of guests was so dense we nearly lost one another several times. Even more frequently, shoulders were bumped and feet stepped on. In the heat, this was more irritating. As Richard looked around yet another gilded room, he scrunched his face. "This is like the Trump Towers of the 1700s," he said.

After a few hours at Versailles, as we were sitting in the garden eating soggy sandwiches from the snack bar, Taite said what we were all thinking: "This place Ver-sucks."

Back in Paris that evening, we found a cozy Provençal restaurant where natural light poured into the dining room, which was filled with distressed wood hutches and crisp white tablecloths. As the owner began placing grilled chicken and potatoes on the table, Taite suggested we play a game in which we go around the table and ask questions about each other. Taite coined the term "quames" for this game of questions. Three hours later, we learned we could all envision Richard as John Lennon's best friend (and florist). We thought Tom would be best cast on *Glee*, and that in a few years, Katie could be mistaken for a botanist. I also learned that eating two desserts on top of a gourmet meal is not impossible if I focused really hard on the incredible taste instead of my tightening waistband.

The next day was a universal crowd pleaser. Richard led us through the *Dynamo* exhibition—a sprawling display of modern art experienced through light and space—at the Grand Palais.

Dozens of geometric light sculptures shared space with black-and-white designs that appeared to change form. Richard was especially taken with a room that was filled with blue fog, and another dotted with bubbled mirrors. The kids howled with delight as they raced through an area where hundreds of blue rubber threads hung from the ceiling like a carwash.

"Pretty great, right?" Richard asked us all. "Did I tell you we'd love *Dynamo*, or what?" I smiled with recognition over our shared familial characteristic, then replied with the only answer that would do.

"This is the greatest and so are you, Richard!"

He smiled at the ribbing. We locked arms and continued out onto the streets with our group, passing posh clothing shops and outdoor cafés.

"Let's play some more quames at dinner tonight," Taite suggested.

"Quames it is!" Richard sang, imitating an English royal.

Katie joined in, sounding like Washington Irving on the Alhambra audio guide. "Quames are completely and utterly marvelous, my little peacock."

On the final day of our Paris trip, Katie and I revisited our favorite museum in the city. The outside of the Museum of Modern Art was still smattered with graffiti, but the inside was far more polished than it was eight years earlier. The space was enormous and bright before, but now had high gloss floors and sleek lights.

The museum was exhibiting the work of Keith Haring, an artist whose distinct pop style brought me back to a time when I was Katie's age. "I remember his chalk outlines in subway stations and paintings on the sides of buildings in New York," I told Katie as we entered the museum.

"I love this guy!" Katie said as we stood in front of murals of Haring's trademark whimsical outline paintings. Nearby was a colossal head of David with bright green hair. Beside that hung a painting of a pig with a snout made from dollar signs, gobbling a mouthful of little people.

In the early eighties, my father and I were walking down

West Broadway in SoHo when I spotted Haring's painting on a warehouse wall. Haring had painted the outline of a crawling baby with shocks of motion pulsing from its body. On another dilapidated building was a second Haring original, this one the outline of a dog, or perhaps it was an alligator. It was hard to tell.

"I'm seeing these everywhere," I told my father. "What are they?"

My father bent his head to light a cigarette then inhaled deeply. "They're art," he said with a shrug.

"Art?" I said skeptically, flipping my hair over the shoulder of my stonewashed denim jacket. "Art is what you see in a museum or a gallery. I was asking what you think this graffiti means."

"It means you're thinking like a very conventional person, JJ," my father said, resting a hand gently on my back. "Why does something need to be approved by the establishment in order to be called art? Some of the best stuff is rejected by society. Van Gogh only sold one painting in his entire life."

"Really?"

"Yeah, really. I think this guy is good," my father said, gesturing to yet another Haring on the wall. "His stuff looks like crime scene outline, but it's also kind of comical."

"Why do you think he's putting it on the sides of buildings, though?"

My father opened his mouth to answer, then stopped

himself. He took another drag of his cigarette. "He puts his art on the outside of buildings because no one's letting him inside."

Even then, I knew we were no longer talking about Keith Haring, but of my father's music career. The gold record he had brought back from Holland four years earlier had not opened doors the way he had hoped. The music scene was shifting in the same direction as the rest of the country, and the days of the ballad-singing hippies were coming to an end. There would always be room for old guard musicians like Neil Young and Bob Dylan, but entertainers like Madonna and Prince were now filling the spots for rising stars. "This guy's got *chutzpa*," my father said, gesturing to Haring's barking alligator. "I don't know what these cartoon characters are all about, but the fact that he's drawing them on the streets is cool. It's like he's saying, 'You can lock me out of your fancy galleries, but you will never stop me from creating and showing my stuff to the world.'" He reached into his cigarette box and lit another smoke.

Soon after Keith Haring's graffiti art lined the subways and streets of New York City, though, gallery doors did open and Haring became an art scene darling. He painted vibrant, colorful canvases, created bold sculptures, and made collages from newspaper headlines. He was hanging out with Andy Warhol and Yoko Ono, lamenting the Reagan Revolution and consumer culture.

Now, thirty years later, my daughter and I experienced Keith Haring's work neatly exhibited in a museum spray-painted with graffiti on the outside.

After a marathon day at the Museum of Modern Art, the Louvre, and the Musée d'Orsay, Katie said that the only other thing she absolutely had to do was climb the Eiffel Tower.

We began our ascent up the steps as the sun dipped beneath the horizon on our last night in Paris. "You ready for this?" Katie asked, double-checking the knots on her shoelaces.

"Probably not, but let's do it anyway."

Katie bounced up the spiral staircase with ease, one of the many benefits of working out with her cross-country team for the last two years. I, on the other hand, had not been as disciplined, and as a result, my lungs began to burn and my breathing was labored as I was nearing the first landing.

"Isn't there a bar up there?" I asked, panting.

Katie was already at the landing and called back to confirm.

"Good, I need water," I said, gripping the rail and catching my breath. A thin layer of sweat coated my back, and my sneakers became leaden as I made it up the last steps and saw a lavender-colored oasis: an outdoor bar illuminated with neon lights that perfectly matched the evening sky. Katie was already asking the bartender for a cold bottle of water.

We continued our climb up the ever-narrowing staircase, looking out at the skeletal structure encasing us and exchanging nods with fellow travelers from every corner of the map. Katie and a Pakistani boy looked at each other's matching buns. We clung to the side of the stairwell to make room for a herd of American teens in yellow T-shirts. I marveled at a woman my mother's age effortlessly tackling the steps. *I really, really need to get back to the gym*, I thought, desperately gulping air.

When Katie and I finally reached the pinnacle of the tower, the sky was black and the city beneath a carpet of starlight. The wind was whipping so hard it was whistling, and my hair was blowing in every direction.

"Thanks for taking the stairs," Katie said, leaning down to kiss my cheek. "I know it was hard for you, but I really appreciate it."

"It wasn't *that* hard," I said, mocking myself.

After a few minutes of taking photos and enjoying the view, I peered over the edge and took in one last look at Paris from this vantage point. I smiled as my eyes settled on the illuminated Ferris wheel at Tuileries Gardens. "Do you remember our first morning in Paris eight years ago?" I asked Katie.

"When you barfed your hot chocolate in the hotel room?" Katie asked.

"I was actually thinking about how we were on that Ferris wheel, looking at this tower."

"Oh yeah, pretty cool," Katie said. We shared a moment in the memory. "Ready to head back?"

"I think so."

"This is the easy part now," she said like a coach. "We got this."

❧

"Ladies and gentlemen, the captain has turned on the fasten seat-belt sign," a calm female voice announced. "If you haven't already done so, please stow your carry-on luggage underneath the seat in front of you or in an overhead bin."

I placed my sleep mask on my head and looked at Katie settled into her seat, white buds and wires falling from her ears.

Shortly after our ascent from Paris, Katie asked if she could use a piece of paper from my travel notebook. I reached into my purse and handed her the book.

Minutes later, Katie tapped my arm. "I feel really bad," Katie said, pointing at a page covered with my writing. "It says here you wanted to explore the eighteenth *arrondissement* and have dinner at an African restaurant."

"So."

"You also wrote that we were going to see the catacombs, take the number fourteen metro from one end of the city to the other, explore the Île Saint-Louis, and visit the sewer museum."

"I was only doing the sewers for you," I told her.

"And there's a line through the Picasso Museum," Katie said.

"Because it was closed for renovation," I reminded her.

"Yeah, but look at all of these other things we didn't do," Katie said. "Because I got sick."

"Katie, I don't have any regrets about this visit, and you have absolutely nothing to feel guilty about, okay?" She nodded. "You are a great travel buddy and I really loved every minute of our trip, even the things that didn't turn out perfectly. As for the sights we left unseen, what can I tell you?" I asked with a Euro-shrug. "We'll come back and do all of those other things."

"We will?"

"Sure, the city isn't going anywhere," I told Katie, then smiled. "We'll always have Paris."

READING GROUP GUIDE

. . . .

1. How does the meaning of the phrase "We'll always have Paris" change for Jennifer by the end of the book?

2. Jennifer describes her desire to travel as a desperate attempt to fill her daughter's mental scrapbook in case she dies young. Do you ever fear dying young, and if so, how do you address your fears?

3. Jennifer describes her home as being in a state of constant disrepair. By making travel a priority, is she enjoying life or being irresponsible?

4. Which of the cities Jennifer and Katie visited was your favorite and why?

5. On the train ride to Granada, Jennifer describes a dream in which she is holding the hands of her father and daughter "in the middle, staggering to find my footing." What does she mean by this? Do you ever feel caught between generations?

6. Jennifer seemed to have a major revelation about enjoying life when she visited the Anne Frank House in Amsterdam.

But then she makes a poor choice and eats a space cake in front of her daughter. Why do you think she did this?

7. When Jennifer regrets eating the space cake, Katie tells her she has no idea how to forgive herself. Do you agree with this assessment? In what other scenarios might Jennifer show herself more forgiveness?

8. How do you think these trips would have been different if William had joined them?

9. Jennifer seems nostalgic for the New York City of the 1970s. What place and time do you most fondly recall?

10. What was your reaction to reading about Jennifer's stepmother painting the piano while her father's corpse was still in the living room?

11. Many young women choose a man like their father. Jennifer seems to have chosen a man more like her uncle, Arnold. What does that say about how she felt about her father?

12. Jennifer seemed heartbroken when the phony medium was unable to contact her father. Do you believe in an afterlife? Do you ever feel Jennifer's father did send her a sign, but she simply missed it?

13. Did you identify with Jennifer as a mother? As a daughter?

14. Where do you see Katie ten years from now?

Acknowledgments

. . . .

We'll Always Have Paris has been a wonderful journey for me, both in the traveling and the writing. I am so grateful that my family and friends allowed me to write about them from my point of view. Their generosity is greatly appreciated.

I am fortunate to have found an early champion in Scott Miller who was the perfect agent for this book. Special thanks to Stephanie Hoover and the rest of the gang at Trident Media Group. And to Jen Lancaster, who introduced me to Scott: wow, you were so right.

I was also lucky enough to have found the absolute perfect editor in Shana Drehs at Sourcebooks. She and Anna Klenke offered keen insight and helped me zero in on the story. Everyone at Sourcebooks has my gratitude for seeing the potential in my opening chapters.

Thanks to my friends who read the manuscript several times and gave me their candid feedback: Joan Isaacson, Marg Stark, Edit Zelkind (Ketchum), and especially Eilene Zimmerman. I also received valuable editorial feedback from

Rachel Biermann, Milo Shapiro, Phil Lauder, and Leslie Wolf Branscomb.

My husband William is a very private person but let me include him in the book anyway, and I am so grateful to him for that—and for doing more than his fair share of dishes as deadlines approached. Katie is truly the best travel buddy anyone could want. I am so fortunate to share my life with Will and Katie O'Nell.

In writing this book, I began to really understand and appreciate everything my mother, Carol Coburn, went through in our early days together. I am astounded by her strength and grace. I am also eternally grateful to my mother for suggesting I write a travel memoir about my trips with Katie.

Thanks to all of the people we met overseas who stopped to give us help, advice, and sometimes a meal. I don't know most of these people's names, but I will always appreciate their kindness. And to those I do know, big, double-cheeked Euro kisses to Janine DiGiovanni, Bruno Girodon, Luca Girodon, Molly Wischhusen, Megan Gannon, Claudia Trillo, Gianluigi Cassandra, Gerado Trillo, Giuliana Garagnani Trillo, Anna Trillo, Aldo Della Ragione, Mary Duncan, Maxime Dumesnil, Markéta Hancová, Jana Kanêrová, Radka Michâlkova, Eliska Michâlkova, Bill Hampton, Martina Chianese, and Benedetto Crasta.

I am also enormously grateful to the readers who continue

to rock my world by writing, tweeting, and blogging about my books. Thank you, thank you, thank you! I appreciate your spending your reading time with my book.

About the Author

Jennifer Coburn is an award-winning author of six novels and contributor to four literary anthologies. She has written for *UT San Diego*, the *Miami Herald*, *Mothering*, the *Huffington Post*, Salon.com, and numerous other newspapers and magazines.

Jennifer lives in San Diego with her husband William and their daughter Katie. Her next trip will

Photo credit: Katie O'Nell

be a cross-country tour of colleges as the family begins its next great adventure: helping Katie find a school she loves.

For more information about events and releases, visit Jennifer at www.facebook.com/JenniferCoburnBooks or www.JenniferCoburn.com.